D1732977

Comedia
Series editor: David Morley

FREEDOM AND CONSTRAINT

FREEDOM AND CONSTRAINT

The paradoxes of leisure

Ten years of the
Leisure Studies Association

Edited by
Fred Coalter

R

A COMEDIA book
published by ROUTLEDGE
London and New York

A Comedia book
First published in 1989 by
Routledge
11 New Fetter Lane, London EC4P 4EE
29 West 35th Street, New York NY 10001

Typeset by Scarborough Typesetting Services
Printed in Great Britain by
T. J. Press (Padstow) Ltd, Cornwall

British Library Cataloguing in Publication Data
Freedom and constraint: the paradoxes of leisure:
ten years of the Leisure Studies Association. – (A Comedia
book).
1. Leisure. Social aspects
I. Coalter, Fred.   II. Leisure Studies Association
306'.48
ISBN 0–415–00649–X

Library of Congress Cataloging in Publication Data
Freedom and constraint: the paradoxes of leisure:
ten years of the Leisure Studies Association/edited by
Fred Coalter.
p.   cm. – (A Comedia book)
'A selection from the published volumes of conference
papers covering the first ten years': p.
Includes index.
ISBN 0–415–00649–X
1. Leisure.   2. Leisure – Social aspects.   3. Leisure
Studies Association (Great Britain).
I. Coalter, Fred.   II. Leisure Studies Association (Great
Britain)
GV174.F74   1988
306'.48–dc19   88–4381

For Vicki

Contents

Notes on the contributors

Fred Coalter is Director of the Centre for Leisure and Tourism Studies at the Polytechnic of North London. He was formerly Research Director of the Centre for Leisure Research, Research Fellow at the Tourism and Recreation Research Unit, University of Edinburgh, and Vice-Chair of the Leisure Studies Association. He has researched and written on various aspects of the sociology of leisure and social policies for leisure.

Paul Corrigan now works for ILEA, having taught social workers for twelve years. In the past he has written on welfare, education, and poverty.

Chas Critcher is Principal Lecturer in Communication Studies at Sheffield Polytechnic and is co-author with John Clarke of *The Devil Makes Work: Leisure in Capitalist Britain* (Macmillan, 1985). He has published articles on sport and its relationship to the media and has a particular interest in theories of postindustrialism.

Geoffrey Godbey is Professor of Recreation and Parks at the Pennsylvania State University. He is the author of five books and numerous articles concerning leisure behaviour and leisure service organizations.

David H. Hargreaves is Professor of Education at the University of Cambridge. He has written four books, the latest of which is *The Challenge for the Comprehensive School* (Routledge, 1982). After chairing the independent enquiry into secondary schooling for the Inner London Education Authority, which produced *Improving Secondary Schools*, he became the Authority's Chief Inspector.

Daphne Johnson is Honorary Senior Research Fellow in the Department of Government, Brunel University, where she contributes to the postgraduate teaching of education policy and methods of social research. She is also a consultant to the Open University's School of Education. The interrelationship of school and family is one of her principal research interests. Her most recent book, *Private Schools and State Schools: Two Systems or one?* (Open University Press, 1987) explores the coexistence of state and private education from the point of view of those who provide or use the schools.

Ann McGoldrick is Senior Lecturer in Human Resource Management at Manchester Polytechnic, having worked previously in the School of Management at the University of Manchester Institute of Science and Technology. Her interests include changing manpower patterns, older workers, retirement, and pensions. As well as publishing widely in articles, she produced a major report for the EOC, *Equal Treatment in Occupational Pension Schemes* in 1984, and a book on *Early Retirement* (Aldershot: Gower, 1989).

Ian Miles is a Senior Fellow of the Science Policy Research Unit at the University of Sussex, where he is currently working on a project entitled 'Mapping and Measuring the Information Economy'. His interests in the emerging information society – especially developments in work and leisure – is expressed in two books published in spring 1988: *Home Informatics: Information Technology and the Transformation of Everyday Life* (London: Frances Pinter), and *Information Horizons: The Long Term Social Implications of IT* (Aldershot: Edward Elgar).

Graham Murdock is Research Fellow at the Centre For Mass Communication Research, University of Leicester, where he has worked on a number of areas including the political economy of the communications industries, youth culture, and the social impact of new technologies. He is the co-author of *Demonstrations and Communication*; *Televising 'Terrorism'*; and *Mass Communications and the Advertising Industry*; and co-editor of *Communicating Politics*. He has been Visiting Professor at the University of California at San Diego, the Free University of Brussels, and the University of Colima, Mexico.

Noel Parry is Head of Sociology and Dean of Social Studies at the Polytechnic of North London. He has researched, edited, and published in the fields of leisure studies, the professions, social stratifications, and the state. Publications include: *Leisure in Hatfield* (Hatfield Polytechnic, 1973); 'Theories of culture and leisure', in M. A. Smith (ed.) *Leisure and Urban Society* (Leisure Studies Association, 1977); 'Sociology and leisure: a question of root or branch?', *Sociology*, 16, 1982; 'Sociological contributions to the study of leisure', Leisure Studies, vol. 2, no. 1, January 1983; 'Class, culture, and leisure: British and Australian comparisons', Paper presented to the second International Conference of the LSA, 1988, University of Sussex.

Kenneth Roberts is Professor of Sociology at Liverpool University. He is the author of *Leisure* (London: Longman, 1970, revised 1981); *Contemporary Society and the Growth of Leisure* (London: Longman, 1977); and *Youth and Leisure* (London: Allen and Unwin, 1983). His current research is investigating indoor sports provisions, patterns of participation, and the quality of life in urban areas. He is also a member of the core research team in the Economic and Social Research Council's 16–19 Initiative.

Chris Rojek is Senior Editor in Sociology at Routledge Publishers, London. In addition to numerous articles on leisure, sociology, and social work he is the author of *Capitalism and Leisure Theory* (Tavistock, 1985); *Ways of Escape: Leisure and Travel in the Modern World* (Macmillan, forthcoming); editor of *Leisure for Leisure: Critical Essays* (Macmillan, 1988); co-author with Gerry Peacock and Stewart Collins of *Social Work and Received Ideas*, (Routledge, 1988); and co-editor with Gerry Peacock and Stewart Collins of *The Haunt of Misery: Critical Essays in Social Work and Helping* (Routledge, 1989).

Sheila Scraton is a lecturer in sociology and leisure studies at Leeds Polytechnic. She has completed research into gender and girls' Physical Education and has published articles on gender, sport, PE, and leisure. Her current research, teaching, and political interests are in the development of feminist theoretical analysis; gender, sexuality, and leisure; and the development of critical research into gender, race, and class in sport, schooling, and leisure. She is an active member of the Women's Sports Foundation.

Tom Stonier holds the Founding Chair in Science and Society at the University of Bradford. He has been concerned with the interactions between science, technology, and society for many years. Previously he held posts in the United States at Brookhaven

National Laboratory, Rockefeller University, and Manhattan College. He has been a consultant to numerous private and public organizations, and has appeared on many radio and television programmes. His publications include *The Wealth of Information: A Profile of the Post-Industrial Economy* (Thames Television/ Methuen, 1983), and *The Three Cs: Children, Computers and Communication* (John Wiley, 1985), co-authored with C. Conlin.

Jane Streather was Director of the National Council for One-Parent Families when her paper was written. She is now Assistant Director for Community Services within the Social Services Department in Newcastle upon Tyne. She has made numerous contributions to journals in the field of social security and social policy. In 1980 she co-authored a book based on the National Child Development Study, which was published as *Children in Changing Families* (Macmillan).

Harald Swedner has been Professor in Social Work at Gothenburg University, Sweden, since 1977. He has published several books and many papers in such areas as the sociology of culture and leisure, social welfare, housing, and migration, as well as on methods for social research and social theory.

Tony Veal is currently Principal Lecturer at the Kuring-gai College of Advanced Education, Sydney, Australia, having worked previously at the Centre for Urban and Regional Studies at Birmingham University and at the Polytechnic of North London. He is author of numerous research reports and articles in leisure studies and of the book *Leisure and the Future* (London: Allen & Unwin, 1987). He was a founder member of the LSA and was chairman from 1984 to 1986.

George de Vink is a leisure sociologist, now working at the Department of Recreation and Leisure of the Province of South Holland, in The Hague, The Netherlands. His main fields of interest are outdoor recreation in rural areas, recreation management, and future trends. He has undertaken research on developing leisure styles, leisure and work/unemployment, education for leisure, and leisure marketing.

General introduction

The Leisure Studies Association was established in 1975 to provide a forum for discussion and debate on the 'penalties and prizes' resulting from quantitative and qualitative changes in work and leisure. From the outset the LSA was avowedly multi-disciplinary, seeking to bring together academics, researchers, and practitioners to discuss issues of theory, politics, planning, and management. The main methods used to pursue such ends were a series of regional seminars and annual conferences. The papers in this volume represent a selection from the published volumes of conference papers covering the first ten years.

Given the large number of papers and the wide diversity of topics the choices for inclusion were, necessarily, somewhat arbitrary. This selection is not meant to represent 'the best of' the conference papers – in a multi-disciplinary field such a judgement is more than usually difficult. Rather, the intention has been to choose papers which illustrate that any meaningful discussion of leisure involves consideration of a wide range of fundamental social and political issues. Individual papers were chosen because they, explicitly or implicitly, reject the reification of leisure, its treatment as a separate sphere, somehow different and apart from wider social, economic, political, or ideological processes.

The papers in this selection stress that leisure – as a social institution, individual behaviour, or subjective experience – is a product of, and influenced by, more fundamental structures. However this is not taken to imply that the social institutions of leisure are merely residual categories; rather they are seen to be at the very centre of social change. Changes in the institutions of work, family, and education are not only reflected in leisure but many of the authors suggest that the institutions of leisure represent the site of potential solutions to a variety of social and economic problems resulting from such changes.

Few of the writers in this volume subscribe to any simple view of the sovereign 'consumer', seeking to maximize utility through the exercise of freedom and choice in the market place. For them leisure, like most social institutions, is Janus-faced, containing elements of both freedom and constraint.

This paradox, and the constant tension or conflict between the potential and reality of leisure, indicate that the definitional disputes concerning 'the meaning of leisure' (some of which are reflected in these papers) are not mere semantics but are of substantive political and ideological importance. This is because leisure, with its ideological components of freedom, choice, and self-development, is often used as a synonym for social progress and the wider liberalization of society.[1]

Perhaps, as many of these authors imply, the quality of leisure is an index of the quality of society. Although the papers in this collection span a ten-year period, it is a compliment to the authors that the issues raised still remain relevant. But it is perhaps disconcerting to note that most of the questions remain un-answered and the issues unresolved. It is therefore hoped that the publication of the arguments and debates contained in the papers will ensure the wider audience such issues demand.

Note

1 F. Coalter and N. Parry, *Leisure sociology or the sociology of leisure?* Papers in Leisure Studies no. 4, Polytechnic of North London, 1982.

PART ONE

Leisure and social change

Introduction

The chapters in Part One address the implications for leisure of broad processes of social, economic, and technological change. The debate about leisure is essentially a debate about the future and this theme is central to a number of papers in this collection.

The contribution by Miles provides a useful antidote to the often mystificatory sophistication of forecasting techniques. He suggests that, far from being purely technical and objective, much forecasting is inherently political. Rather than simply predicting change, forecasting is often a conscious attempt to influence the direction of change, the balance between freedom and constraint. The consequences of many predictions are to reduce choice by proposing a narrow range of technologically determined futures. For Miles the conflict between freedom and restraint is symbolized by the differences between the rather deterministic, technocratic predictions and a humanistic perspective which suggests that the future is not to be predicted but 'made'. In such circumstances he is proposing a surveyor's approach to evaluating forecasts – before you mortgage your future check the premises!

The paper by Stonier might be described as a form of 'deterministic humanism'. While acknowledging that the greatest threat of new technology is the displacement of labour, he nevertheless proposes an optimistic view of the shift from the mechanical to the 'communicative era'. In this era the education system will absorb large numbers of workers and, via research and the production of new technologies, become the motor force of technological change. In contrast to the humanistic perspective suggested by Hargreaves and de Vink in Part Three, Stonier appears to suggest that education needs to become subordinate to the requirements of technological development and economic growth.

The Rojek paper emphasizes the intimate relationship between work, or rather the social organization of production, and the nature and experience of leisure. He outlines the more pessimistic view of neo-Marxist thinkers who suggest that the processes of de-skilling and increased control inherent in the capitalist labour process, are reflected in the increasing commercialization and commodification of leisure. Such leisure is not 'free' but is 'forced', directly serving the reproductive needs of capitalism. Rojek ends by questioning the reductive and deterministic nature of this analysis, suggesting that many of the processes are not specific to capitalism and proposing that any approach to the study of leisure must be situated within the context of an understanding of historically specific social processes of regulation, legitimation, and negotiation.

Some of these themes are present in the paper by Critcher who rejects the technological determinism of many of the theories of post-industrial society, arguing that they suppress the roles of political, economic, and cultural factors. Such predictive determinism can be countered, and the dynamics of purposive social behaviour grasped, by adopting an historical perspective. Such an approach serves to emphasize the duality of leisure as containing both elements of control and development, that its content and meaning are often not determined but are the result of conflict and struggle and that new forms of leisure are rarely devoid of influences from the past.

Roberts offers a sceptical antidote to the more idealistic themes about the emergence of a 'society of leisure'. He questions the use of quantitative indices of increased recreational behaviour as a basis for deducing that we have entered a society of leisure. For Roberts (and Critcher) this is to confuse doing with being, because any analysis of the changing significance of leisure would require an examination of the meanings of activities within the wider context of family networks and social relationships. The society of leisure might require more fundamental indices than increased participation in recreational activities.

This scepticism is also central to Godbey's paper. Adopting a humanistic perspective, he suggests that if 'real' leisure is concerned with autonomy and freedom then what we have at present is 'anti-leisure' – behaviour which is undertaken compulsively, instrumentally, and with a high degree of time consciousness and anxiety and a minimum of personal autonomy. Godbey suggests that this is because leisure has failed to become an autonomous sphere but instead directly reflects wider social and economic processes and demands. Factors such as the life-style requirements of professionals, styles of work invading the sphere of leisure and limitless materialism all serve to undermine the essential properties of leisure.

1

Predictions, portents and paradigms (1976)

IAN MILES

The functions of forecasting

Why do we forecast? It is easy enough to answer that it is simply part of human nature to attempt to anticipate the future. Such an answer begs many questions: why are elaborate techniques of forecasting being developed and employed by some people, while others throw up their hands in horror at the thought of 'futurology' or even of 'planning'? What sorts of problems are the subject of forecasts? How are the terms in which forecasts are made formulated? What are their effects?

At least four possible functions of forecasts might be distinguished. First, a forecast may be concerned with anticipating significant events in one's operating environment so that one may *adapt* to these changes. Second, a forecast may be again concerned with anticipating environmental events, but this time so one may *avert* or *assist* their fulfilment. Third, a forecast may be aimed at creating an image of a possible future environment, so that one may develop the means to *achieve* that future. And finally, a forecast may be more concerned with *influencing the present* than accurately portraying the future; with the audience than with the substantive content of the forecast. It may be employed more as a means of producing some impact on people's action and attitudes than as a valid insight into the future. (In this case a manifest forecast will conceal a latent forecast concerning the evolution of people's action and attitudes and the impact of the manifest forecast.)

These different functions need not be entirely exclusive of each

6

other, of course. What I have done here is draw distinctions between what Popper[1] calls prophecies and technological predictions, between what Jantsch[2] calls exploratory and normative forecasts, and between prophecies, predictions, and plans on the one hand and propaganda on the other.

'Coping' forecasting is a strategy that would be necessitated by a lack of control over one's operative environment. Not being able, for example, to influence the increase in car ownership in the population at large, the authorities in charge of a recreation area may want to know its future levels in order to cope with potential increases in traffic flows.

Anticipating changes may aid the rational development of policies appropriate to environmental change. 'Changing' forecasting is possible where some degree of control over the environment may be exercised. For example, Galbraith[3] argues that the growth of powerful giant corporations in recent times has meant that industry can now manipulate consumer demands and government economic policies to a much larger extent than could the small businesses of the past, which were forced to adapt. Likewise state authorities, of course, may use forecasts of population growth or of car ownership either to cope with these contingencies or to attempt to influence them (for example through family allowances and taxation policy).

What I might here have called 'creative' forecasting – the creation of images of particular futures and the delineation of how they may be achieved – is more generally known as *normative forecasting*. This is sometimes described as if one started off with a blueprint for an ideal future, and then traced a path backwards from that future to the present. In contrast the 'exploratory' approaches outlined above start from the present and project particular images of the future out of particular trends or developments. In practice, however, normative forecasts are not simply plans or blueprints: it is not possible to control every single parameter of a complex system, and some exploratory projections are required for those aspects of the environment that cannot be controlled. Thus Jantsch[4] points out that present levels of need are often inadequate as goals for the future: instead the future levels of these needs should be considered where future levels of provision are being normatively forecast. If the size and age distribution of the population are changing, it is ill-conceived to think of futures in which new recreation facilities are being provided to meet the unsatisfied (age-related) demands of the present population.

Forecasts may also, as I pointed out above, be intended as propaganda for a particular cause. This need not mean that the forecast involved has no validity as a forecast, although in many cases it is likely that an image of the future is propagated to secure particular ends, without its sponsor having much faith in it. Recent doomsday forecasts may be employed to encourage people to submit to austerity or erosions of civil rights. Forecasts of economic growth, by way of contrast, have been used to counter demands for greater economic equality, by promising painless redistributions of wealth in the future. Technocrats may advance the notion of a 'post-industrial society' in which their own colleagues will guide social change by means of new intellectual technologies.[5] A forecast can serve to mystify or legitimate social change. Unpleasant presents are the price of progress, investments for the future; social costs are necessitated by 'technological imperatives' rather than resulting from human decisions.

As may be inferred from this I am by no means advocating that futures studies are inevitably a good thing. Many forecasts and images of the future are produced on behalf of specific groups, and may serve to advance their cause at the expense of others. However, if we agree that some human interests are worth advancing, it is difficult to see how this could be accomplished without some forecasting of future contingencies. Futures studies may actually help people articulate and advance their interests. This does not necessarily mean that existing forecasting techniques should be taken from the most up-to-date literature and feverishly applied: techniques developed for one set of purposes may not apply to other ends or circumstances.

Teleology and techniques

An adequate history of the future has yet to be written. Perkin[6] has argued that there have been three main eras in social forecasting, if forecasting is considered to be a logical construction of the future from past events. Macro-forecasts, holistic views of future society, he considers to be a product of the Enlightenment, whether imbued with the notion of progress (which he traces through to Marxian and Fabian socialism) or that of Malthusian pessimism. These macro-forecasts were, according to Perkin, intuitive and highly aggregated. In contrast micro-forecasts, increasing in influence from the early demographers and actuaries to the development of government economic planning after the First World War, are analytical and disaggregative. Micro-forecasts involve the study and projection of individual components of social change, and achieved prominence after the Second World War with econometrics, operational research, and social planning. More recently there has been a revival of macro-forecasting, which he sees as stimulated by awareness of exponential growth, limited natural resources, continuing massive international disparities, and the overturning of many micro-forecasts by unprecedented events such as the 'energy crisis' – which showed that basic assumptions of economic micro-forecasts, and the hosts of forecasts derived from these, might be overturned by changes in international politics and other areas. The new macro-forecasting strives to integrate different areas and analyses using sophisticated methodologies in place of intuition: once again the ideas of progress and decline loom large.

Without being a historian – perhaps because I am not – I would disagree with many of Perkin's assessments, while still finding his three-stage analysis useful. In contrasting earlier with modern macro-forecasts, he raises some interesting points. While it is unfair to describe all of the earlier macro-forecasts as intuitive – Adam Smith and Karl Marx did derive their prescriptions from detailed formal analyses – these did share the property of being holistic. In contrast, many contemporary macro-forecasts consist of a combination and interconnection of micro-forecasts. To expand on this point, we have the spectacle of elaborate computer models built up from a combination of essentially unrelated subsystems (population, economy, social change, etc.), rather than from a consciously integrated social theory. Often we find that the different subsystems of models used in urban planning, as well as in forecasting the world's future, are not themselves based on explicit theories, but simply attempt to replicate empirical regularities.

Possibly the changing character of futuristic activity that Perkin points to can be understood in terms of the needs of the three eras concerned. I would like to offer some suggestions as to how this might be conceived, while stressing the need for further study of these issues. The nineteenth century was a time of industrialization and empire-building, and the economic dogma of the ruling class was *laissez-faire*. Why plan when the invisible hand is in action? The functions of images of the future led to three types of forecast.

First, there were forecasts of growing wealth, welfare, and rationality, which were employed by conservatives to postpone

9

state intervention and by reformers to demonstrate the feasibility of amelioration of the worst excesses of industrialism. Second, there were the revolutionary forecasts of Marx and his colleagues, which proposed that the unregulated capitalist economy would inevitably break down under its own internal contradictions. Third were the reactionary forecasts of Malthusians, using a pessimistic image of limits to the expansion of human society as an argument against social reformers and in support of the waning landed aristocracy. In each case macro-forecasts were advanced, although for widely different purposes and in the interests of different people.

Macro-forecasts were of the essence because what was being established in the nineteenth century was a new kind of society. These images of its future were employed in the hope of mobilizing support or opposition to industrial capitalism. With such holistic concerns, it is no wonder that micro-forecasts were less prominent (although they played some role in ameliorative social policy).

As the twentieth century developed, however, the emerging society took on a different form. In particular, technology made vast strides and the competition of small industries was increasingly displaced by large-scale enterprises, while the Western countries engaged in bitter feuds over overseas territories, investments, and resources. These conflicts erupted into the First World War in which state intervention became vital. Large national interests were increasingly to require support from national governments in the form of planning. In America the pioneering work of William F. Ogburn[7] in the interwar years anticipated much contemporary futures research. (He was an early exponent of sophisticated trend extrapolations and regression analyses, and impressively antedated the 'social indicators movement', technological forecasting, and technology assessment.)

But, as Perkin points out, the Second World War was the occasion for micro-forecasting to 'take off'. This took several forms as the technology of computing, the techniques of operational research, the experience of wartime national planning and the Keynesian revolution in economics all added to the development of analytic capabilities. Planning on the part of government was used to ward off further depressions and maintain employment and economic growth. Industry too required its materials, manpower, and markets. With the growth of expenditure on education, health, armaments, and nationalized industries, micro-forecasts of population employment structures, regional growth, transport, and so on became increasingly sought.

Yet such micro-forecasts themselves prove insufficient as we move towards the present. Perkin has chronicled the failure of highly specific forecasts to achieve reliability in such cases as educational and manpower forecasts. There are other factors creating a demand for new syntheses, however. These are prominent where managers and planners are simultaneously concerned with multiple aspects of complex systems such as cities, nations, and international systems.

The 'social indicators movement' and the 'systems movement' arose.[8] Urban forecasting developed as a rapid growth area in planning research, stimulated by developments in computing and financial incentives from central government, which latter policies reflected an attempt to cope with the environmental and social problems of industrialization and the motor car (viz. the large number of transportation studies).[9] Local authorities have been both pragmatically and legally driven to engage in long-term forecasting and planning as population and industry have shifted and transformed.

Forecasting for national planners took several turns. There was the development of econometrics, as Keynesian management was seen as needed to stimulate investment and build infrastructures for industry. However, more important precursors of contemporary futures studies sprang out of military growth (which was itself justified by Keynesian theories). Techniques of model-building and systems analysis, which were soon to be brought to bear on urban planning and social policy, were developed as the military and the aerospace industries turned to complex problems of co-ordinating technological and human systems that could not be handled simply by extrapolations. The less formal techniques of scenario-building and gaining were also reared in this environment.

For many years following the war, multinational corporations were growing in a relatively unrestrained way. While there was much interest in applying Keynesian and other theories to forecasting and planning development in the poor countries, the future of the whole world was not so much a topic for macro-forecasts. More recently, however, there has been turbulence in international relations, especially as European and Japanese-based companies arose to challenge American ones, as the monetary system gradually broke down, and as some producers of raw materials (notably oil) began acting in a concerted way to secure revenues. One consequence of this is that multinational corporations have been turning *en masse* to macro-economic modellers for short-term forecasts of inflation, exchange rates, and markets in different countries.[10]

Concurrently there has been a revival of concern in forecasting the future of the whole world system. The few images of the world future produced by academics in the 1960s stem from either the tradition of strategic forecasting of technological and international changes, mixed with notions of state management of the post-industrial society (e.g. Herman Kahn's work),[11] or the early environmental movement (e.g. Paul Ehrlich's work).[12] More recently, and particularly since the 'energy crisis', there has been a number of attempts to tackle the problems of the world in what is described as a 'holistic' way, bringing the techniques of systems analysis and computer modelling to bear.

While several computer models of the world are in existence,[13] the best-known models are those of the Club of Rome.[14] These forecasts revive Malthusian ideas, and, not surprisingly, some commentators have seen the Club of Rome as an organization speaking for those organizations whose power is waning in the international arena.[15] Their 'Limits to Growth' study, sponsored by the Volkswagen Foundation, was heavily promoted internationally; members of the Club have admitted that its doomsday forecasts were propagated so as to achieve a dramatic impact on the public and politicians even though they did not necessarily subscribe to the predictions offered themselves. At present the Club is busy selling a more sophisticated model to various governments as a planning tool, and is trying to influence the debate over setting up a new world trading system with its project on the 'Revised International Order'. These new models of the future – whose holism is more the aggregation of various micro-forecasts than the product of integrated social theory – are focused on physical limits to world development, and are accompanied by pleas for organization and moral regeneration to combat economic disorder. They are used to support proposals for international regulation of resources and stabilization of prices, for the guaranteeing of rights over the seabed, for educating the public to accept declining living standards, and for acceptance of massive continuing inequalities between rich and poor countries.

Appraising forecasts and techniques

In this section I will describe some conclusions that I have reached about futures research, and situate these conclusions within an account of the STAFF programme within which I have been working.[16] (STAFF is acronymous for Social and Technological Alternatives for the Future.)

The Science Policy Research Unit was set up in 1966 by members of the University of Sussex, both natural and social scientists, who were interested in problems of science policy such as the 'technology gap', the transfer of technology from rich to poor countries, processes of innovation, and so on. In 1971 the STAFF programme was begun, and this currently (1976) consists of a core group of six workers with relevant research and inputs provided by up to twenty others. The genesis of this programme lay in the realization that studies of science policy and technological forecasting that were to have any practical significance for policy-makers must take into account the patterns of future social changes.

The forecasting team decided in 1971 to concentrate first on examining existing futures studies and techniques. This took the form of attempting to evaluate the different approaches to the future that were available, and to understand exactly what were the debates about the future of the world. At this time the initial publicity for the first Club of Rome reports was building up, so it was thought useful to focus the efforts of the team on appraising these works.[17] This provided an opportunity for co-ordination of members of the group working mainly on: systems analysis and modelling, economics, food and agriculture, materials and natural resources, energy, pollution, population, and social dynamics. Hindsight studies of the accuracy and limitations of past forecasts in several of these areas were undertaken, as well as analysis of the assumptions underlying the MIT computer models under scrutiny.[18]

The subsequent methodological analyses carried out by the STAFF group have taken several paths, of which several have been reported in book form. First has been detailed analysis of all the major efforts at understanding world problems by computer modelling.[19] Second has been a more general study of available methods in social and technological forecasting.[20] Third has been a study of images of the future in social science, which particularly investigates claims that we are moving towards a post-industrial society in which extensive knowledge about future possibilities will be yielded by quantitative social research.[21] Rather than describe the contents of these volumes and associated work, I will attempt to show some of the general conclusions about forecasting which I would draw from them. I will subsequently outline the approach to studying the future which the STAFF group has itself taken in consequence of these analyses.

The first conclusion, which is so basic as to be an assumption for all that follows, is that we cannot predict the long-term future. The future is to be made, not to be observed through scientific instruments. The only useful predictions are conditional predictions, which are statements along the lines of 'if x, then y will happen'. Conditional predictions may be straightforward assumptions or even truisms about the causal relationship between x and y, or they may be the conclusions of lengthy analysis. They may be tentative or definite, inputs for further study, suggestive formulations, or policy evaluations.

When considering social forecasting, I have elsewhere[22] used the term 'prediction' to describe forecasts which project a single broad image of the future, which assume that the future is narrowly banded by deterministic parameters. For example, many social scientific studies of the future rely upon historicist notions of a single trend in the evolution of societies, attributing future changes in social organization to technological causes. Indeed, technological determinism is a recurrent approach in contemporary futurology. Even technology assessment is more generally considered to be an approach to making choices between technologies on the basis of their potential impacts on society rather than to be a possible aid to designing technologies on the basis of desired goals for society. More generally, one consequence of attempting to make forecasting predictive, is the development of images of at best a narrow range of futures (reflecting, perhaps, the consequences of adapting in different ways to an inevitable environment) rather than a set of exploratory alternative futures, or of desirable normative futures and the routes to them.[23]

Perhaps this is a good place to consider trend extrapolation. This is of course the most familiar exploratory forecasting technique. An example relevant to the theme of this conference is Leicester's projections of world tourist flows.[24] Applying an exponential curve to historical growth rates in tourism he obtains the figure of 1,700 million tourist arrivals in the world by the turn of the century (as compared to the 1970 level of 200 million). This curve assumes continuation of the rapid historical growth rate. In contrast, by application of a logistic curve, which assumes that a ceiling will be attained, he suggests an alternative projection of 300 million arrivals.

This example highlights the impact and problems of extrapolations. On the one hand there is the dramatic forecast that if current apparently exponential trends persist, that if the processes generating them continue to act in the same way, then some horrendous and unlikely future will materialize.[25] A logistic curve is one way of avoiding such problems of extrapolating growth; many social phenomena have been found to follow logistic-type paths. But the problem is then shifted to one of specifying the manner in which decelerating forces will operate, the levels of growth at which a ceiling is likely to be reached. Sometimes limiting cases can be found: the number of holidaymakers at any one time cannot exceed the total population!

Over the course of this century, and especially since the last war, economic growth in the west has proceeded at an unprecedented rate (although by no means uninterruptedly). During these years, many social phenomena concerned with leisure have shown exponential growth trends.[26] Others have shown periods of declining activity after initial exponential growth as their functions have been replaced by other phenomena: for example, cinema by television. It would generally seem that trend extrapolation will be more reliable the greater the past experience that is being drawn upon, and the shorter the time-span being forecast.[27] It must be borne in mind that vital aspects of this past experience may lack continuity into the future (for example, economic growth), and that past experience may be a poor guide to competitive innovation. The vulnerability of a trend to perturbations from outside factors must be considered, which essentially means taking into account the casual processes generating the trend. Of course these strictures apply to the use of extrapolations in forecasting, rather than in using data to shock people.

More sophisticated exploratory forecasting techniques do not simply relate changes in one variable to time, but attempt to relate together different variables as they change over time. Changes in income, in car ownership, and in vacation time might be related to future patterns of visiting holiday resorts or parks, by employing multiple regression, causal path analysis, and so on. While making a real step beyond simple extrapolations, such approaches raise problems of their own: the need for adequate data (often long-term forecasts are based upon data that is largely collected from only one point in time, often surrogates for important variables are employed), the selective attention paid to quantified variables (which is often reflected in the attitude that the only impacts of change that need be worried about are 'hard', numerically expressed effects), and the assumptions of continuity both within the relationships between the variables involved and in the environmental inputs to the forecast.

Rather than treat each of a wide range of techniques separately, I will present some more conclusions drawn from the study of such techniques. We have already seen that predictions are insufficient, that some understanding of the causes of change must replace pure empiricism in forecasting,[28] and that we need to go beyond straightforward technological and economic determinism. Further to this, futures studies often mystify rather than expose the problems they are dealing with. For example, in Delphi studies the judgements of 'experts' are combined to yield predictions about the most likely dates of particular changes or events occurring. The sorts of assumptions that these 'experts' are using are often masked in this procedure. So, also, is the judgement of what 'expertise' actually is, when social forecasts are being made. Delphi forecasts are often reflections of nothing more than the crudest forms of technological determinism.

Mystification is particularly prone to happen when high methodology is being employed. The 'Limits to Growth' study really tells us no more than a back-of-the-envelope calculation would: that an exponential curve will always intersect a straight-line trend at some point. The Club of Rome commissioned an expensive computer study in order to utilize the authoritative aura of modern technology to sell this conclusion – and, in the process, to disguise assumptions about the essential invariance of these two trends. More recent computer models are vastly more complex, and it can take detailed analysis to reveal the numerous hidden assumptions that inform their forecasts and policy prescriptions.

The more recent Club of Rome work (by Mesarovic and Pestel),[29] for example, comes to pessimistic conclusions about the abilities of Third World countries to feed their populations. If one investigates the bases for these, it turns out that very questionable assumptions are involved in the model – very low estimates of potentially arable land and high specifications of subsistence nutrition levels are among the factors combining to give these results.

It can be almost impossible for the audience of such a forecast to understand what assumptions and value-judgements are built into it without spending much effort on highly technical investigations. Yet we may be sure than any model of a large social system, whether it be of a city or a planet, will contain controversial and essentially political assumptions. We need to stimulate informed debate about such issues, which might perhaps initially proceed through the mutual criticism of independent forecasting groups. What is also required is to demystify expertise itself in this area.[30] People need to be encouraged to question 'purely technical' decisions, and to assert the role of values in futures creation. To this end public debate about alternative futures is vital, and this debate should take forms above that of simply choosing between different options handed down by experts and policy-makers.

Related to these problems of mystification and expertise, and the associated technocratic flavour and practice of much futures research, are other limitations on the ability of futures research to contribute to the creation of a more human future. For example, there is the frequent overselling of methods and studies. Delphi technique is a particular example of a dubious methodology that has been widely promoted but sparsely evaluated. Forecasts have often been promoted with little admission of the tentative nature of their conclusions. I suspect that the net outcome of such circumstances is often a kind of fatalism, in which people decide that there is no way of attaining any more valid insight into the future beyond their 'native' optimism or pessimism. Associated with the emphasis upon single methods and techniques is often the restriction of forecasting to quantitative approaches. The image of the future is defined purely by numerical variables – and, in the extremes of cost-benefit analysis, these variables are all transformed into monetary values (calculated in a purely technical manner by the best experts of course). One common consequence of this is a humanist revulsion against the idea of bringing rationality into policy-making by the use of long-term forecasting. Unfortunately this often leads to a relinquishing of any image of the future to the technocrats.

Alternative futures

I want to conclude by briefly describing the ways in which the STAFF programme has developed its futures-orientation in the light of these conclusions.

A central feature of our approach is that it is explicitly normative and focused on alternative futures. Research into the future is inevitably value-laden, and need be no less rigorous for confronting this fact. One role of a forecasting group can be to stimulate and improve the level of discussion about the future, to enter the ongoing debate about where the world might or should go, and to try and make it possible for more people to play a meaningful role in this debate.

Two values have informed much of our work on world futures. The first is the value of material welfare, that people's basic requirements for food, shelter, clothing, and security should be met. This has meant looking at the question of economic growth: is high economic growth desirable? Are we destroying the world with industrialization and technology, or are these the only ways to meet the needs of the human race? The second is the value of equality, in the sense of reducing the disparities between and within nations. Are inequalities functional or inevitable components of the world system? Can people effectively participate in creating their future if they are underprivileged in respect of economic power, and can futures reflect broadly human needs if they have been created largely by a minority of the world's inhabitants?

These values have meant that we have been drawn into two debates: the debate about economic growth, and that about world development. We have tackled this problem by looking at four alternative profiles of the future, taking a long-term view of up to a century. The first is a world of high economic growth in which current international equalities are maintained or even increased, the sort of picture that might emerge from extrapolating postwar trends. We also consider a high-growth world in which inequalities are significantly reduced; a low-growth egalitarian world; and a low-growth inegalitarian world. Futures which fit into each of these four profiles can be found in the contemporary futures literature.

We believe that it is necessary to look at questions of the long-term future options in order to provide a context for short-term choices. For example, looking at these four profiles of the future gives us insights into conditions under which exploratory forecasting techniques might become invalid: the circumstances when a given extrapolation ceases to hold, for example. I should add that in consequence of our review of forecasting techniques we concluded that no single method was suitable for all our needs, and that different problems call for different combinations of methods. Likewise our work has inputs from a large number of disciplines, so that we may hope to avoid crude determinisms in our forecasts.

Three sectors of the world economy are vitally relevant directly to questions of material welfare and, indirectly, through trading and other links, to questions of world equality. These are food, energy, and materials resources, and members of the programme are involved in the study of the social questions and technological possibilities in each sector. Alternative courses of action in each sector are being assessed in terms of their social and environmental impacts and pre-requisites, and the contribution that they might make to attaining each of the four profiles. More specific work is also carried out on other sectors: transport, military technology, climatology, health, and communications, for example. This work is of value in giving the Unit a problem-centred, interdisciplinary approach, and in allowing workers to bear in mind both long- and short-term issues.

Working with eclectic techniques and a range of specific sectors, we have found in the four profiles of the future a means of integrating our work. However, the four profiles are clearly too oversimplified to serve as viable images of the future. On the basis of our review of forecasting methodologies[31] we were drawn to the generation of scenarios – future 'histories' – as a means of illuminating alternatives and critical choices, of making futures studies comprehensible and free of the mystique of high methodology, and of simply opening our own and others' minds to wider horizons.[32]

Moving from these four profiles of future worlds to scenarios, in which the way in which these worlds could come about and their detailed appearance, is a big step. It involves taking into account not only the considerations raised by analysis of the three economic sectors, but also social and political possibilities. Yet there is no consensus among social scientists as to how the world works. Our approach has been to identify three major world-views, or paradigms, from the social science literature – especially drawing upon macroeconomics – and to consider what possibilities exist for moving towards each profile if the world were actually to operate along the lines these suggest.[33]

In the economic literature these world-views go under the labels of the neoclassical, Keynesian, and Marxist approaches. The fundamental assumptions of these approaches are shared by particular sociological schools and traditions of political analysis. Functionalist theory in sociology shares the view of a consensual society, social evolution by diffusuion of the most adaptive ideas and technologies, and an ideal of *laissez-faire*, that is held by neoclassical economics and pluralist political theory. A vision of society as containing the conflicts of many interest groups, and of needing regulation and mechanisms of countervailing power if social problems are not to accumulate is shared by Keynesian economists, political liberals, and sociological theorists of post-industrial society. Marxism is a self-consciously holistic theory, extending throughout social science disciplines with its focus on the dialectical interplay of ideology and class conflict.

Our recent work, then, has involved studying the contours of four views of the future through these three perspectives, and contrasting the idealized images of the future found in the literature of social and political theory with the possibilities and constraints identified in socio-economic sectors. We are thus trying to avoid the problem of developing pseudo-holistic alternative futures by the aggregation of micro-forecasts which may rest upon different theoretical bases. Instead the three paradigms offer three distinctive broad world-views that subsume the different 'subsystems' of international relations, trading patterns, institutional changes, population, social conflict, choice of technologies, and so on. Our aim is to develop images of alternative futures that are openly tied to assumptions of fact and value, and thus to encourage and help people to evaluate their own assumptions about the future of the world and to play a part in creating their own futures.

Notes

1 Karl Popper, *The Poverty of Historicism*, London, Routledge & Kegan Paul, 1957.
2 Erich Jantsch, *Technological Forecasting in Perspective*, Paris, OECD, 1967. The distinctions drawn between coping, changing, and creating attitudes to the future have been inspired by some ideas presented by Warren Ziegler at the World Futures Studies Federation Conference in Dubrovnik, April 1976.
3 John Kenneth Galbraith, *The New Industrial State*, London, André Deutsch, 1972.
4 Jantsch, *Technological Forecasting in Perspective*.
5 Galbraith, *The New Industrial State*.
6 H. Perkin, 'The history of social forecasting' in Christopher Freeman, Marie Jahoda, and Ian Miles, *Progress and Problems in Social Forecasting*, London, SSRC, 1976.
7 I have described Ogburn's work in chapter 4 of *The Poverty of Prediction*, Farnborough, Saxon House, 1975.
8 I have described the contemporary social indicators scene in chapters 4 and 5 of *The Poverty of Prediction*, and also in Solomon Encel, Pauline K. Marstrand, and William Page, *The Art of Anticipation*, London, Martin Robertson, 1975, chapters 11 and 12.
9 See Marcial Echenique, 'Urban development models: fifteen years of experience', in Richard Baxter, Marcial Echenique, and Janet Owers, *Urban Development Models*, Hornby, The Construction Press, 1975.

10 For example, see 'The trouble with forecasting world economies', *Business Week*, no. 2429, 26 April 1976.

11 Herman Kahn, *Thinking About the Unthinkable*, London, Weidenfeld, 1962; Herman Kahn and Anthony Wiener, *The year 2000*, New York, Macmillan, 1967; Herman Kahn and Brian Bruce-Biggs, *Things to Come*, New York, Macmillan, 1972.

12 Paul Ehrlich, *The Population Bomb* New York, Ballantine, 1968; Paul Ehrlich and Ann H. Ehrlich, *Population/ Resources/Environment*, San Francisco, W. H. Freeman, 1970.

13 For the critical overview from the STAFF group, see John Clark and Sam Cole, *Global Simulation Models*, Chichester, John Wiley, 1975. This volume contains some interesting insights into the technical and sociological aspects of computer modelling.

14 Dennis Meadows, Donella Meadows, and Jorgen Randers, *The Limits to Growth*, London, Earth Island, 1972; Mihajlo Mesarovic and Edward Pestel, *Mankind at the Turning Point*, New York, Dutton/Readers Digest Press, 1974.

15 See especially Robert Golub and Joe Townsend, 'Malthus, multinationals and the Club of Rome', reading 21 in *Systems Modelling, Readings*, Open University, Milton Keynes (a publication for the Third Level Course in Technology); and Emma Rothschild, 'How doomed are we?', *New York Review of Books*, 26 June, 1975.

16 The account of the STAFF programme here provided is not an official account agreed upon by all members of the team. It is a partial account which I offer so as to illuminate the ideas on forecasting which I am here presenting. Contributions to the development of these ideas have been made by every member of the team, in which a lively debate is continuing about the nature and role of forecasting.

17 An early publication from the Club of Rome, anticipating the Meadows' work in method and conclusions, was Jay W. Forrester, *World Dynamics*, New York, Wright-Allen Press, 1971.

18 The results of this study were published in H. S. D. Cole *et al.*, *Thinking About the Future*, London, Sussex University Press, 1973. An American edition, *Models of Doom* is published by Universe Books, New York, and contains a reply by Dennis and Donella Meadows.

19 Clark and Cole, *Global Simulation Models*.

20 See Encel, Marstrand, and Page, *The Art of Anticipation*.

21 See Popper, *The Poverty of Prediction*.

22 ibid.

23 Even Herman Kahn's apparent abundance of scenarios boils down to one 'surprise-free' image of the future, and a number of largely catastrophic deviations from this trend.

24 Colin Leicester, 'Tourism in 2003 A.D.', presented to the BTA seminar on strategic planning, November 1973.

25 'Some forces must be operative to produce a marked or regular trend, especially if it has been long continued. Even if these forces are not fully known, yet they must exist and presumably will continue to be effective.' M. Clawson and J. L. Knetsch, from their study 'Economics of

outdoor recreation', quoted in Thomas L. Burton, *Experiments in Recreation Research*, London, George Allen & Unwin, 1971. Burton provides an interesting discussion of recreation forecasting techniques.

26 Or to be more precise, successive epochs of exponential growth. See Robert L. Hamblin, R. Brooke Jacobson, Jerry L. L. Miller, *A Mathematical Theory of Social Change*, New York, Wiley-Interscience, 1973. Tables 5.5 and 6.3 are concerned with leisure systems in the United States. This book discusses in detail social change processes which may be described in terms of exponential, logistic, and other trends.

27 In lieu of genuine time-series data, cross-sectional information on how, for example, younger or richer or better educated people behave is sometimes used as a basis for extrapolations. See chapter 11 of *The Art of Anticipation* for a discussion of this approach. In social forecasting and marketing it is often implicitly employed when more affluent countries are taken to provide an image of the future of poorer countries.

28 The point has been made that the variables most useful in predicting change need not always be those most relevant to understanding it. For example, voting intentions may be a better predictor of actual voting than other variables such as class and age. This sort of situation is likely to arise when very short-term forecasts are involved, rather than in the long term.

29 See Mesarovic and Pestel, *Mankind at the Turning Point*.

30 See David and Ruth Elliot, *The Control of Technology*, London and Winchester, Wykeham Publications, 1976.

31 See Encel, Marstrand, and Page, *The Art of Anticipation*.

32 One member of our group has done much to advance the methodology of scenario-construction in a more limited field, namely the future of UK passenger transport systems and the potential of electric vehicles. See J. I. Gershuny, *Toward a Social Assessment of Technology*, London, HMSO, 1976. Carried out for the Programmes Analysis Unit, Harwell.

33 Many sources were used in the identification of world views. Among these are: Michael Barret-Brown, *The Economics of Imperialism*, Harmondsworth, Penguin, 1975; David and Ruth Elliot, *The Control of Technology*; Robert Gilpin, 'Three models of the Future', *International Organization*, Winter 1975 (vol. 29); Paul Lazarsfeld, *Main Trends in Sociology*, London, George Allen & Unwin, 1973; Ralph Miliband, *The State in Capitalist Society*, London, Weidenfeld & Nicolson, 1969; Irving Zeitlin, *Rethinking Sociology*, New York, A.C.C., 1973.

Note

The study described in the final section was published as C. Freeman and M. Jahoda (eds), *World Futures: the Great Debate*, London, Martin Robertson, 1978; for a later approach, see S. Cole and I. Miles, *Worlds Apart*, Brighton, Wheatsheaf, 1984.

2

Technological change and the future (1980)

TOM STONIER

Introduction

The decade from the mid-1960s to the mid-1970s saw the emergence of a public concern over a constellation of problems which were perceived to threaten human survival. These problems included pollution, impending shortages of critical resources, overpopulation, nuclear annihilation, and repression of personal liberties by increasingly centralized governments. It is the purpose of this paper to point out that although these problems deserve continuing concern, their threat is declining under the impact of advances in science and technology. At the same time, a new set of problems is emerging, of which the most important is the accelerating displacement of labour by the new 'information' technology. Both the problem, and a potential solution, are considered in greater detail.

Environmental accounting

By the late 1960s, there had emerged in most of the western (OECD) countries an environment movement able to articulate its concerns in three basic areas: pollution, potential resource shortages, and overpopulation. Pollution was affecting the air, water, and land with a variety of man-made, or man-caused products such as industrial wastes, chemicals, and sewage, by excessive fertilization and DDT, or just plain litter. On a global scale, DDT, nuclear proliferation, or atmospheric catastrophes threatened the world. Included among these were the destruction of the ozone layer, the possibility of an ice age from too much fine dust in the stratosphere, or conversely, too much carbon dioxide, creating a 'greenhouse effect' which would melt the polar ice caps. A similar polar melt-out could result if sufficient spills from oil tankers reached the polar caps. These concerns, representing a broader, global ecosystems approach, received much impetus, by the publication of Rachel Carson's book *Silent Spring* in 1964.[1]

The second area of concern, shortages of critical resources, included minerals and fuel as well as clean air, water, and good farmland. These concerns became systematized by the publication of *Limits to Growth*[2] and their potential danger was driven home dramatically by the Arab-imposed oil sanctions in late 1973. Finally, overpopulation as a threat was backed by statistics from the UN and other sources, and brought forcefully to the public attention by Paul Ehrlich.[3]

Unlike the more traditonal 'conservation movements', which date back to early in the Industrial Revolution and which involved mainly the rich, the environment movement became broadly based, though still predominantly middle-class. Its primary response to the combination of environmental threats, can be summed up by E. F. Schumacher's phrase 'Small is Beautiful',[4] which served as a paradigm for a whole generation of students.

The environment movement was vital in bringing awareness and public pressure to deal with these problems. As a result, increasingly stringent legislation reduced air and water pollution and severely restricted the use of DDT. Nuclear energy developments slowed and increasing sums of money became available for developing alternative energy sources. At the same time, industry, government, and individuals were motivated to begin serious energy conservation schemes. In addition to these victories, the environment movement could not have foreseen the further technological developments such as computer-based control systems which reduced the requirements for energy and materials. Nor were they able to predict the technologically feasible exploitation of undersea oil reserves and deep ocean minerals. Under the impact of science and technology, the problems have receded in importance and the forecasted critical time span has been pushed back. The breathing space has been enhanced by the fact that a number of western countries have achieved zero population growth.

This does not imply that the problems are solved. Much work remains to be done. Along with the new knowledge of population dynamics and existing resources, technology needs to continue to explore alternative solutions such as solar, wave, and fusion power. Technology now involves substituting information flows for energy and materials: one example involves the use of the telephone instead of the mail or making visits. Another involves reducing fuel consumption by microprocessor-controlled fuel injection systems in automobiles. A third which may develop significantly over the next two decades involves 'telecommuting' by means of home-based computer terminals, by which business can be conducted with the office or even with foreign offices, without leaving the home.

Creating substitutes, such as coal processed into oil, and re-placing copper cables with optical glass fibres, should be considered as prototypes for solving shrinking materials resource problems. Technology can develop other new resources, including a vast expansion of food production in the form of coastal fish farming and making the deserts bloom. As a result of a massive expansion of productivity, sufficient wealth can be produced around the world to effect a demographic shift and permit the attainment of a stable population.

1984

The threat of overpopulation, of pollution, and of resource shortage are not the only problems which face global society. Political repression and nuclear war must also be added to the list of concerns when dealing with the future. Paradoxically, inherent in the very technology which has created these threats lies the solution.

Societies which have undergone the 'electronic revolution' are emerging into a new era, the *communicative era*.[5] One of the parameters for determining whether a country has moved into the communicative era is that the majority of its households possess radio, television, and telephone. Modern transportation facilities, plus the combination of electronic communication and printed word media, yield a highly efficient information network, which becomes very difficult to control from the centre. Add to this an increasingly complex society run by increasingly sophisticated information operatives, and it becomes apparent why an expanding, advanced information network presses one country after another into in-creased democratization. As the communicative era overtakes the Soviet Union and Eastern bloc countries, corresponding changes in the political structure will be observed there as well.

The institution of war

Perhaps the most important shift in the economy of the communicative society relates to the increasing specialization of the global economy, made possible by modern communications and transportation technologies, resulting in a trans-national web of production and services. The economies of the communicative society are having the same impact on the political organization of the globe today, as the rise of mercantilism a few hundred years ago had on the political organization of Western Europe. The present shift from national policies to supra-national policies, as exemplified by the European Community, reflects the fact that national economies are no longer primarily closed systems. The change is accelerated by the shifting military technology. Just as the shift from feudal to nation-states a few hundred years ago was accelerated by gunpowder and other military inventions, so have the traditional defences of the contemporary nation-states been breached by the nuclear missile technology.

Associated with the replacement of the nation-state by larger political units is the decline of large-scale warfare as an institution. Here again the situation is analogous to the decline of that other ancient institution, slavery, which disappeared with the advent of industrialization. The primary social motivation for slavery involved the need for maintaining an extensive economic infrastructure through the use of coerced labour. That noxious social institution could not survive when society found an improved technology, namely the combination of machines and wage labour. A comparable process is taking place today, as nations move from the national economies of the mechanical era into the trans-national productive web characterizing the communicative era. Although it is often couched in ideological terms, the primary social motivation for war always has been the extension of resources (with secondary motivations involving such other factors as status, defence, or revenge). In recorded historical times, whenever one group was sufficiently powerful to deprive another of valuable resources, it was merely a matter of time before that deprivation came to pass. This is no longer true. The vast productivity of technologically advanced societies makes the extension of resources through technological ingenuity not only possible, but much more reliable. It becomes easier to substitute synthetics for raw materials or to grow crops more efficiently than to enter into foreign conquests with the immense destructive risks associated with advanced military technology.[6]

The new threat

The greatest threat to western society at the moment is the rapid displacement of labour by technology. Present trends in unemployment do not represent a mere downturn in business activity or a temporary recession, which will in time correct itself. Jobs in the manufacturing sector are, and have been for some time, on the way out. What we see now is an acceleration of a historical process which can be traced back at least a couple of centuries, a process which involves a shift in the principal economic activities from manipulating land, to manipulating machines, to manipulating information.[7]

At the beginning of the eighteenth century, over 80 per cent of the workforce laboured on farms to feed the rest.[8] Today, it takes less than 3 per cent in the US to feed not only the rest of the country, but much of the world as well.[9,10] This dramatic shift reflects the effective coupling of new technologies to better informed farm operatives. The American farmer works no harder than his forefathers. He sits in an air-conditioned tractor, listening to a transistor radio, while he pulls a combine harvester. However, he is doing as much work as fifty men breaking their backs using a sickle. He has at his disposal the use of fertilizers and pesticides, information on the weather, hybrid seeds, and world market conditions. The modern farmer is highly productive because he is a highly skilled operative who has available to him a wide variety of technological back-ups.

Over the past three centuries, largely as a result of this increased efficiency in agriculture, the bulk of the labour force shifted from farms to the manufacturing industries. The new job market was created by the Industrial Revolution. That revolution in turn was marked by the invention of the steam engine, not just another piece of technology but a 'metatechnology'.[11] Steam coupled to existing machinery made it many times more powerful. Coupled to a loom, it became a power loom; coupled to a wagon, it became a locomotive. Ultimately, the increasing mechanization in industry, largely over the last hundred years, brought about a further shift in labour from the manufacturing to the service industries. Today an even more dramatic shift is taking place as a result of a new technology.

The new metatechnology

The appearance of the microprocessor is having a profound effect on labour patterns. The microprocessor does nothing radically different from its progenitor, the computer. But it does it faster, more

27

reliably and more cheaply. Coupled to existing machinery it greatly increases productivity.

A new technology displaces an older one as a function of how much better it is. If a new technology is only 10 per cent better, it displaces existing technology very slowly, if at all. If it is 50 per cent better, then it begins to make inroads, although the process may take decades. When it is many times better, as clearly the new microprocessor technology is, then it moves very rapidly indeed.

Among the new microprocessor-based technologies emerging are industrial and office robots. Industrial robots, once they become cheap enough, have enormous advantages. They can operate in dangerous situations and under inhuman conditions. Moreover, a welding robot, for example, can be 'shown' how to weld a wing on to a car in an assembly line by having the motions traced for it *once* by a master welder (the perfect apprentice). From that point on, it carries on the function 24 hours a day, 365 days a year, without going on strike, tea-break, or sick leave (unless designed badly). Investment costs can be recouped in a year and a half. Additional robots monitor lining-up procedures and are programmed to signal difficulties or to shut down production. Indeed, there already exist entire sections of such plants in Western Europe and Japan, virtually devoid of human operatives. Other robots can monitor stocks and, by means of terminal links with suppliers, re-order parts. Specifications for cars can also be received directly from retailers, thus eliminating many middle-line managers as well as workers on the shop floor.

Equally startling will be the displacement in offices; as recent experience has shown, typing pools can be cut in half, and achieve an overall 300 per cent increase in output. The corporation's investment in this case may be zero, since the microprocessor can be bought on time, out of the savings on staff.[12]

The effect of these changes is evident in the statistics of, for example, the textile industry. In Bradford, an annual production of £200,000,000 (approximate current prices) of wool 100 years ago took 20,000 to 30,000 workers.[13] Compare this to the synthetic fibre plants at Teesside where the same volume can be produced by 600 to 1,000 workers. That is, it takes only about 3 per cent of the amount of labour to produce comparable amounts of wealth in manufacturing industries. That 3 per cent figure in terms of labour requirement is almost the identical figure which we have seen in the US in terms of farm labour. As the electronic revolution proceeds with the microprocessor at its core, comparable statistics will be attained throughout all the manufacturing industries. It is highly probable that by early in the next century it will require no more than 10 per cent of the labour force to provide us with all our material needs, that is, all the food we eat, all the clothing we wear, all the textiles, appliances, etc. In the near future, the vast majority of labour will be engaged as information operatives, that is, workers who make their living by creating, organizing, applying, or transmitting information: scientists, managers, engineers, librarians, computer programmers, technical salesmen; all those in formal education and the mass media, etc. As a result of the burgeoning information technology, industrial labour is now shifting to adapt to the new productive systems, which require greater mental and less manual effort. This shift in labour is parallel to the historical one from farm to factory.

Modern productive systems are becoming less dependent on land, labour, and capital for their primary input. Instead, they become increasingly dependent on organized information. The displacement of labour in the form of technology has already been referred to. Similarly, the requirement for land, both for agriculture and housing, becomes reduced by advancing technology such as skyscrapers, multi-storey chicken farms, and mechanical farming. The advent of the tractor released millions of acres used for growing horse fodder. The acreage released will be even greater with the advent of single-cell protein to feed cattle. Finally, capital moves today not in terms of the transfer of large sums of gold or even money, but in the transmission of credit information. Post-industrial economies are run primarily on credit, rather than cash transactions. In modern post-industrial society, where labour requirements are beginning to shrink in manufacturing as they did in industrial society for agriculture, the primary input is knowledge, and the most important single resource the post-industrial society has is its human capital and the skills and knowledge it can harness. At the base of all technological skills and back-up is a history of education, and research and development. This trend will accelerate such that in the next century education will become the number one industry and employ about half the total workforce. The education industry will include far more than schools and universities.

The new wealth producers

The Department of Education and Science and its local partners and subsidiaries should begin planning now, how they can become the nation's primary employer. All government departments should begin to develop policies to aid in the shift from farm, and industrial and machine operatives to information operatives by an expansion of the education system.

In order to effect such a change, we must understand that applied science and technology is the major producer of wealth. About 1,000 years ago, northern Europe was a fairly barbaric part of the world. Compared to the Mediterranean, it was poor and backward, largely because it did not have the economic base the Mediterranean area possessed. Northern Europe did, of course, have enormous potential in terms of the fertile grasslands, but these could not become a major resource until the invention of the deep plough and ancillary technology.[14] It was the so-called agricultural revolution of the ninth and tenth centuries which set the stage for wealth creation. This was followed by the rise of mercantilism and the beginning of the ascendancy of northern Europe over Mediterranean Europe. The emergence from the Dark Ages became a reality because technology made into a resource something which had not been a resource before, fertile land. We can say the same thing about North Sea oil. We all know that the British economy (as reflected by the value of sterling) turned around because of the presence of North Sea oil. That oil has been there a long time. It was there before the Battle of Hastings; it was there before there was a Europe; it was there long before there were humans. But it was not a resource. It became a resource only when a sophisticated consumer technology appeared and made oil a valuable commodity, then developed a technology for exploring and finally, extracting oil from under the sea. Here again, technology based on knowledge (organized information) developed a new area of wealth.

By the mid-1980s, we will see a similar phenomenon as we begin mining the deep oceans for manganese, nickel, copper, and other elements. It was not very long ago that elements such as manganese and nickel were not considered particularly valuable, nor for that matter were aluminium and magnesium. Technology is probably *the* most important single factor in increasing capital for any society. Yet the new knowledge is always based on previous knowledge transmitted from one generation to the next, principally by the education system. And that education system is maintained at public expense. The PhDs who develop a new chemical process or electronics system, the engineers who design the plant, the technicians who help in the construction, all will have had their education paid for only to a small extent by the industries which use them. We must understand that the government is not merely important as a political institution, or even as a social institution. It is also a major, perhaps the major economic institution. Much of what passes as profligacy, 'wasting the taxpayers' money by creating huge edifices of government', is really good economics: the government is the only institution able to co-ordinate modern post-industrial economies. In fact, in modern post-industrial systems, the national government may no longer be adequate. Thus, just as we see a drift of firms becoming multinational, we see a similar drift of national governments becoming regional governments such as in the EEC. By the next century, that process should lead to a global association and our children and our grandchildren will all be very grateful for it. The answer to the unemployment problem is to accelerate the shift away from manufacturing and into the information sector of the economy.

The most sensible way to achieve that shift is by a massive expansion of the education system. We should seriously consider doubling the education budget by the mid-1980s and then redoubling it again by the mid-1990s. There are several reasons why this would be both practical and desirable. First, education is labour-intensive and can provide hundreds of thousands of jobs. It is one of the few areas in our society where it makes sense to be labour intensive. A teacher responsible for only twenty students is at least twice as effective as one responsible for forty, and only ten pupils is twice as good again.

The second reason why a massive expenditure on education will solve the unemployment problem is that the bulk of the unemployed are youngsters. To give a figure, between early 1975 and late 1977, those in the under-26 age group unemployed in the EEC jumped from about half a million to two million.[15] Many youngsters who are out of work have been turned off the education system, usually when they were at about middle-school level, some earlier, some later. They can't wait to get out. Simply forcing them to stay in for another year is probably of very little help to them, their classmates, or the teachers. If we designed a truly attractive system, many, hopefully most, young people would stay in education perhaps right through university level. By expanding further and community education, we could attract more mature individuals back into education as well, thereby relieving the welfare rolls still further. Thus the bulk of the unemployed would be constructively engaged, in accordance with a well-established historical tradition (over the last 100 years) in which the average educational level has been rising steadily. Relying solely on such a historical process is inadequate. We need to engage in a deliberate policy of accelerating the up-grading of education for all people, so that it matches the acceleration of labour displaced by technology. Such a policy is crucial for social and economic health.

In addition to expanding education, the government must also expand research and development. It is no good churning out a lot of PhDs and then having no jobs for them. On the other hand, if research and development is coupled to an up-graded education system, then the country can begin to generate new technology and new sources of wealth which will pay for the whole system. Consider the following possibilities.

Current economic analyses are dominated by the assumption that Britain must export manufactured goods, because it must import food. That assumption is not valid if one were to develop technologies which could make Britain a net exporter of food. A combination of single-cell protein production and coastal fish farming could probably make Britain such a net exporter of food.

ICI has a plant in operation now, producing a single-cell protein for cattle supplement.[16] This technology is still in its early stages. The product is as good as, or better than, other feed supplements. However, the price of the single-cell protein is such that it is cheaper than fishmeal or soya-bean meal when soya beans are expensive, but cannot compete when soya beans are cheap. A good deal of Britain's food imports involve food for cattle. More than half of all the cereal consumed in this country is eaten by cattle.[17] Perhaps even more important in the long run is the possibility of coastal fish farming. This is practised to a very limited extent now but could be expanded enormously once we know enough. The technology appears to require much greater inputs of basic knowledge in fields such as limnology, marine biology, ecology, etc.

North Sea oil is needed for the production of energy and of petro-chemicals. Britain is an island on the leeward side of a highly energetic ocean. At the moment, the enormous energy provided by the waves hitting that island goes to waste. The energy is sufficient to provide about fifty megawatts per kilometre.[18] This would be a major source of electrical energy if the existing technology could be made economic. Not only would it provide large amounts of energy, it would provide a large number of jobs in the shipyards, constructing the necessary machinery. This would first have to fill a domestic market, and then, if Britain were first in the field, would be a major export item. Secondly, the technology which converts coal into oil is also quite far along, but only marginally economic. There is no reason why, as the world runs out of oil, and the chemical processes converting the carbon of coal into hydro-carbon of oil become cheaper, that Britain's large coal reserves should not become an important source of wealth. Thus, there are substitutes which could have enormous economic benefit for Britain and the world after the oil runs out.

Envision now that we have developed those four technologies and in consequence Britain becomes wealthy as it continues to be an energy exporter, now also becoming a food exporter.

The function of developing new technologies and industries is not to produce jobs – some jobs will be produced – but the main function is to produce wealth. That wealth generates revenues for the government, which allows it to pay its employees. At present, more than one out of five of us work for the government.[19] In the next century perhaps half, possibly three-quarters, will. The reason is that the labour required to operate the primary and secondary sectors of the economy (foodstuffs, raw materials, and manufacture) will require no more than 10 per cent of the labour force as the processes of mechanization and automation accelerate. The other 90 per cent will be involved either in private entrepreneurial service sectors or (the bulk) working for the government. There is no contradiction in this economically, because what we are achieving in the post-industrial society is the creation of material wealth by robots. Boring work should be left to robots. Human beings should spend most of their time working with each other. Whether that is in the health services, in the education system, or in some other capacity is irrelevant. In any case, the post-industrial society will shift the labour force away from manufacturing, just as the industrial society shifted the labour force away from farming.

Conclusion

The biggest problem confronting British society at the moment is how to transfer labour from the manufacturing industries, where jobs are shrinking at an alarming rate, into the knowledge industries, which need to be subsidized by the government. The most sensible way to do this is through a massive expansion of the education system, which is first of all labour intensive, producing ultimately millions of jobs; secondly, it would keep the young off the labour market; and thirdly, it would create a more versatile labour pool. It would also encourage a more creative use of leisure time, and, finally, it would help to develop the new industries, which would produce the wealth necessary for sustaining the process. The adroit use of technology could make Britain a net exporter of food and energy (even after the North Sea oil runs out). Thus a massive expansion in education, coupled to research and development, becomes a true investment in the future, not only in social terms, but also in pay-back economic terms.

Notes

1   R. Carson, *Silent Spring*, Boston, Houghton Mifflin, 1962.
2   D. I. Meadows, D. H. Meadows, J. Randers and W. W. Behrens, *The Limits to Growth*, New York, Universe Books for Potomac Associates, 1972.
3   P. R. Ehrlich, *The Population Bomb*, New York, Ballantine, 1968.
4   E. F. Schumacher, *Small is Beautiful*, New York, Harper & Row, 1973.
5   T. Stonier, 'The natural history of humanity: past, present and future, Inaugural lecture, University of Bradford, 17 February 1976.
6   T. Stonier, 'Economic and technological prerequisites for achieving political and military stability' in D. Carlton and C. Schaerf (eds), *Arms Control and Technological Innovation*, London, Croom Helm, 1977.
7   T. Stonier, 'Materials production labour requirement in post-industrial society', working paper commissioned by Central Policy Review Staff (Cabinet Office) as reported by K. Owen, *The Times*, 13 November 1978.
8   P. Deane, *The First Industrial Revolution*, Cambridge, Cambridge University Press, 1965.
9   US Department of Commerce, *Statistical Abstract of the United States*, US Government Printing Office, 1977.
10 US Department of Agriculture, *Statistical Bulletin 233: Changes in Farm Production and Efficiency – A Summary Report*, 1970.
11 T. Stonier, 'Changes in Western society: educational implications', in J. Megarry (ed.), *World Yearbook of Education 1979*.
12 J. Franklin and F. M. Jones, 'Word Processing takes Bradford into jet-age', *Municipal and Public Services Journal 1978*, 18 August 1978, pp. 833–5.
13 C. Richardson, *A Geography of Bradford*, University of Bradford, 1976.
14 L. White, *Medieval Technology and Social Change*, Oxford, Clarendon Press, 1962.
15 J. Palmer, 'Their future behind them?', in *The Guardian*, 17 October 1977.
16 D. G. MacLennan, J. S. Gow and D. A. Stringer, 'Methanol-bacterium process for scp', *Process Biochemistry*, June 1973.
17 Ministry of Agriculture, Fisheries, and Food, *Output and Utilisation of Farm Produce in the United Kingdom 1969–70 to 1975–76*, HMSO, 1977.
18 S. H. Salter, D. C. Jeffrey and J. R. M. Taylor, 'The architecture of

nodding duck wave power generators', *Naval Architect*, January 1976, pp. 21–4.

19 Central Statistical Office, *National Incomes and Expenditures 1966–76*, HMSO, 1977.

3

De-skilling and forced leisure: steps beyond class analysis (1984)

CHRIS ROJEK

Neo-Marxist writers are making an important attempt to develop leisure theory within the context of the general de-skilling process, said to be characteristic of capitalist relations of production.[1] However, although their main observations are sound I wish to suggest that the presuppositions and deductions of many of these writers are faulty. By illustrating such deficiencies I will set out an alternative position on the theory of leisure relations under capitalism.[2]

Marx and the cardinal principles of capitalist production

The first imprint of a systematic theory of de-skilling and forced leisure is made by Marx in *Capital*. In that work he submits that the capitalist productive process obeys three cardinal principles:

(1) The governing purpose of management is the accumulation of profit for the capitalist class.
(2) The fragmentation, standardization, and regimentation of the labour process is geared to produce a docile, efficient, and productive workforce.
(3) Capitalist industry and science aims to convert living labour power into capital goods, i.e. mechanized productive power.

Capitalism de-skills labour, and it works the better the more labour it de-skills.

The idea of forced leisure crops up in the context of Marx's discussion of commodity consumption under advanced capitalism.[3]

36

Workers, he argues, engage in two forms of commodity consumption. These are:

(1) Productive consumption, in which the worker consumes commodities in the labour process, for example in expending labour power the worker uses up raw materials and other resources supplied by the capitalist entrepreneur.
(2) Individual consumption, in which the worker allocates the money paid to him for his labour power for his means of subsistence.

Productive consumption assists capital accumulation in a two-fold way. It (a) converts the resources consumed by the worker into commodities with a higher exchange value, and (b) creates a demand for the renewal of expended resources which is supplied by other branches of capitalist industry. It is, therefore, easy to see why Marx classifies productive consumption as an integral part of the general process of capitalist accumulation. It is less easy to see why individual consumption warrants the same conclusion: after all, individual consumption appears to involve the worker in free choice. No one forces the worker to buy the goods and services which the capitalist lays before him. No one obliges the worker to plough back his wages into a system which enslaves him and his family.

Marx supplies at least two counter arguments to forestall this interpretation. First, individual consumption is required for the perpetuation of the working class, and is therefore a necessary condition for capitalist production. Second, what the individual consumes is determined by what the market supplies. Since the market is controlled by the capitalist class, it follows that freedom, choice, and self-determination at the level of individual consumption are illusory. The market will supply only those goods and services which enhance the power of capital. Oppositional forms of collective production and consumption which spring up in the midst of the workers will be treated as mere targets for the forces of capital to attack and colonize.

For Marx then, de-skilling and forced leisure are joined together in a circuit of class exploitation. The capitalist class de-skills workers in the production process in order to maintain and reproduce working-class subordination. At the same time, the capitalist class ensures that workers' disposable income and leisure time is sufficient to (a) replenish their energies, (b) meet the requirements of civil order, and (c) provide a ready market for capitalist entrepreneurs. In sum, working-class leisure is organized and financed by the demands of capitalist accumulation.

De-skilling and forced leisure: the view from Braverman

Marxists certainly do not have a monopoly over the concepts of de-skilling and forced leisure. On the contrary, many non-Marxist writers have recognized and examined the causal connections between unsatisfying work and leisure pursuits.[4] Even so, it is perhaps only Marxist writers who have pursued the links between the connections and class power to their end point. Thus, Adorno and Horkheimer deny the reality of spontaneity and self-determination in leisure because 'the man with leisure has to accept what the culture manufacturers offer him'.[5] Gorz makes a similar point in trying to explain increased working-class leisure time and spending on related goods and services in the post-war period. 'Capitalism', he writes, 'civilizes consumption and leisure to avoid having to civilize social relationships. Alienating men in their work, it is better equipped to alienate them as consumers; and conversely it alienates them as consumers the better to alienate them in work.'[6]

In recent years the Marxist position on de-skilling and forced leisure has perhaps been most powerfully expressed by Braverman.[7] Echoing Marx's analysis in *Capital*, Braverman argues that modern capitalism applies three principles of design and organization in the workplace:

(1) The dissociation of the labour process from the skills of workers, i.e. the attempt to constantly reduce capital's dependence on the abilities of workers by automation, the scientific division of labour, computerization and so on.
(2) The separation of conception from execution, i.e. the monopolization of work knowledge by management and the reduction of work tasks to simple instructions provided and determined by management.
(3) The use of the monopoly over work knowledge to control each step of the labour process and its mode of execution, i.e. the predetermination of work instructions in order to maintain and reproduce the subordination of workers.

Braverman, then, presents a picture of the development of capitalist society in which de-skilling in the workplace becomes ever more systematic and thorough.

His view of leisure relations under capitalism corresponds to his position on de-skilling. Leisure is exploited by the capitalist entrepreneur as a major source for accumulation. 'Corporate institutions', he declares, 'have transformed every means of entertainment into a productive process for the enlargement of capital.'[8] His analysis contains at least three senses in which leisure relations in advanced capitalism may be said to be 'forced':

(1) Choice and self-determination in leisure activities in capitalist society are merely illusory. Leisure practice is determined by the amount of resources, including time and finance, released by the market. In the long run, the market supports only those leisure forms which are consistent with the profit motive. Leisure forms which cannot be commercialized, or which offer an inadequate return on investment, are confined to the margins of society.

(2) Popular forms of leisure which oppose capitalist values are colonized and converted to the *status quo*. 'So enterprising is capital', writes Braverman, 'that even where the effort is made by one or another section of the population to find a way to nature, sport or art through personal activity and amateur or "underground" innovation, these activities are incorporated into the market insofar as possible.'[9]

(3) The imposition of the profit motive onto leisure forms produces 'mediocrity and vulgarity which debases popular taste'.[10] Commercialization forces the quality of mass leisure experience to the 'lowest-common-denominator' level.

Critical commentary

The Marxist tradition on de-skilling and forced leisure focuses on a number of important features of modern leisure relations. Among the most noteworthy are: the false equation of leisure with free time and freedom; the ideological significance of leisure as a release from, or reward for hard work; the incessant commercialization of leisure relations; the lack of excitement in many mass leisure forms; the unequal distribution of leisure resources; the increasing fragmentation and mechanization of popular leisure forms; and the passive, undemanding aspects of many leisure pursuits. These features are explained in terms of class dialectic. Class is held to determine the kinds of jobs people do, the leisure time they have at their disposal and the leisure activities they participate in. By the same token, the development of the productive force of capitalism is fated to expose the real exploitative basis of capitalist society. When the working class becomes conscious of itself, as a class, it will marshal its collective might and create the conditions for a classless society.

All of this is very familiar. But Marxists are often unequivocal about what it actually means for the study of leisure in capitalist society. If the notion that the history of leisure is the history of class struggle means anything, it means that leisure practice is structurally determined. Thus, for example, each clash between working-class youths and the police on the football terraces exposes the axis between working-class subordination and the forces of the state apparatus. Every time the masses slump into their armchairs and tune in to the latest soap opera or format thriller they fulfil the hidden design of capital. The (capitalist) development of the silicon chip hastens Albury's dystopian vision of 'leisure based on computerised war games for unemployed youth, centrally controlled educational curricula for isolated desocialised learning, microprocessor based homemaking gadgets to expand the working day of the woman who works in the home'.[11]

This kind of analysis is explicitly reductive. Everything points to the monotonous reproduction of class surbordination in capitalist society. Against this a powerful Marxist lobby exists which emphasizes the capacity of the working class to manipulate what the capitalist leisure industry grinds out.[12] Leisure practice is examined as a crucial register of the economic and cultural contradictions of capitalism. As such, it is defined as a key agency for raising working-class consciousness and challenging capitalist values. At first sight, this position appears to signify a major and important critical departure from the first view. But what exactly is being claimed here? The control aspect of capitalist leisure forms is recognized. However, in conjunction with it is an apparently conflicting sensitivity to the relative autonomy of leisure relations from the economic base. On the one hand class control, on the other relative autonomy: it is, in short, an untenable position.[13]

The great strength of Marxist theory is that it defines relations of leisure as relations of power. This is in sharp contrast to the dominant tradition in the field which identifies leisure with choice, freedom, spontaneity, and self-determination.[14] The main weakness of Marxist theory, in all of its many forms, is that it prioritizes the class relation and, *ipso facto*, neglects the significance of analytically distinct types of power relation. It is important to be clear about this point. Leisure practice in capitalist society *is* shaped by class struggle. But it is also shaped by other structural forces, notably sexism, racism, nationalism, and the 'requirements' of civilization.

Steps beyond class analysis

In this concluding section I want to outline, in a fairly stark form, an alternative position on leisure theory. It derives from selected strands pulled together from the traditions of figurational sociology, psychoanalytic criticism, structuration theory, and the *Annales* school of historiography.[15] I would be the first to acknowledge that these traditions do not amount to a unitary view of history, society, and leisure. On the contrary, they exist in a situation of open rivalry with each other and, in addition, with other powerful traditions in the field, e.g. Marxism and social formalism. Nevertheless, what I think is common to all of them is a *realist* stance on social relations: i.e. social relations are seen as irreducible to their component parts. In this view, social integration, conflict, and development cannot be fully explained by the will or design of individuals, classes, and nations. Rather, they must be studied as the intentional strategies and unintentional consequences of the manifold and multi-dimensional relations of power which divide and unite social actors.

The main points I wish to make can be most simply expressed in summary form:

(1) Leisure may be structurally defined as a set of rules, resources, and conventions which order the use of time and space. Leisure studies are therefore essentially concerned with how (leisure) time and space are demarcated, regulated, transformed, and mediated in social life.

(2) Types of leisure are effects of historically specific systems of legitimation. These systems *both* constrain and enable leisure relations, i.e. they set the conditions for practice, but at the same time practice presupposes that they exist. For example, in the societies of the west, a complex system of rules and conventions exists which enables social actors to distinguish between the playworlds of children and legitimate/illegitimate adult leisure practice.

(3) Systems of legitimation in leisure are themselves aspects of wider ensembles of historical, social, economic, political, and geographical relations. These relations both shape leisure

forms and are shaped by them. The interplay of leisure relations with these wider ensembles means that forms of leisure cannot be treated as isolated, unified subjects which have a definite beginning, middle, and end.

(4) The development of leisure forms is relatively open-ended. Leisure is not mechanically produced and reproduced. It does not inevitably progress to an assigned maturity of type, e.g. leisure in mass society, pluralistic industrialism, communism, etc. Rather, systems of legitimation consist of *ambiguous* rules, resources, and conventions. They do not simply determine leisure practice. On the contrary, they may be exploited and manipulated by social actors as resources for experiment and innovation.

Capitalist society does de-skill workers, and it does press people into forced leisure pursuits. But it is not unique in either of these respects. The socialist societies have de-skilling and forced leisure processes of their own.[16] More generally, it is likely that wherever advanced urban-industrial societies exist, large sections of the population will be de-skilled and driven to participate in leisure forms which foment feelings of anonymity, impersonality, and meaninglessness. This is because all urban-industrial societies are based in the constant revolutionizing of production and the requirements of international competition. Whatever changes one might like to see in the ownership and control of property within individual nation-states must be understood in this general context. Given this, the Marxist view that de-skilling and forced leisure can be transcended is as much an ideological statement as the opposing conventional wisdom which associates current leisure practice with freedom, choice, and self-determination.

Notes

This is a revised version of a paper entitled 'The deskilling thesis and forced leisure' given in the seminar on 'Theorizing Leisure' in Sussex University on 6 July 1984. I am grateful to all seminar participants and conference delegates who commented on my paper.

1 See, in particular, H. Braverman, *Labor and Monopoly Capital*, New York, Monthly Review Press, 1974; J. Alt 'Beyond class: the decline of industrial labor and leisure', *Telos* 28, 1976, pp. 55–86. D. Albury 'New technology – the quantity and quality of work and leisure', in T. Veal, S. Parker, and F. Coalter (eds) *Work and Leisure*, London, Leisure Studies

Association Conference Paper no. 15, 1982; A. Gorz *Paths to Paradise*, London, Pluto Press, 1985.

The term 'neo-Marxist' is used because while these writers belong to the Marxist tradition they are explicitly critical of many aspects of Marx's original theory.

2 For a more extensive treatment of this position see C. Rojek *Capitalism and Leisure Theory*, London, Tavistock, 1985, esp. pp. 13–23, 173–81.

3 See, in particular, K. Marx *Capital vol. 1*, London, Lawrence and Wishart, 1977, pp. 43–144; 535–8.

4 See, for example, H. Wilensky 'Work, careers and social integration', *International Social Science Journal* 4, 1960, pp. 343–560. J. E. Champoux 'Perceptions of work and non-work', *Sociology of Work and Occupations*, 5(4), 1960, 401–23; G. Staines 'Spillover versus Compensation: a review of the literature on the relationship between work and non-work', *Human Relations* 33(2), 1980, pp. 111–25; S. R. Parker *Leisure and Work*, London, Allen and Unwin, 1983.

5 T. Adorno and M. Horkheimer *Dialectic of Enlightenment*, London, Verso, 1979, p. 124.

6 A. Gorz 'Work and consumption', in P. Anderson and R. Blackburn (eds) *Towards Socialism*, New York, Cornell University Press, 1965, p. 249.

7 Braverman, op. cit.

8 ibid., p. 279.

9 ibid.

10 ibid.

11 Albury, op. cit., p. 23.

12 See, in particular, S. Hall and T. Jefferson (eds) *Resistance Through Ritual*, London, Hutchinson, 1976; G. Stedman Jones 'Class expression versus social control? A critique of recent trends in the social history of leisure', *History Workshop Journal* 4, 1977, pp. 162–70; H. Marcuse *The Aesthetic Dimension*, London, Macmillan, 1978.

13 For a more detailed critical discussion see Rojek, op. cit., pp. 128–37.

14 This tradition is represented by J. Dumazedier *Towards a Society of Leisure*, London, Collier Macmillan, 1967 and *The Sociology of Leisure*, Amsterdam, Elsevier, 1974; K. Roberts *Contemporary Society and the Growth of Leisure*, London, Longman, 1978; and *Leisure* (2nd edn), London, Longman, 1981; J. Neulinger *To Leisure: An Introduction*, Boston, Allyn and Bacon, 1981; S. R. Parker 'Choice, flexibility, spontaneity and self determination', *Social Forces* 60(2), 1981, pp. 323–32 and *Leisure and Work*, op. cit.

15 These approaches are represented as follows:

(i) Figurational sociology

Elias, N. (1978) *What is Sociology?*, London, Hutchinson.
—— (1978) *The Civilising Process vol. 1: the History of Manners*, Oxford, Blackwell.
—— (1982) *The Civilising Process vol. 2: State Formation and Civilisation*, Oxford, Blackwell.

Dunning, E. and Sheard, K. (1979) *Barbarians, Gentlemen and Players*, Oxford, Martin Robinson.
Goldsblom, J. (1977) *Sociology in the Balance*, Oxford, Blackwell.

(ii) Psychoanalytic criticism

Derrida, J. (1977) *Of Grammatology*, Baltimore, Johns Hopkins Press.
—— (1978) *Writing and Difference*, London, Routledge & Kegan Paul.
Lacan, J. (1977) *Ecrits: A Selection*, London, Tavistock.
Foucault, M. (1970) *The Order of Things*, London, Tavistock.
—— (1972) *The Archaeology of Knowledge*, London, Tavistock.
—— (1981) *The History of Sexuality vol. 1* Harmondsworth, Penguin.
Barthes, R. (1973) *Mythologies*, St Albans, Paladin.

(iii) Structuration theory

Giddens, A. (1976) *New Rules of Sociological Method*, London, Hutchinson.
—— (1979) *Central Problems in Social Theory*, London, Macmillan.
—— (1981) *A Contemporary Critique of Social Materialism* London, Macmillan.
Bashkar, R. (1979) *The Possibility of Naturalism*, Brighton, Harvester.
Bourdieu, P. (1977) *Outline of a Theory of Practice*, Cambridge, Cambridge University Press.

(iv) The Annales school

Braudel, F. (1973) *The Mediterranean and the Mediterranean World in the Age of Philip II*, (2 vols), London, Fontana.
—— (1982) *The Wheels of Commerce: vol. 2 of Civilisation and Capitalism 15th–18th Century*, London, Collins.
Le Roy Ladurie, E. (1974) *Montaillou: Cathars and Catholics in a French Village 1294–1324*, London, Scolar Press.

16 For a discussion of de-skilling and forced leisure in the socialist countries, see R. Bahro *The Alternative in Eastern Europe*, London, Verso, 1978; C. Rojek 'The limits of "the new industrial relations" ', *Industrial Relations Journal* 15(2), 1984, pp. 66–71, and 'Typologies of education and the capitalist world system', *British Journal of Sociology of Education*, vol. 5, no. 3, 1984, pp. 213–25.

4

The politics of leisure: social control and social development (1980)

CHAS CRITCHER

Introduction

The focus of this chapter is almost wholly theoretical: it is concerned to develop an argument, one which seems essential but which has often been ignored by contemporary writers. This problem is approached in three ways: first, by looking at the more general ways in which the understanding of leisure can be improved by utilizing the perspectives of 'control' and 'development'; second, by taking a broad view of the nature of the historical approach; third, by trying to fuse these two strands of evaluation by tracing the relationship between the nature of contemporary leisure and the leisure of 100 years ago. The general tenor of the argument is relatively straightforward: to establish that leisure is a political arena, where struggles over access to free time, adequate resources, and cultural meanings, are continuously taking place, even (and perhaps especially) where leisure appears to be a most private and individual undertaking.

The concepts of control and development

That a human activity may take the form of individuals seeking to evolve and express their own identities (development) and of one group seeking to induce another to adopt what activities they see as desirable (control) is not unique to leisure. In social work, for example, the debate continues as to whether social workers are primarily agents of social control or agents of caring.

It seems doubtful whether the argument is useful, unless or until it is specified in particular ways. What is important is not to agonize morally over the general principles involved but to specify the conditions under which either the care or control element comes to predominate. One of the aims of this paper is to extend that argument to leisure: to see development and control as character-istics of leisure which need to be identified in terms of concrete human practices within a dynamic historical perspective.

There is one other important connection to be made between social work and leisure. It is that much social work strategy is directed towards leisure activity, a target recognized even more explicitly by various forms of youth and community work. For some client groups, notably the elderly and the handicapped, the provision of leisure activities – clubs, outings, and holidays – is an end in itself. The problem of such people is often defined in terms of an excess of leisure. Because they are outside the normal rhythm of wage or domestic labour they are burdened with too much spare time. Here the emphasis would seem to be on the development aspect of leisure, giving those involved an opportunity for meaningful social intercourse they would otherwise not have. It is of course a peculiar and, some would argue, an indirectly controlling feature of these activities that those involved mix only with others of the same kind, thus producing segregated leisure institutions which paradoxically are claimed to be a means of social integration.

Even more ambiguous is social work's intervention in the leisure-time activities of young people, whether they are defined as deprived or depraved. A transparent example is the innovation of Intermediate Treatment which, as its name implies, is intended to provide some form of treatment (a word embodying both care and control) falling between leaving the young to their own devices and institutionalizing them. Directed mainly, though not exclusively, at boys, Intermediate Treatment involves a whole gamut of activities: regular group meetings (similar to specialized youth clubs), involvement in good deeds for the old and handicapped, and weekend camps often with an emphasis on outward-bound type activities. A number of objectives are stated: to let those involved let off steam, to develop social skills within their peer group, to relate positively to adults.

Implicit in this whole enterprise is what might be called a 'spillover' theory: that if proper habits and attitudes can be inculcated during leisure time, these will be carried over as the basis for a general code of conduct at home. The approach is directly analogous to that adopted by sections of the ruling class with regard to working-class leisure in the nineteenth century.

It is always a real difficulty in leisure analysis that controllers seek to express their objectives in developmental or moral terms. What is being advanced is not described in terms of the interests of the controllers but in the interests of the controlled. Measures are justified by reference to a set of morally or socially desired values. Part of the problem of the analysis of contemporary leisure is that control is even further disguised by the appeal to consumer choice as the ultimate arbiter. But it is not necessary to go very far back in history to reveal this disguise.

The case for the historical perspective

Two quotations illustrate how historical observers have seen leisure as a source of, respectively, control and resistance. The first is from 1920, though with some changes of tone and language it could be applicable today – as indeed, so could the second which is written some twenty years later:

> We all know – many of us to our sorrow – that there is a wave of unrest sweeping over this – and other – nations. Now my contention is the unrest and discontent are not bred while a man works but during his leisure activity. During the week a big manufacturer and employer of labour was showing me over an excellently equipped sporting and recreation ground which his firm has provided for the work people. The place must have cost a considerable sum and I asked him whether he did not think he was paying rather dearly for the recreation of his work people. 'It's the best investment I've ever made' was his reply. He went on to tell me that his experience was that the people who played well were those who worked best . . . what they laid out in providing for the leisure of the workers they got back in more and better work. . . . Our legislators pay a lot of attention to the workers at work but none of our big social reformers seem to think the leisure of people worth a second thought.[1]

> Another English characteristic which is so much a part of us that we barely notice it . . . is the addiction to hobbies and spare-time occupations, the privateness of English life. We are a nation of flower-lovers, but also a nation of stamp-collectors, pigeon-fanciers, amateur carpenters, coupon-snippers, darts-players, crossword-puzzle fans. All the culture that is most truly native

centres round things which even when they are communal are not official – the pub, the football match, the back garden, the fireside and the 'nice cup of tea'. The liberty of the individual is still believed in, almost as in the nineteenth century. But this has nothing to do with economic liberty, the right to exploit others for profit. It is the liberty to have a home of your own, to do what you like in your spare time, to choose your own amusements instead of having them chosen for you from above.[2]

I am not for the moment concerned with the historical accuracy of these arguments. Nor do I seek to indulge in spurious parallels between the 1930s and the 1980s, though the nature of the current economic crisis makes the interwar period seem less far away than it did twenty or even ten years ago. What I am concerned to do is to argue that the framework of development and control still has validity. Such a perspective is too easily suppressed by facile generalizations about social change. Whether society is seen as having been transformed by affluence and the privatization of the family or by the service economy and the microchip, it is rarely specified exactly what the nature of these changes is or how they reverberate through society as a whole. In particular their implications for leisure are assumed rather than analysed: that because people have more money, place more emphasis on family life or do less menial jobs, therefore their leisure activities will automatically change. This is not to deny that such changes may well have far-reaching implications for leisure. But it will not be possible to understand what these are, nor understand how and in what ways the balance between development and control is shifting, unless there exists a greater rather than a lesser sense of history. It is impossible to predict without invoking one or other theory of social change. For example, to emphasize the role of technology is to favour an explanation of social change in terms of *technological determinism*. The role of political, economic, and cultural factors is actively suppressed in this version of history. I wish to argue that the more gross generalizations about the 'post-industrial society' or more elaborate models of how society might change are not required. What is needed is a proper sense of history. History is not advocated, in this sense, as a discipline or a catalogue of events, but as a perspective for grasping the dynamics of social behaviour. This operates at an empirical as well as a theoretical level. Thus one historian, justifying his concentration on the period 1780–1880 as crucial for the development of leisure, has this to say:

The politics of leisure

Two points need to be made about these dates. First, unlike some other historians, I cannot see any particular year or event as peculiarly vital in the history of leisure; hence I am reluctant to tie myself down to any very specific starting or ending dates. But, secondly, the century I have chosen to study does have a coherence. It starts with the beginning of the Industrial Revolution. Despite the continuity with, and impact of, the past – which it is one of my objects to stress – the Industrial Revolution affected leisure as much as it affected work, initiating changes as a consequence of which the meaning and experience of leisure were transformed. In 1780 no one could have predicted the shape of leisure a century ahead. In 1880, by contrast, the lines of development are clear. Since then the time and money available for leisure have increased, technology has changed the form of leisure activities, and there has been a growth of the leisure industries and of governmental provision of facilities. But there is nothing in the leisure of today which was not visible in 1880. Thus for England the century 1780 to 1880 stands out as crucial in setting terms to the meaning and experience of leisure in advanced capitalist society.[3]

This is clearly a tendentious statement. It would not be difficult to make substantial objections to it by arguing that some important subsequent influences on leisure, such as car ownership or the electronic mass media, could not be seen in quite such a straight-forward fashion. But this argument can be – and often is – taken too far by seeing such related influences as having revolutionized leisure. The continuities are real and may be as important as any changes. It is precisely because of the need to specify, rather than generalize about, change and continuity in leisure that the historical perspective is invaluable. The next move is to identify the most useful levels of analysis.

Yesterday, today and tomorrow: levels of historical analysis

Having tried to establish the nature of leisure as a form of both social control and social development and to make a general case for a historically dynamic view of leisure, I conclude by bringing the two concepts together, to indicate – albeit briefly and crudely – how such a fusion can help to reveal elements of control and develop-ment in the past, present, and future. This is done under three headings:

(a) the overall determinants which shape the characteristics of leisure;
(b) the collective and individual meanings sought from leisure;
(c) the organizational forms assumed by leisure activities.

But first a brief note on the advantages and disadvantages of the historical perspective. One of the great advantages of historians is that no one expects them to make policy recommendations, a demand invariably placed upon sociologists and other social scientists. Nor do they have to encounter the demand for the kind of proof too often thought to be guaranteed by surveys and questionnaires. Partly as a result of this methodological autonomy, historians do not see the category of leisure as self-evident or achievable by the process of abstract definition. Rather, leisure is seen as a social construction; the idea of leisure is seen as inextricably bound up with the revolution of industrial capitalism. What now seems to us a static sphere of life – free time – appears to the historian as the end-product of a struggle over both the amount of free time and the permitted uses of it. These two considerations – leisure as social construction and leisure as struggle – are fundamental to the analysis of control and development.

There are of course disadvantages also. One of the greatest is a reliance upon written records; by definition these are the monopoly of the educated and literate, who do not always take great interest in the leisure activities of the common people in the nineteenth-century – or, if they do, are more concerned to attack than represent them. Less explicable is the curious tendency of historians to avoid relatively recent periods of history. If we look at the body of leisure history to have emerged over the last ten years – specialist or general, documentary or oral – there is an almost exclusive concern with the latter half of the nineteenth century, rarely going beyond 1914. As noted by two historians, who reviewed leisure research on the interwar period, there is probably a broader and deeper understanding of leisure in Victorian times than in the 1930s.[4] Perhaps one explanation, other than rather arbitrary conceptions of the boundaries of academic disciplines, was evident in the earlier quotation: a sense that the middle to late nineteenth century set quite distinct parameters for the subsequent development of leisure. So a crucial question is what these parameters were and the extent to which they have changed.

Parameters and determinants

The crucial historical period is 1780 to 1880, in which Britain was transformed from a rural agrarian society into an urban industrial one. That much is agreed. There are, however, fierce arguments about the nature of this transition, in particular its effect on leisure: whether pre-industrial forms died a natural death or were murdered; whether the attack on popular culture early in the century was significant or successful; whether the result was the bleak age vividly described by the Hammonds;[5] how far the distinctive leisure patterns which emerged in the third quarter of the nineteenth century were genuinely new or involved traditional elements; the relative weight to be placed on reform from above or agitation from below in the reduction of working hours; the significance of relative economic prosperity in producing the demand for leisure. Essentially these arguments can only be reviewed and resolved by the detailed consideration of empirical evidence – which cannot be done here. It is possible, however, to identify the implications of these historical debates for analysis of contemporary leisure.

In the 1870s and 1880s a pattern of mass leisure emerged which combined a number of very different elements. Some were very traditional with roots in pre-industrial culture: the pub, fairs, race meetings. Some were the outcome of middle-class initiatives which were responded to in ways which were not intended: for example, football and working men's clubs. Other evolved from what had initially been the wholly repressive influence of religion: choirs and bands, Sunday School outings and excursions. Still others involved the development of originally indigenous and informal working-class leisure activities through the intervention of small-scale entrepreneurs: music hall, betting. Lastly there was evidence of new technology and capital investment combining to produce the first truly mass media: the popular press.

In the following years it was to be entrepreneurship and technology aimed at the mass audience which were to be the driving forces in leisure innovation and development. Yet even before this became the dominant institutional pattern it was possible to discern common characteristics across a whole myriad of leisure activities, whether religious or secular, sober or drunken, self-governed or commercially sponsored. This was the fact that, in a remarkably short period of three-quarters of a century, the nature of leisure had changed dramatically. Where previously there had been custom now there was commerce; where work and leisure had been intermingled now they were sharply differentiated; where the rhythm of life had been set by the agricultural cycle now it was structured by the unvarying routine of the industrial week; where previously activities had been chaotic now they were disciplined; where once had been anarchy now were codes of conduct. Leisure looked very much as it would be defined and recognized today: something which went on outside working hours; at regular times; in specially provided places (where frequently one person's pleasure was another's profit); unequally distributed between classes and sexes. If no more is to be learnt from the history of leisure than that these developments were not inevitable, or necessary by definition but were generated by the conditions of industrial capitalism, then much will have been learnt which has escaped many analysts of contemporary leisure.[6]

The above is meant to do more than merely repeat the common-place assertion that leisure as it is now known is a product of the Industrial Revolution. The above assessment tries to specify the particular conditions under which leisure existed and still exists, as well as the variety of initiatives – often producing effects quite different from those intended – which led to the establishment of particular leisure institutions. This author would assert that there is as much, if not more, evidence of continuity as there is of change in the parameters of leisure as laid down by economic, political, and cultural influences. If there have been changes, they have taken place *within* the category of leisure, but the category itself remains largely as it was by the end of the nineteenth century.

Cultural meanings and leisure

It might be argued that, even if the time and space allotted to leisure have remained the same, the meanings and expectations people bring to it have changed. New leisure groupings appear to have emerged, most noticeably teenagers, who bring to leisure a set of experiences and expectations quite different from any previously known. Again, it is possible to take a contrary view. Youth, too, has its own history which goes farther back than Elvis Presley.[7] Youth culture also remains shot through with influences of class and ethnicity often reflected in different styles of music.

The question then is whether the meaning of leisure is located randomly in the individual's own preference and choices, or whether it remains deeply affected by membership of socially stratified groups. Much sociological work attempts to fuse the two by producing a set of variables in a matrix and situating the individual or group at some point where several variables – say, sex, age, and social class – intersect. But this is to reduce the influence of social stratification to the interplay of free-floating variables, a coincidence of otherwise independent social statuses. Again it is necessary in this paper to foreshorten the argument and simply state that the enduring power of major forms of stratification – gender, age, class, and race – cannot be grasped in this way.

That such factors continue to be of crucial importance may be illustrated by a consideration of those groups – especially housewives and the unemployed – for whom leisure hardly exists; the demographic and cultural trends underlying the emergence of so-called leisured age groups – not only young adults but also the retired; the fact that at any one time most British households do not consist of parents and children though many have yet to enter, and others have passed through that stage; the largely unacknowledged influence of ethnicity providing some distinctive leisure subcultures; the durability, despite all attempts to wish or measure it away, of class membership. Each of these has a history; each history interacts with the other; together they produced not a set of variables but the framework of social stratification. It is not that a black unemployed teenage girl and a white professional middle-aged man happen to be at opposite ends on one continuum or another. It is that such hypothetical examples illustrate the polarities of stratification from which leisure is no more immune than other aspects of life-style.

Leisure forms

There are two ways of thinking about leisure forms, both of which benefit from the historical perspectives. Firstly, it is possible to look at defined forms of leisure – what people actually see as their leisure. In some instances the historical lineage is relatively clear. Part of the problem now being experienced by professional football lies in the apparently decreasing relevance of the image and reality of working-class masculinity on which it rests. Attitudes towards violence, on and off the pitch, seem to have no underlying code of any kind. Saturday afternoons no longer fit a routine of working mornings, pubbing through the lunch time and going to the match. These are historical questions about changes in cultural patterns over time.[8]

Other examples identify new leisure forms, but framed by a more long-standing context. Bingo is an instance: a largely working-class female activity triggered off by the increased availability of money within that group. Yet historically, just as bingo halls are frequently converted cinemas, so the cinema was the precursor of bingo's function as a female night out. And in the same way it was framed – in part if not in substance – by the husbands' view of what was an appropriate leisure activity for their wives. This meant that a group of women should get together in circumstances where there would be no danger of meeting other men; an activity in short, which did not threaten their roles as wives and mothers. Certainly bingo is a form of gambling; but it is other things as well, which only an understanding of the history of female leisure can give us.[9]

Even if an example is made of such an unprecedented leisure form as television, then the connections with pre-existent forms of entertainment are still evident. Though television may produce some new forms of entertainment, it is primarily a means of transforming, visualizing, and amalgamating other forms of entertainment existing outside it. Thus we expect a good amount of television to be feature films and sport; comedy and variety programmes draw heavily on music-hall traditions; series and serials may have the audience agog for the next development as pulp magazines did some hundred years ago; definitions of what constitutes news may draw on the long-standing journalistic tradition of Fleet Street.[10]

New forms of leisure, then, are rarely without more or less important influences from the past. Leisure forms in the other sense – the forms of organization taken by leisure activities – also provide a sense of continuity. Much leisure in and around the home is, of course, completely informal as the earlier Orwell extract pointed out. It is also difficult to appreciate the amount of time and effort put into voluntary leisure organizations of one kind or another. The author's own experience of park football teams and leagues suggests that this may be immeasurable. Much voluntary effort depends upon the provision of some sort of facility, however basic, by a local or public authority. With the advent of the Sport and Arts Councils, innovation is encouraged and funded by public bodies.

Yet all this pales into insignificance before the massive turnover of commercial leisure organizations, whether they are selling serrvices or consumer goods. Ever since the realization at the end of the nineteenth century that large-scale leisure consumerism could produce massive profits by multiplying a small profit margin by thousands or millions, the nature of leisure has been determined by commerce. Yet this is curiously ignored by many social scientists. So concerned are they with the extension of consumer choice, the need for rational planning, or the relationship between leisure and human values, that they forget that leisure is subject to the laws of the market and that the need to control now appears – to the boards of diversified oligopolies at any rate – as the need to control demand. For it is not the case that the commercialization of leisure removes political and moral constraints and allows development to reflect the wishes of the majority, because this would interfere with the maximization of profits. Any acceptance of this myth ignores history: that leisure's primary status as a commodity does not indicate a degree of freedom or choice but demonstrates the extent to which leisure remains the leisure of capitalist society: in its definition, its temporal and spatial locations, its institutional forms, its profitability, and its disguise of economic control as consumer development.

Notes

1 Birmingham Sports Argus Junior column, 24 July 1920.
2 George Orwell, 'England your England' (1940) reprinted in *Inside the Whale and Other Essays*, Harmondsworth, Penguin, 1962, pp. 63–90.
3 Hugh Cunningham, *Leisure in the Industrial Revolution*, London, Croom Helm, 1980.
4 A. Howkins and J. Lowerson, *Trends in Leisure, 1919–1939*, London, Sports Council and Social Science Research Council, 1979.
5 J. L. Hammond and B. Hammond *The Bleak, Age* (revised edn), West Drayton, Pelican, 1947.
6 Chas Critcher and John Clarke, *The Devil Makes Work*, London, Macmillan, 1985.
7 John Gilles, *Youth and History*, New York, Academic Press, 1974.
8 Chas Critcher, 'Football since the war' in John Clarke, Chas Critcher and Richard Johnson (eds), *Working Class Culture Studies in History and Theory*, London, Hutchinson with Centre for Contemporary Cultural Studies, 1979, pp. 161–84.
9 Centre for Contemporary Cultural Studies, 'Bingo', in *Fads and Fashions*, London, Sports Council and Social Science Research Council, 1980, pp. 13–19.
10 Raymond Williams, *Television Technology and Cultural Form*, London, Fontana, 1974.

5

The society of leisure: myth and reality (1975)

KENNETH ROBERTS

The aim in what follows is, firstly, to endorse the view that there has been a continuing growth of leisure in modern society. Secondly, and more centrally, I want to separate some of the fact and theory from the myth and ideology liable to be associated with the notion of a 'society of leisure'. Specifically, I intend to query the relationship between certain contemporary trends, particularly the recent 'explosion' in participant recreation, and the broader, continuing pattern of historical change. Thirdly, pursuing the above argument will lead to some critical suggestions concerning methods of conceptualizing and analysing leisure.

The growth of participant recreation

Taking a broad historical perspective it is difficult to deny that, in some senses at least, since the early industrial era there has been a growth of leisure. Since the nineteenth century, for the employed population in Britain, hours of work have generally and consistently declined. Further, simultaneous demographic changes have been compressing the demands of child-rearing into a relatively short part of the life-span, and childhood, adolescence, and retirement have become institutionalized as periods of life free from the demands of work. All these trends have contributed to the creation of more leisure time, alongside which economic standards of life have been rising, enabling people to exercise more choice and develop new tastes.

Together with these changes in its scope, shifts in attitudes towards leisure have also occurred. By the mid-nineteenth century the meaning of leisure had been recast by industrialism; rather than a total style of life, it had come to mean a distinct part of life. It was then a compressed and subsidiary sphere, which aroused fears that it might be misspent, and provision for leisure emphasized character-training, self-discipline, and controlled competitiveness – as was also the case in education and the youth movements. During the twentieth century, however, a 'fun ethic' has become more prominent. Today the principle of public support for the arts, countryside recreation, and sport simply to allow people to enjoy themselves is scarcely controversial.

More recently, since the 1950s, there has been a dramatic upsurge across a number of fields that can be collectively described as 'participant recreation',[1] and it is perhaps misleadingly easy both to see the broader historical growth of leisure embodied in these trends,[2] and to infer that the quality of life in the immediate future will depend upon resources being provided to permit these recent trends to continue. It is this inference that I intend to query but, before doing so, a summary of the trends in question is required.

Sport is one field in which a current upsurge in participant recreation is evident. Attendances at some major spectator sports may have been declining during recent decades, but this trend is not reflected in the numbers playing. The traditional team games are holding their popularity, but the most dramatic growth rates are being recorded elsewhere; across what have previously been regarded as select, minority sports. With sailing, golf, squash, badminton, and horse-riding, for example, the indications are of greatly increased participation within the space of a decade.

Other types of participant recreation also appear to be entering a boom era with parallel developments in more casual forms of outdoor recreation. More people are visiting the countryside regularly, in some cases just to drive around, for many 'trippers' do not venture far from their vehicles. But all the indications point to more people walking, climbing, and camping in the countryside, and queueing for leisure can now be observed not only outside football grounds and cinemas, but also at municipal golf courses and, in season, at the foot of some of the better-known climbs in Snowdonia and potholes in Yorkshire. Countryside recreation is changing from a solitary to a gregarious activity.

Alongside this there is a more general growth in tourism. More people are taking more holidays in Britain and abroad, and a significant feature is that the trend is not towards hotels, but towards do-it-yourself holidays. The major growth areas in tourism are in caravanning and camping. Camping in particular has become popular throughout a much wider range of age groups and social classes: indeed, the higher socio-economic strata are now over-represented amongst campers.

This growth in participant recreation is most evident in, but is by no means confined to, vigorous and athletic activities. The same trend appears across a range of what are conventionally termed 'cultural' pursuits. Sales of classical music records, attendances at art galleries and museums, enrolments at non-vocational evening classes, and loans of books from public libraries all show the same upward trend.

Participation in certain fields is not increasing at the expense of others; rather an all-round growth is under way.[3] As in macro-economics, there appears to be a multiplier effect operating in the leisure field. As a result of the contacts and interests that it creates, involvement in one type of recreation can stimulate interest in others. Hence there seems little need to argue the case for camping versus football, or painting against music. Obviously in the final analysis resources are limited, but rather than competing against each other, current upward trends in participation in different fields appear mutually supporting. Needless to say, this same multiplier effect can conversely trap less advantaged sections of the population in a circle of impoverishment.[4]

These trends are well known, and while social scientists may have been slow to react, other occupational groups have been less inhibited. Provision has been institutionalized and the providers are becoming professionalized. Baths attendants are now increasingly styled as managing leisure centres, and park-keepers as administering recreation complexes.

Teachers of physical education, art, and music have found a new justification; they tell us that they are 'educating for leisure'. Commercial interests are no less responsive to current trends than established pressure groups sponsoring sport and the arts, and the professionals in these fields are enhancing their status with diplomas buttressed by specially designed courses, conferences, and textbooks.

None of this need be deplored, but it should serve as a reminder that statements about leisure, as much as remarks about social class, can serve or threaten the interests of various groups. The line between fact and ideology, myth and reality, is never more than loosely drawn. Fifty years ago the relevant professionals were already alert to the challenge of leisure. However, the talk was then about the threat of free time that needed to be channelled into innocuous uses. Public provision was justified in terms of deflecting energy away from what were seen as reprehensible activities, and talk of 'keeping the kids off the streets' has far from completely disappeared. Today, however, leisure is a theme capable of furnishing ideas which are more glamorous but which still serve as a basis for decisions regarding policy and provision.

Once institutionalized and professionalized, every activity gains a built-in momentum for growth; this is very evident with the current thrust of participant recreation. Its recent growth has produced a vocal 'leisure lobby', and in such a situation social science has a contribution to make in charting the boundaries between myth and reality. It is deceptively simple to equate the emergence of a 'society of leisure' with the growth of participation in sport and the other fields outlined above, and to allow this equation to lead into a plea for resources to satisfy this seemingly inexorably growing demand. Whilst not completely dismissing this equation, the intention below is to offer a challenge by querying some of the assumptions underlying the body of apparently objective research that is now accumulating, and which not only fails to challenge but offers support for equating the historical growth of leisure with the development of participant recreation. This research deserves a more sceptical reception than it is likely to receive from its professionally interested audiences. To the extent that we are moving towards a society of leisure, this must mean that the options are somewhat wider than the voices of those lobbying on behalf of already institutionalized forms of recreation might indicate.

Leisure systems

Research on leisure has been less directly influenced by sociological thinking than the frequent attention paid to 'sociological' variables might suggest. The major large-scale investigations into uses of leisure in Britain have been facility-oriented and principally concerned to measure and predict demand for different types of provision.[5] Researchers have attempted to identify socio-demographic variables associated with participation in specified types of activity, and from these studies age, sex, marital status, and a series of factors linked with social class, including occupation, education, income, and car-ownership, have emerged as useful predictors enabling plausible assessments of future trends to be made. It is these assessments that have produced apparently objective evidence pointing to a continuing growth in demand for virtually all the facilities that have been the objects of the enquiries.

While it is no part of this argument to suggest that these studies have nothing to contribute, it is worth entertaining a measure of scepticism regarding some of their presuppositions. Is the emphasis placed on specific activities, interests, and pursuits really justified? To what extent does leisure actually consist of individuals deciding to do particular things?

Having been responsible for scores of interviews asking respondents what they did last night, I have been made aware of how inappropriate the question often is. Similarly, having invited informants to name their favourite leisure activities, I have confirmed that most people can obligingly supply an answer, but their manner of doing so often suggests that 'favourite activities' are only acquired in the presence of an investigator.

People can spend a great deal of time doing 'nothing in particular' though survey techniques may report them as reading or watching television. And doing 'nothing in particular' need not be a reprehensible waste of time. A great deal of leisure comes in inconvenient batches such as a couple of hours per evening when there may not be time to do anything in particular, and these 'leisure occasions' are often surrounded by jobs and domestic responsibilities after which individuals may not wish to do anything other than relax and recuperate while 'doing nothing'.

Checklists of activities may not adequately describe how people spend all their leisure time. In addition to this, however, there is a more basic point; namely, that individuals' lives possess a 'holistic' quality to which there is a 'being' in addition to a 'doing' dimension. The 'golfers' and 'swimmers' whom surveys identify, mostly participate in these activities for only a fraction of their leisure time, though their propensity to participate may influence and be influenced by their behaviour on other leisure occasions. The implication therefore is that individuals do not so much engage in ad hoc miscellanies of activities as develop wider *systems of leisure behaviour* consisting of a number of interdependent elements and related to the yet broader life-styles of the individuals concerned. Hence, instead of starting with facilities, measuring their use and identifying their users, an alternative approach would focus upon the systems of leisure behaviour that people develop, maintain, and change, and would set their participation in various specific activities within such a broader context.[6]

There is a lesson to be learnt from the history of mass media research, one of the longer established fields of enquiry encompassing leisure behaviour. In its early stages media research concentrated upon identifying audience characteristics, thereby at least partly satisfying the curiosity of media men, but with the accumulation of such evidence its limitations gradually became apparent. More recently social scientists have been proposing research aimed at identifying the underlying processes linking predictor variables to audience behaviour. For example, Dennis McQuail has urged a move away from simply tabulating audience characteristics towards probing in greater depth the uses and gratifications that individuals derive from the media. This call has been taken up in the enquiries of McQuail himself and those of several other investigators including Rosengren and Windahl, Meyersohn, and Musgrave.[7] One thing that has become clear is that the same media programmes can offer contrasting gratifications to different people. Conversely, different individuals may derive similar gratifications from different activities. The broader implication is that individuals who patronize different facilities and superficially appear to use leisure in quite different ways may nevertheless be involved in very similar overall leisure systems.

The notion of 'leisure systems' draws attention to an intermediate level of analysis between specific activities on the one hand, and total *life-styles* on the other, and the point being argued is that we need to treat leisure as a whole if we are to explain both how leisure relates to the rest of life, and how more specific leisure interests and activities are developed and maintained. The leisure system concept is an attempt to approach the holistic properties that authentic leisure possesses and that tend to be by-passed in facility-oriented research.

Most previous attempts to typify whole leisure systems have been unilineal, focusing, for example, upon the degree of interconnectedness between leisure and work[8] or the level of participation in community associations.[9] However, as part of an investigation recently conducted on Merseyside,[10] based upon interviews with 474 economically active males, we attempted to operationalize the leisure systems concept multi-dimensionally. We collected information about respondents' uses of five recent leisure occasions and processed the resultant data to distinguish types of leisure behaviour which tend to be *complementary, independent,* and *substituted* for one another. Obviously, the more time an individual devotes to any one interest, the less time will be available for all other uses. However, in practice, high levels of involvement in certain areas tend to diminish involvement in some distinguishable alternatives rather than others. The classification of uses of leisure contained in Tables 5.1 and 5.2 on p. 65 condenses the relevant findings. When uses of leisure are categorized into (a) watching television, (b) being 'entertained' in other ways such as at concerts, cinemas, and theatres, (c) pursuing specific 'activities' including sports, reading, and hobbies, and (d) 'social' behaviour such as meeting friends or relatives, televiewing is shown to vary inversely mainly with consumption of other forms of entertainment and diffuse social behaviour, whilst the latter also varies inversely with involvement in activities.

Treating leisure as a whole in such a manner is desirable in order to adequately test propositions about how it relates to the rest of life. Social life contains such variety that there is nothing easier in social science than discovering relationships between variables, and in the case of leisure it is rarely difficult to uncover differences between any two or more populations, irrespective of the basis upon which they are distinguished. It is tantalizingly easy to discover leisure differences because there are so many hundreds of specific leisure interests and alternative ways of measuring them upon which attention can be focused and, needless to say, the greater the discrimination with which any phenomenon is examined, the greater the likelihood of differences becoming evident.

Hence the importance of not looking for differences too vigorously; we need to pay equivalent attention to constant features of leisure across different populations, and treating whole leisure systems is a way of ensuring an appropriately balanced perspective. When the influence of individuals' occupations upon leisure as a whole rather than upon carefully selected aspects is analysed, an appreciation of the functional autonomy of leisure within contemporary societies is obtained. Rather than being shaped by the constraints and opportunities associated with different types of work, as will be illustrated below, leisure systems are much more sensitive to variations in the structure of the family and individuals' roles in this.

Leisure systems and social change

If it is desirable to treat leisure systems as wholes when studying relationships with the rest of life, the same applies equally to the analysis of trends over time. In particular, the recent growth of participant recreation needs to be placed in this type of broader context. Comprehensive statistical data are not available, but one thing that is clear is that alongside the recent upsurge in participant recreation, there are equally impressive elements of stability.

In terms of time devoted, televiewing is far and away the most popular single leisure pursuit in contemporary Britain. This is true at all levels in the social hierarchy and, with the exception of adolescents, amongst all age groups. Furthermore, the popularity of television extends across national frontiers.[11] Compared with television, the amounts of leisure time devoted to all forms of participant recreation are minuscule, and current trends derive an 'explosive' appearance only on account of their very low take-off points. Thinking of leisure in terms of participation in sports and other out-of-home activities is misleading. Leisure is more typically spent less actively, at home, watching television.

Television is relatively new; it took Britain by storm during the 1950s but its impact upon the population's overall uses of leisure has been less dramatic than is often imagined. Surveys conducted during the 1950s found that television was displacing mainly the cinema and radio and, to a lesser extent, spectator sports and magazine reading while participation in sports, clubs, and hobbies was virtually unaffected.[12] Television replaced mainly other similarly 'passive' ways of spending free time which, in all probability, formerly played equivalent roles in individuals' broader systems of leisure behaviour.

In an earlier historical period, between the two world wars, the cinema and the radio were innovations upon the leisure scene, and contemporary studies showed that they were displacing mainly the music hall and the public house, but again, membership of clubs and participation in sports were virtually unaffected.[13] At the beginning of the century, before the advent of the mass media, drinking was the population's staple form of recreation. Particularly for men, the 'pub' was usually the first resort on any occasion of high emotion, misery, or distress, and drink remained by far the most important object of recreational expenditure in Britain until the First World War.[14]

Since time immemorial, changes in recreational behaviour have been accompanied by forecasts of social collapse and moral decay. Before the Second World War the 'social' type of youth club catering for both sexes was a highly controversial innovation, whilst the advent of 'modern' dancing with its physical contact between couples evoked fears about promiscuity and the dissolution of the family.[15] The concern recently aroused by 'pot' and pop festivals is well precedented. Likewise television has been blamed for virtually everything from trends in delinquency to the decline in church-going. The major effect of television however, at two historical removes, has probably been to increase the sobriety of the population.

From television and its antecedents, there is evidence of a 'like replacing like' process operating in the leisure field. New fashions can be absorbed and bring about dramatic changes in the super-ficial face of leisure, whilst the balance in overall leisure systems may swing less sharply. Hence the need for caution when inter-preting the current growth in participant recreation. Facility-oriented research that focuses on specific activities is likely to present a misleading picture. Uses of leisure are undoubtedly changing, but the shifts are more subtle and the trends less explosive than crude counts of participants in selected activities indicate. It is extravagant, therefore, to infer that we are entering a society of leisure in which the quality of life will depend, above all else, on provision for out-of-home recreation. Our society of leisure, if it deserves the title, remains solidly anchored around home, family, and television.

Social networks

Leisure is often less a matter of doing things than of being with people, and this implies a further reservation about research that seeks to explain why individuals engage in particular activities. If focusing upon your specific activities is a questionable practice, the same is equally true of the 'individuals' in the equation. Leisure behaviour is often group rather than individual conduct, hence the futility of attempts to explain uses of leisure simply by relating them to attributes of individuals such as their education, incomes, and occupations. It is often more meaningful to relate leisure pursuits to the types of participating groups. For example, no matter how assiduously individuals' motivations and gratifications are explored, it remains difficult to explain the apparent recre-ational preferences of car trippers who drive for miles into the countryside but never venture on foot beyond the perimeter of a lay-by. Examining the function of the trip for the participating group is a more promising procedure.

Table 5.1 *Associates (%)*

Use of leisure	Alone	House-hold	Relations	Friends	Total
Television	8	51	9	3	32
Other					
entertainment	2	3	5	9	4
Activities	65	14	17	27	24
Social	11	15	58	55	25
Other	15	17	11	7	14
n =	317	1,215	127	425	2,084

Table 5.2 *Use of leisure (%)*

Associates	Tele-vision	Other enter-tainment	Activities	Social	Total
Alone	4	6	40	7	15
Household	93	42	34	34	56
Relatives	2	7	4	14	6
Friends	2	45	22	45	22
n =	669	86	510	517	1,782

Note: In these tables respondents are reported as having been 'alone' on some occasions that are classified as spent 'socially'. This is not due to coding errors so much as to an almost inevitable degree of arbitrariness in allocating responses to a limited set of categories. For example, it is possible for a person to go out alone to meet friends in a public house.

In the Merseyside enquiry referred to earlier we related uses of leisure to characteristics of individual respondents and inevitably uncovered a large number of relationships, but none were as clear-cut as the associations between uses of leisure and types of participating groups (see Tables 5.1 and 5.2). Television accounted for 32 per cent of the leisure occasions investigated, and as many as 93 per cent of these occasions were spent with other members of respondents' households. Televiewing rarely occurred in any other type of company. Respondents were more likely to engage in particular 'activities' when alone than when they were with any type of associates, whilst general 'social' intercourse tended to predominate on occasions spent with relatives and other friends.

The above data may appear to merely confirm what is only common sense, but even common sense requires verification for otherwise it is all too easily ignored. The point being argued is that instead of treating variations in leisure behaviour as expressing differences between individuals' preferences, it can be more fruitful to conceive uses of leisure as arising from various types of *social networks*. This concept refers to the total systems of social relationships in which individuals are involved, and these networks can possess many bases including family, kinship, work, localities, and education. These bases will vary in their potency depending, for example, upon the types of work and family situations in question and hence the type of social network within which every person is enmeshed will depend upon his or her type of job, education, and so on.

Variations in total systems of leisure behaviour are closely related to the various types of personal social networks that are characteristic among different sections of the population. Because the family accounts for such a large proportion of the adult populations's total leisure time, variations in the composition of, and members' involvement in the family have important effects on leisure behaviour. Whether or not individuals are married, have children, and the degree of mutuality present in the conjugal relationship affect the prominence of the family in individuals' personal social networks and hence, for instance, the proportion of leisure time spent watching television rather than being entertained in other ways and enjoying more general social intercourse. For example, with age held constant, Table 5.3 shows how marriage is related to changes both in the types of persons with whom individuals associate and the ways in which leisure time is used.

This type of analysis also draws attention to the importance of education as a factor influencing uses of leisure and, more importantly, it helps to identify the underlying processes. Table 5.4 summarizes the relevant data for two 'extreme' groups of respondents in white-collar occupations (the blue collar sample's educational histories were more homogeneous, and therefore education was less important as a discriminating factor). We asked all respondents to name the two people, other than members of their own households, with whom they most frequently spent their leisure, and then sought various types of information about these associates including where they were initially met. A prolonged full-time educational career was related to a relatively high proportion of adult associates having been initially met at school or

The society of leisure

Table 5.3 *Marriage, networks, and leisure (%)*

| | | Aged 18–30 | |
		Single	*Married*
Associates			
Alone		11	15
Household		23	63
Relatives		2	5
Friends		64	17
Uses of leisure			
Television		20	33
Entertainment		7	3
Activities		21	19
Social		43	26
Other		9	19
	n =	249	173

college, and also to a relatively high proportion of associates having been met 'socially'. Hence, in relative terms, the family was a less prominent base in the social networks of our most highly educated respondents; at the time of the investigation they were spending less time only with members of their own households and more time with friends, and consequently were less preoccupied with television and more involved in 'social' uses of leisure.

Other illustrations could be given, but the aim of this paper is not to present a comprehensive analysis of the interrelationships between social networks and systems of leisure behaviour. Rather the object is to argue out some general implications of the approach in question; namely, that in explaining uses of many leisure occasions, the people whom individuals are with are just as relevant as the things they do.

At first it can be a surprise to interview people who tell how they have spent virtually the whole of the weekend and nearly every evening the previous week watching television, and then state that they do not particularly enjoy it. The question itself may be of doubtful relevance but, for what it is worth, television is rarely named as a 'favourite leisure activity' despite the amount of time that it commands. Cases of exceptionally heavy televiewing often involve individuals who are trapped in the self-reinforcing circle of impoverishment referred to earlier, and it is often sheer economic

Table 5.4 *'White-collar' respondents: education effects (%)*

		Left school at 14 or 15 No subsequent education	Left school at 16 or over Full-time further education
Source of leisure companions			
Education		3	13
Work		17	19
Family		32	15
Neighbourhood		15	17
Socially		33	37
	n =	65	47
With whom 5 recent leisure occasions were spent			
Alone		13	14
Household		59	54
Relatives		8	5
Friends		18	26
Other		2	1
	n =	196	146
Uses of 5 recent leisure occasions			
Non-leisure (e.g. sleeping)		17	13
TV		30	17
Other entertainment		3	4
Activities		18	17
Social		19	31
Other		12	18
	n =	239	168

hardship or physical disability that makes escape difficult, but the hold of television cannot be entirely explained in these terms. Television's appeal owes a great deal to its extrinsic features; it is convenient and cheap. In addition, however, televiewing is usually a group activity, nearly always a household occupation, and to explain its apparent attractiveness reference needs to be made to its compatibility with the functioning of this particular group.

Other types of leisure behaviour are susceptible to similar illumination. For example, the attraction of drinking in pubs and the game of golf may be understood by regarding them not as ends in themselves, but as providing milieux which will support the groups in which individuals wish to spend their leisure.

One implication is that in seeking explanations for trends over time in leisure behaviour we need to pay attention to changes in the types of social networks in which members of the public are involved. Changing patterns of family life, changes in the social cohesiveness of neighbourhoods, developments in education and the strengthening or weakening of occupational communities are all likely to have important ramifications.

A further implication is to alert us to the possibility of there being more flexibility in the uses of leisure that individuals can find satisfying than might otherwise be imagined. Not only are the participants in leisure pursuits rarely solitary individuals. In addition to this, leisure associates are only exceptionally groups who associate together solely because they wish to engage in a particular activity. Leisure itself is only a minor source of the social relationships in which leisure is spent. More typically leisure activities appear to be selected from among a range that will support systems of social relationships rooted in other spheres of life, and trends such as the growth of participant recreation need to be set in this context. If we supply the resources to allow this growth to continue we may to some extent be catering for individual enthusiasts who are especially attracted to the activities in question. However, to a probably greater extent we shall be providing milieux for groups that would otherwise discover alternative supportive environments.

The society of leisure

As yet there are no good reasons why philistines should be persuaded to change their ways. Push-penny is as good for people as poetry until someone proves otherwise and the proof has yet to be delivered. Despite recent experiments with 'social indicators', we have made little headway towards measuring the quality of people's lives. The blunt but available techniques of measuring 'well-being' still await use in assessing the human value of different uses of leisure.[16] Despite the heated debate surrounding the issue as to whether a 'high culture' is being preserved, submerged, or diluted, we still know little about how life's overall quality varies depending upon whether people attend symphony or pop concerts.

Given this situation, then, as in other spheres there is plenty of scope for planners' and providers' values to act as a 'social filter in the leisure field'.[17] Upon what other basis for example, does the Arts Council dispense patronage? The sport and outdoor recreation lobbies can claim that they are campaigning on behalf of an independently growing public demand, but how persuasive is this argument? It is easy to latch on to ongoing trends and to presume that they indicate areas of 'need', but is this necessarily so?

It cannot be simply assumed, though it may sometimes be the case, that as constraints are removed as a result of more free time and higher incomes, individuals will automatically adopt increasingly satisfying ways of life. Cohen has pointed out that there can be an anomia of success in addition to an anomia of failure.[18] There is no originality in arguing that the leisure activities individuals 'voluntarily' adopt may not be entirely satisfying, but hitherto such arguments have been rehearsed mainly in relation to the more easily consumed forms of mass entertainment. It is with such activities in mind that de Grazia has argued that so much of modern leisure is deformed with people compulsively searching for distractions and seeking new ways of filling time.[19] Likewise Meyersohn has argued that, particularly for the poor, television is often no more than a time-filler, whilst Rosengren and Windahl have suggested that this same medium often serves as an agency of 'para-social involvement' indicating impoverished lives rather than functioning as a positive source of enjoyment.[20] In relation to mass entertainments these arguments have an immediately plausible ring. However, it could just be that they also apply to some visitors to the countryside, sports centres, art galleries, and museums. So if additional facilities are provided for these tastes to be indulged, will the quality of life be enhanced? At the moment the only honest answer is that we do not know.

It is always tempting to try to see around the corner and into the future. Are we on the verge of a golden age of leisure or threatened by a wilderness of boredom? Before taking such questions too seriously we should remind ourselves that social science is not really in the prediction business. Social science may clarify past and present trends, and may thereby actually influence the future, but it is simply impossible to write history in advance.

Since the nineteenth century there has been a growth of leisure, and one of its recent manifestations has been the upsurge of participant recreation described earlier, but there is no necessary reason why this upsurge should continue into the future. It could equally prove to be a very temporary manifestation.

Leisure is not synonymous with fun and euphoria. Indeed, whether leisure has grown in response to popular demand is questionable. It may be more realistic to regard present-day leisure as an unplanned and equivocally received by-product of industrialism. Adolescents are an age group exceptionally endowed with free time. Whether in education or employment, they tend to work shorter hours than adults, and prior to marriage their domestic responsibilities are usually minimal. So young people possess plenty of leisure, and therefore tend to be heavily represented amongst those involved in virtually all branches of out-of-home recreation. Yet every recent study of young people at leisure has concluded that their lives, on their own admission, are often drab and desultory.[21] 'What to do' tends to be a recurrent topic of peer group conversation, and young people are not loath to experiment. Trying out new leisure activities is a prevalent feature of adolescent life[22] and if we look around the youth scene we find experiments under way with various alternative life-styles.[23] And these are not deviant aberrations. Indeed, they have as much claim as the queues outside golf courses for recognition as symptoms of the growth of leisure. This growth has created possibilities that mainstream society has hardly begun to explore, some innovators are beginning to try out the options, and it is not inconceivable that they will pioneer what may eventually become institutionalized alternatives to the television and the car trip to the coast.

How frequently leisure is regarded as a *central life interest* depends on how broadly leisure is defined, but the available evidence suggests that out-of-home recreation and the presence or absence of the relevant leisure facilities are rarely considered critical determinants of the quality of life.[24] So the 'society of leisure' could mean more camping and canoeing, or it could equally lead to the evolution of new forms of 'communal' life, or to more widespread involvement in political processes, not necessarily through conventional channels. Such responses are no less inherently compatible than participant recreation with the growth of leisure, and may eventually prove to be the more satisfying alternative.

David Riesman was among the first to argue the need to develop new bases for satisfying modes of life in the emergent post-industrial society,[25] and eventually current trends may themselves contribute to a re-casting of systems of leisure behaviour. There may be no absolute shortage of land in Britain, but there is pressure upon the more attractive and accessible locations, there is a physical limit to our ability to cater for sports that require outdoor space in or near urban areas. Inland water sports are already pressing close to physical capacity, and it seems doubtful whether provision can hope to keep abreast of the current growth-rate in demand for indoor sports facilities. This must reinforce scepticism as to whether any society of leisure that we might be entering will involve simply more of the same.

Portraying the advent of leisure in terms of the continued growth of those forms of participant recreation that have already become institutionalized is a resort to ideology rather than theory, though it offers an image of the future that will inevitably appeal to professionals with vested interests in existing modes of recreation. Research that limits itself to asking which individuals engage in which (currently popular) activities, and uses the evidence as a basis for future prediction may generate data that the leisure industries embrace but its product will be little more than a folk-science. To understand the current state of leisure and future possibilities, social science will be of greater service if it applies itself to sketching the alternative systems of leisure behaviour that may be constructed within the types of social networks available to various sections of the public. While the above analysis does not claim to have achieved this, it has aimed to offer a reasoned plea for the type of exercise in question.

Notes

1 For a more thorough discussion of evidence relating to the trends under review see T. L. Burton, *Recreation Research and Planning*, London, Allen & Unwin, 1970.

2 This type of equation is strongly implied in A. Patmore, 'The busy world of leisure', *Observer*, 1 December 1974.

3 See the analysis in M. Young and P. Willmott, *The Symmetrical Family*, London, Routledge, 1973.

4 For an elaboration of this argument see R. Meyersohn, 'Television viewing and other uses of leisure', *Public Opinion Quarterly*, 32, 1968.

5 British Travel Association University of Keele, *Pilot National Recreation Survey*, report no. 1, 1967; K. K. Sillitoe, *Planning for Leisure*, London, HMSO, 1969.

6 This type of approach is also explicitly advocated by A. A. C. Phillips, *Research into Planning for Recreation*, Cheltenham, Countryside Commission, 1972.

7 D. McQuail, *Toward a Sociology of Mass Communications*, London, Collier-Macmillan, 1969, and 'The audience for television plays', in J. Tunstall (ed.), *Media Sociology*, London, Constable, 1970; D. McQuail *et al.*, 'The television audience: a revised perspective', in D.

McQuail (ed.), *Sociology of Mass Communication*, London, Penguin, 1972; K. E. Rosengren and S. Windahl, 'Mass media consumption as a functional alternative', in ibid; Meyersohn, op. cit.; P. W. Musgrave, 'How children use television', *New Society*, 20 February 1969.

8 For example, S. Parker, *The Future of Work and Leisure*, London, Paladin, 1972; G. Salaman, 'Two occupational communities: examples of a remarkable convergence of work and non-work', *Sociological Review*, 19, 1971, pp. 389–407.

9 R. J. Havighurst and K. Feigenbaum, 'Leisure and life-style', *American Journal of Sociology*, 64, 1959, pp. 396–405.

10 This enquiry was supported by a Social Science Research Council grant.

11 See I. Cullen, 'A day in the life of . . .', *New Society*, 11 April 1974.

12 For a summary of this evidence see W. A. Belson, *The Impact of Television*, London, Crosby Lockwood, 1967.

13 See *New Survey of London Life and Labour*, London, King, 1930.

14 J. Myerscough, 'History and philosophies of the use of leisure time', *Symposium on Leisure*, University of Edinburgh, 1972.

15 See F. Rust, *Dance and Society* , London, Routledge, 1969.

16 This refers to the techniques developed by L. Srole, 'Social integration and certain corollaries: an exploratory study', *American Sociological Review*, 21, 1956, pp. 709–16; M. Seeman, 'the signals of '68: alienation in pre-crisis France' *American Sociological Review*, 73, 1972, pp. 385–402; D. L. Phillips, 'Social participation and happiness' *American Journal of Sociology*, 1967.

17 This phrase is taken from I. Emmett, 'The social filter in the leisure field', *Recreation News Supplement*, 4, 1971, pp. 7–8.

18 H. Cohen, 'The anomia of success and the anomia of failure', *British Journal of Sociology*, 23, 1972, pp. 229–43.

19 S. de Grazia, *Of Time, Work and Leisure*, New York, Twentieth Century Fund, 1962.

20 Meyersohn, op. cit.; Rosengren and Windahl, op. cit.

21 P. Jephcott, *Time of One's Own*, Edinburgh, Oliver & Boyd, 1967; J. Leigh, *Young People and Leisure*, London, Routledge & Kegan Paul, 1971.

22 For relevant evidence see the surveys conducted for K. Roberts *et al.*, *The Character Training Industry*, Newton Abbot, David & Charles, 1974.

23 As described, for example, in A. Rigby, *Alternative Realities*, Routledge, 1974, and R. Mills, *Young Outsiders*, London, Routledge, 1973.

24 J. Hall and N. Perry, 'Aspects of leisure in two industrial cities', *Occasional Papers in Survey Research*, 5, SSRC, 1974.

25 D. Riesman, 'Leisure and work in post-industrial society', in E. Larrabee and R. Meyersohn (eds), *Mass Leisure*, Glencoe, Free Press, 1958.

6

Anti-leisure and public recreation policy: a view from the USA (1975)

GEOFFREY GODBEY

In 1974, sociologist Joffre Dumazedier made the following statement concerning leisure. I quote it here in full since my paper is
in basic opposition to his conclusions:

> First of all, leisure time is obviously the result of the appli-
> cation of discoveries in technical science. This progress has
> come about by a double play; that of the trade unions, which
> insist on salary increases and shorter working hours, and that
> of businesses which need to extend the time of consumption in
> order to use up their products (the consumer must consume
> vast quantities and it takes time to consume).
>
> However, this technological-economical component does not
> explain everything: a socio-ethical component must come into
> it, and I call this a decline in institutional control over indi-
> viduals. This means that society's fundamental institutions
> (family, socio-religious, socio-political) control time less and
> that free time is used especially in leisure activities. This
> decline is related to the youth and feminist movements against
> the all-important family and conjugal duties, to religious move-
> ments which insist on lay responsibility and to citizen's move-
> ments against totalitarian politics.
>
> Leisure has been introduced by means of a profound mu-
> tation of the being which means that a new relationship is
> established between the individual and his or her exterior
> nature, and the individual and his or her inner being. This
> results in leisure becoming the framework of a kind of cultural
> revolution.[1]

This statement is in many ways typical of many other social scientists who believe that leisure has become a central feature of the post-industrial society. Some scholars have written that the rise of leisure in the post-industrial society is 'indisputable', or has been proven beyond disagreement. Allow me to disagree. It appears to me that during the last few decades leisure has not increased, whether we refer to leisure in a residual sense, as surplus time after work, sleep, and other necessary activities; leisure in a prescriptive sense, as a condition of the soul; or leisure in a normative sense, as time free from work and other duties which may be used for relaxation, diversion, social enrichment, or personal development.[2] What has increased in post-industrial societies, particularly during the last decade, is *anti-leisure*. By anti-leisure I refer to activity which is undertaken compulsively, as a means to an end, from a perception of necessity, with a high degree of externally imposed constraints, with considerable anxiety, with a high degree of time consciousness, with a minimum of personal autonomy, and which avoids self-actualization, authentication, or finitude.

My purpose is briefly to explore the sources of anti-leisure and to examine the implications of anti-leisure for public recreation policy. The focus of this analysis is primarily the United States but I believe that a similar case can be made for Britain and other post-industrial societies. While many reasons could be given for the rise of anti-leisure, I have dealt here with (i) the increasing demands of labour, (ii) the decline of pleasure, (iii) limitless materialism, (iv) increased societal complexity and change, and (v) the increasing need for self definition.

The increasing demands of labour

Several recent labour analyses indicate that there has been no decrease, and even an overall increase, in the amount of work activities.[3] One basic reason for this has been a 70 per cent increase in people employed in service occupations during the last decade, while the corresponding rise of those producing goods has been minuscule. Services are devourers of time because service workers are less efficient, live performance and personal contact are involved, and capital cannot easily be substituted for such labour. Since the production of goods is increasingly dependent upon the production of services (legal, financial, governmental) the very efficiency of the production of goods creates a need for the production of services.

The amount of overtime by wage-earners has also been increasing and it is expected that the rate of dual job holding is going to increase. Additionally, one time-budget study of housewives showed that the total time used for home-making has not decreased during the last forty years.[4] Add to this the increasingly time-consuming journey to work, the 'homework' required for 'continuing education' and life-style requirements of professionals, government's new commitment to controlling pollution and improving the quality of life, and the increasing attention to food production, and it is difficult to argue that work is waning.

The decline of pleasure

Not only has work become more pervasive for many in our society, but increasingly the goals, methods, and styles of our institutions of work are spilling over to our institutions of leisure. In much of our 'leisure' activity, no less than in our 'work' activity, we place a high value on advanced planning and goal setting, competition, incremental improvement through the mastery of special knowledge and technique, the efficient utilization of time, and, of course winning; always winning. What has emerged, as Wolfenstein notes, is a 'fun morality' in which, 'at play, no less than at work, one asks: "Am I doing as well as I should?" [5] This seriousness of approach has led to the decline of many forms of pleasure. Consider, for instance, the consequences of the desire to use time 'efficiently' on leisure behaviour.

Many forms of pleasure take time and there is no way for their time requirement to be shortened. A love affair takes time, preparing and enjoying a good meal takes time, writing a poem takes time, as does enjoying a game of darts. Today, however, many such pleasures have become anti-leisure due to the increasing scarcity of time. Economist Steffan Linder's explanation for this is that, just as we have become more efficient and productive in our work and our work time has become more scarce, we have also sought to become efficient and productive in our leisure and it has also become scarce at least in terms of perception.[6] Today, in the United States, the 'fast food' restaurants represent nearly 25 per cent of the total restaurant trade.[7] Instant Breakfast – add milk and drink it – is selling very well. Many people in the United States eat lunch in fifteen minutes or less.

In regard to romance, the practice of taking a mistress has largely died out because it is too time-consuming. It has been replaced by the 'one nighter'. Linder believes that today's sexual promiscuity is primarily due to the desire to speed up the courtship process and achieve what intimacy can be achieved in a very short period of time. Linder suggests that extra-marital sex may actually be declining due to lack of time to make contacts.[8] Research by Humphreys indicates that increasing numbers of men who are not homosexually inclined are seeking sexual outlets with homosexuals in public restrooms. Humphreys believes that such behaviour is a sexual response to the time famine – as is the practice of prostitutes meeting their clients in parked cars in indoor parking garages for 'quickies'.[9]

Many other leisure activities today have been designed primarily to save time. You can learn to do oil paintings by number, you can tour an entire country in three days or less, learn to skydive and jump the very first time up, learn to play songs on the guitar in three easy lessons, or visit a number of commercial zoos and animal habitats without even getting out of your car. The format of such activities, however, conveys the importance of saving time to the participant and increases his awareness of time, and perhaps, his anxiety.

Limitless materialism

Anti-leisure behaviour has been increased by our inability to satiate our material desires. As Linder points out, the acceleration of consumption has found no limits, even though we have no societal justification for it, such as the eradication of poverty or a rise in the level of humaneness and culture.[10] The sequence goes like this: if I have no television set, I want a small black and white set. If I have a small black and white set, I want a large black and white set. If I have a large black and white set, I want a small colour set. If I have a small colour set, I want a large colour set. If I have a large colour set, I want a second small black and white set, *ad nauseam*. The acquisition, maintenance, and use of a vast number of material goods takes time and increases the activities we are compelled to undertake to sustain our life-style.

Increased societal complexity and change

Anti-leisure has also been on the increase due to the new costs of our society. Decisions have become more complicated and time consuming in a society where planning and regulation by government are increasingly necessary, and where citizens expect a greater role in that process.

Today the individual citizen is being forced to absorb more and more information, at an increasingly accelerated rate. Such information is often of a highly technical nature. There is evidence that we are near our limit to absorb it. A recent report to UNESCO by Dr Ivan Khorol indicates that millions of people are suffering from 'brain overloading' due to the increased tempo of everyday life, the political, technical, and moral changes to which we must adapt, and the length of time taken up by education and training, which is accompanied by constant strain. Unlike the computer, Dr Khorol says, the human brain is a one-thing-at-a-time machine. When several problems must be solved at once, the brain pays with mental strain, or even pathological alterations in its structure.[11] Approximately 125,000 Americans are hospitalized each year for depression, 200,000 undergo treatment in outpatient clinics, four to eight million need psychiatric assistance and 50,000 commit suicide. This phenomenon, although on a smaller scale, is also true in other post-industrial societies.

While there is always the danger of romanticizing the past, nevertheless previous generations were born into, and died in a world whose dimensions they understood. My grandmother has described her childhood and the simple pleasures of being a member of a large family in a rural area. She spent long silent watches in the woods or chased rabbits with two dogs. In spring, her job was to find the nests of turkeys and to herd them home so the foxes would not get them if they failed to come home at night to roost in the large trees. At night she sat around the log fire with her brothers and sisters and listened to stories. As she said: 'Each member of [my] big family felt near to each other member and was interested in them. Sometimes I wonder if that might not be some of the problem of youth today. Not enough interest and love, one for another, in our present day families. Too much hurry and rush and the entire time and life of the child planned and taken up by school and other activities outside the house.'[12]

The need for self-definition

Our modern philosophical notions have contributed largely to anti-leisure. Logical positivist beliefs in the notion of progress through science and rationalism have been tempered by the calamities of this century: unnecessary war, unnecessary poverty and famine, and an inability to define a suitable relationship with nature. Man is less sure that his nature is fixed and inherent. Existence precedes essence. Existential man is coming more and more to believe that 'an authentic life is not handed to us on a platter but involves our own act of self-determination (self-finitization) within our time and place.'[13] He believes, in short, that he is not born in God's image or in anything else's. He is not one of the lilies of the field. He has lost his assurance of an inherent relationship with the macrocosm.

One indicator of the increasing importance placed on what an individual does is the dominance of achieved statuses over ascribed statuses in our society. The first thing Americans ask when meeting a stranger is 'What do you do?', since this is considered to be the most important thing to know about the person in order to determine who he is. In a highly competitive meritocracy, one cannot afford to be bad at any activity because he is being defined and judged by others through his activity, regardless of whether he is playing tennis, fixing a dessert, or selling shoes.

Because of these situations, acting has become necessary, even compelled, regardless of whether the acting generates income or not. Time is scarce for people who have little sense of an historical self-concept to fall back on. When there is no human nature every human must re-invent it at considerable cost. Anti-leisure is a major cost. While the need we are discussing is psychological and theological rather than physiological, it is no less real than the pain of the hypochondriac.

Some implications for public recreation

What are the implications of anti-leisure for public recreation policy? Before attempting an answer, let us look at the function of public recreation and parks. Basically, the public recreation and park movement came about in response to urbanization. The rise of technology brought about a concentration of the means of production, a division of labour, and a rigid scheduling of work hours. This resulted in the formation of urban areas as people moved closer to the industries where they worked. The land-based forms of recreation they had previously enjoyed were no longer feasible. Government involvement in recreation and parks came about in response to this situation: as an attempt to get children off the streets, to make possible many traditional land-based forms of recreation, and to help the worker adjust to urbanization.

Today, in the United States, recreation and parks are an accepted responsibility of government. Nine major Federal agencies operate under legislation which permits them to sponsor and fund public leisure services. The creation of the Bureau of Outdoor Recreation in 1962 marked a turning point in Federal assistance to states in planning for outdoor recreation and the co-ordination of Federal programmes dealing with outdoor recreation. Each of the fifty states currently has some agency with direct responsibility for outdoor recreation and a myriad of other agencies with some involvement in recreation or park services.

Much anti-leisure behaviour has occurred as a result of a frantic search for pleasure. Public leisure service organizations, therefore, must address themselves to the question 'What is worth doing?' rather than 'What is pleasurable?' Some worthwhile activities are pleasurable at the time they are done; some are not. Some pleasurable activities are worthwhile; some are not. This is not said to negate the importance of pleasure; just as an admission that the issue of pleasure is not the primary one. Additionally, many activities which the individual believes are worthwhile produce pleasure as a by-product, even though the actual performance of the activity is not pleasurable. Learning to ski may not be fun. Campaigning against a government policy can be painful. Weeding a vegetable garden can be drudgery. If these activities come to have meaning to the individual, however, the question of direct or immediate pleasure becomes less important. While it may be argued that what one does during leisure is automatically an expression of what one believes to be worthwhile, it should be remembered that television viewing is the single most time-consuming leisure activity in post-industrial societies, yet research indicates that many viewers themselves place a low value on it.

Public leisure service agencies might well learn from this example. 'Participation' as a goal in and of itself is an insult, as is 'keeping kids off the streets'. These are goals of the anti-leisure society. It is not enough for government-sponsored leisure activities to be 'wholesome' if they are also innocuous. Many arts and crafts programmes for adults, for instance, involve little real originality, creativity, or investment of self. Paul Goodman has discussed this situation in challenging the model of successful use of leisure put forward by the National Recreation Association (now the National Recreation and Park Association). Suppose, he said, the goals of the NRA were realized:

There would be a hundred million adults who have cultured hobbies to occupy their spare time – some experts on the flute, some with do-it-yourself kits, some good at chess, some square dancing, and all playing athletic games. . . .

Now, even if people were indeed getting deep personal satisfaction from these activities, this is a dismaying picture. It isn't important. There is no ethical necessity to it, no standard. One cannot waste a hundred million people that way.[14]

Goodman believed NRA's mistake is to conceive of recreation as 'any activity participated in ... merely for the enjoyment it affords'.[15] Enjoyment, Goodman said, is not a goal; it is a feeling which accompanies important on-going activity. Pleasure depends upon function. No new culture can emerge from such activity unless there is some communal necessity. Public recreation organizations can help foster a sense of community and an evolving culture, but not without experimentation, taking risks and a belief in the importance of leisure. Ironically, government agencies concerned with leisure often act as if they place little importance on what happens to the individual in the leisure experience. Their goals, like the goals of many businesses, are sometimes only to keep the consumer of the services consuming. This goal is an anti-leisure goal which produces one more form of mindless consumerism. Public recreation and park agencies must attempt to justify their role more in terms of the meaning of participation rather than its fact. Data concerning behavioural and environmental change have got to be used to justify expenditures in recreation and parks. Do greenbelts or neighbourhood parks decrease noise levels? Do they provide opportunity for people to contemplate in a relatively natural environment? Do people who receive instruction in a specific leisure skill continue to use that skill? Often the answer is not known.

A final implication of anti-leisure for public recreation concerns the preparation of those who work in public recreation and park agencies. Currently, recreation and parks is emerging in North America as a distinct profession, in which college or university preparation is a pre-requisite. During the last three years the number of students enrolled in curricula specialized in recreation and parks or leisure services in North America has increased from less than 17,000 to an estimated 35,000.[16] Much of the preparation of these students emphasizes public management techniques and is slowly beginning to utilize the sociology and psychology of leisure

and other related theory and research concerning leisure behaviour. In most curricula, however, the student has little opportunity to understand those who have traditionally *had* leisure in
our society: the philosopher, the artist, the theologian, the musi-
cian. If students are later to combat anti-leisure behaviour as
recreation and park professionals, they must understand that
there are alternatives to anti-leisure, and experience such alternatives for themselves. The ironic cliché of the work-driven recreation
and park professional is usually quite accurate. If public recreation
and park agencies are going to change anti-leisure, they must lead
by example.

In summary, it may be said that our institutions of leisure have
been dominated by our institutions of work. Public recreation came
about in response to industrialization and is an extension of our
work ethic. For this to change, it will be necessary for such
organizations to promote different values from those of work
organizations, and to renew attention to the individual meaning of
those services they provide.

Notes

1 J. Dumazedier, *Loisir Plus*, reprinted in *Recreation Canada*, no. 32,
May 1974, p. 55.

2 G. Godbey and S. Parker, *Leisure Studies and Services: An Overview*,
Philadelphia, Saunders, 1976.

3 See, for instance, R. Carter, 'The myth of increasing non-work versus
work', *Social Problems*, vol. 18, Summer 1970; G. Burck, 'There'll be
less leisure than you think', *Fortune*, March 1970; P. Drucker, 'Workers
and work in the metropolis', *Daedalus*, vol. 97, Autumn 1968; D.
Dempsey, 'The myth of the new leisure class', *New York Times
Magazine*, 26 January 1958.

4 K. Walker, 'Homemaking still takes time', *Journal of Home Economics*,
vol. 61, 1969.

5 M. Wolfenstein, 'The emergence of fun morality', in E. Larrabee and
R. Meyersohn (eds), *Mass Leisure*, Glencoe, Free Press, 1958, p. 93.

6 S. Linder, *The Harried Leisure Class*, New York, Columbia University
Press, 1970.

7 J. Morgenstern, 'The roadside gourmet: pop goes the food', *Newsweek*,
25 September 1972.

8 Linder, *op. cit.*

9 L. Humphries, 'New styles in homosexual manliness', *Transaction*,
March 1971.

10 Linder, *op. cit.*

11 Dr Ivan Khorol, quoted by S. Koo, *Associated Press*, 20 October 1974.

12 Z. Godbey, letter to editor, *Mansfield Advertiser*, Pa., 19 March 1969.

13 W. Barratt, *Irrational Man: A Study of Existential Philosophy*, New York, Doubleday Anchor Books, 1962, p. 271.
14 P. Goodman, *Growing Up Absurd*, New York, Vintage Books, 1956, pp. 234–5.
15 *ibid.*, p. 235.
16 T. Stein, 'Recreation and park education in the United States and Canada – 1973', *Parks and Recreation*, vol. 18, 1974, pp. 32–3.

PART TWO

Leisure and social structure

Introduction

The chapters in this section emphasize the necessity to recognize the relationship between constraint and choice, between structure and agency in analysing leisure meanings and behaviour. All reject the individualizing approach contained in the ideology of the market and consumer choice, suggesting that issues of constraint are as important as the exercise of freedom in understanding leisure.

Murdock draws on the work of Pierre Bourdieu to propose that a more sophisticated understanding of leisure choices, behaviour, and meaning would be gained by exploring the relations between class structure and cultural consumption. From this perspective leisure behaviour is not simply to be understood in terms of individual satisfaction but as part of a deeper process which sustains and reproduces broad structural inequalities. Murdock suggests that differential patterns of cultural consumption (leisure behaviour) reflect and reinforce the differential distribution of class-based cultural competences and meaning systems. Therefore the importance of class, family, and education in structuring and delimiting choice sets real, structural limitations on the democratization of culture and extension of opportunities.

The continuing importance of class-based culture and meaning systems is emphasized by Swedner in his paper on leisure policy in Sweden. He questions the popular image of Sweden as possessing a uniform culture and uses research findings to illustrate the continuing importance of class differences in leisure time and behaviour. In describing a series of municipal initiatives to extend the community use of libraries he illustrates both the possibilities and limitations of cultural change. Swedner suggests that the extension of opportunity and the democratization of culture require the rejection of the 'marketing perspective' with its rigid producer/consumer relationships, and the adoption of more humanistic 'therapeutic' and 'social change' perspectives which reject the divisions between 'finkultur' and everyday life, between culture and leisure.

Whereas Murdock and Swedner are concerned largely with the effect of class stratification on leisure, the other three chapters in this section offer varying perspectives on the importance of gender-stratification. Parry and Johnson offer a critique of the liberal, evolutionist perspective which suggests that a process of 'stratified diffusion' is leading to diminishing constraints on women and the reduction of segregated sex roles, thereby leading to an increase in leisure time for women. More fundamentally they propose that there are inherent conflicts between the gender-biased demands of the familial ideology and the notions of individual choice and freedom contained in ideologies of the market. Such a conflict will become increasingly obvious as the process of sex-role desegregation proceeds.

The conflict of definitions and ideologies is also central to Scraton's analysis of the processes whereby young women reject PE and sporting activities and sexual stereotypes are reproduced. She raises doubts about simple biological explanations and, drawing on the cultural studies tradition, seeks to provide a more thoroughly social explanation of these processes. In line with Roberts' contention that leisure behaviour and meanings can only be understood by situating them with social relationships, she emphasizes the necessity of analysing young women's attitudes and 'the culture of femininity' in order to understand their rejection of PE and sport. Many of the elements of PE – the emphasis on 'suitable clothing', discipline, and control – conflict with their emerging definitions of femininity. Paradoxically, where the curriculum is made more relevant it means that young women are both saved by and trapped in the culture of femininity. What is required is a redefinition of PE within a broader context of redefining femininity and increasing women's control over their own bodies and health and the development of a greater self-confidence. Scraton suggests that attempts to use PE as a preparation for leisure are very problematic (and often recognized as such by young women) in the light of evidence on the constraints on the leisure lives of women.

The issue of constraints is central to the paper by Streather who looks at a particular group of women – single parents. She illustrates how the social position of women interacts with changes in the family to produce greatly constrained and deprived leisure lives. Drawing on research findings she illustrates how one-parent families not only suffer from low incomes but also from social isolation and social stigma. Such problems, which serve to undermine self-esteem, are exacerbated by the low status of women's work, the pressures of the dual role of wage-earner and single parent, and the general lack of child-care facilities. Here we have another paradox of leisure – those parents who need it most (as relief from social isolation, for developing self-esteem, or as an escape from constant demands of children) are those who have the fewest leisure opportunities and resources.

However, despite arguing for policies to increase leisure opportunities for one-parent families, Streather sounds a note of caution shared by many of the contributors to this volume. She warns against offering leisure solutions for social problems, suggesting that policies for leisure and 'palaces of fun' will achieve little if the pressures of poverty, poor housing, and social isolation remain.

7

Class stratification and cultural consumption: some motifs in the work of Pierre Bourdieu (1977)

GRAHAM MURDOCK

Introduction

It has often been remarked that the sociology of leisure in Britain has tended to become somewhat isolated from the mainsteam of sociological theory and argument, including contemporary debates about the nature and dynamics of class stratification in advanced societies.[1] By and large, sociologists of leisure have not been particularly interested in exploring the general relations between class structure and cultural consumption, preferring to focus instead on the narrower and rather more manageable problem of the links between work situation and leisure activity. They are certainly not alone in their neglect however. Leading sociologists of class such as Giddens, Parkin, and Poulantzas have also paid very little attention to the areas of leisure and consumption. There are a few exceptions to this pattern of reciprocal neglect however, and one of the most notable is Pierre Bourdieu. I want to sketch here some of the basic themes in Bourdieu's work and to outline some of the directions they suggest for future research in the sociology of leisure.

Bourdieu can lay claim to being one of the most fertile and productive figures in contemporary sociology. Over the past decade and a half he has conducted a series of substantial investigations into various aspects of the relations between class stratification and leisure consumption which have produced a wealth of fascinating empirical material. For this contribution alone he deserves serious consideration from anyone interested in the sociology of leisure. But Bourdieu has done much more. He has attempted to explain and account for his empirical results by developing a general theoretical perspective which points to the ways in which leisure and consumption are locked into, and help to reproduce, the prevailing system of class inequalities. His work on leisure then is part of a wider attempt to tease out the relations between the economic and symbolic dimensions of class stratification. Whether or not you are finally convinced by his evidence and his arguments (and I have a number of reservations) his work is valuable on two counts. First, it forcefully reconnects the sociology of leisure with the central currents of contemporary debate in the subject, and secondly, it throws up a whole series of neglected questions for further consideration and research.

Basic themes in Bourdieu

Stratified consumption: cultural capital and cultural competence

One of the pivotal concepts in Bourdieu's work is the notion of *cultural capital* by which he means the stock of cultural goods which are 'socially designated as worthy of being sought and possessed'.[2] On this definition, cultural capital obviously includes those activities and artifacts which are usually thought of as 'Cultural' with a capital 'C' – listening to classical music, attending concerts, going to the theatre, ballet, and opera, reading 'serious' fiction, and so on. But cultural capital is not simply another term for the traditional constituents of 'high culture'. It also includes those elements of avant-garde and popular culture which have been defined as worthy and legitimate and been incorporated into the pantheon of status-conferring cultural activities. Hence our current stock of cultural capital includes not only the plays of Shakespeare and Pinter and the music of Beethoven and Britten, but the films of directors like Buñuel and Bergman, the television plays of David Mercer and Denis Potter, and the music of Duke Ellington. The conferral of legitimacy on recent and contemporary forms is signalled in various ways; by their presentation in traditional élite milieux like the National Theatre and the Festival Hall; by extended critical consideration in 'serious' journals of opinion and comment; and above all by their incorporation into the official curriculum of the élite sectors of the education system.

According to Bourdieu then, there are two kinds of wealth circulating in society – economic wealth and symbolic wealth. Both forms can be inherited and accumulated and both are highly unequally distributed, with the lion's share of each going to those at the top end of the class structure.[3] Why is this? Why are those richest in cultural capital as indexed by participation in prestigious cultural activities overwhelmingly drawn from the middle and upper classes? Bourdieu's answer is that the possession of cultural capital presupposes the possession of skills and competences which are concentrated among the non-manual strata. Although nominally offered to everyone equally, Bourdieu argues, access to the legitimated stock of cultural capital only really exists for a person who has the means to appropriate it, or in other words to decipher it, and access to the requisite knowledge and competence is systematically maldistributed.[4]

The idea of *cultural competence* is an extension of the sociolinguists' notion of communicative competence by which they mean mastery of the basic ground rules of the language and of the habits and attitudes surrounding its use.[5] Cultural competence therefore, can be broken down into three basic components – knowledge about the legitimate stock of cultural capital, mastery of the intellectual and social skills surrounding its consumption and use, and the ability to deploy this knowledge and skill to advantage in social situations. Some concrete examples may make this a bit clearer.

According to Bourdieu, competence consists first and foremost in mastering the prevailing systems of cultural classifications. The more competent the person the more complex and subtle the subdivisions in his classificatory schema.[6] Take Van Gogh's celebrated painting of sunflowers. An incompetent person in Bourdieu's terms would classify it simply as a picture of flowers. A slightly more competent person would be able to specify that it was by Van Gogh and provide some minimal contextual background – that he also painted a pair of old boots, that he cut off his ear and sent it to his girl friend, and that he eventually committed suicide. A truly competent person however, would be able to place the picture in relation to Van Gogh's total oeuvre, to compare his subject matter and technique to other artists of the period, to say that it was expressionist rather than impressionist, and so on. Competence in this sense means mastering the dominant vocabulary of classification and criticism; it means knowing what's in the catalogue and the programme notes without having to look it up. But full competence consists not only of knowing about the works themselves, but also of knowing how to respond to them. This is particularly crucial in situations like theatres and concerts where responses are subject to public scrutiny.

While at school I was once taken to a classical concert provided by the London County Council for the elevation of the secondary school population. The centrepiece was a violin concerto. After the first movement had finished there was a burst of enthusiastic clapping and a few ragged shouts of 'more'. Some of this was clearly sarcastic, but a lot had to do with simply cultural incompetence. Most of the audience had only ever heard live music at local dances or in pop and blues clubs where you are expected to clap after each number. Nobody had bothered to tell them that most classical pieces are in three or four segments and that you wait until the end of the last one before applauding.

All cultural activities, 'popular' as well as 'élite', require their own particular kinds of competence. Becoming a bona fida football fan, for example, entails knowing how to read the game and comment knowingly on the run of play, being able to make telling comparisons with other games and teams, past and present, and learning the ritualized forms of match behaviour – the chants, stylized insults, and so on. However, Bourdieu argues, access to competence is highly structured by class location. The specialized knowledge and skills involved in competences are part of the wider patterns of collective meaning and response developed by particular class segments – they are embedded in specific class cultures. Differential patterns of cultural consumption and leisure participation are therefore rooted in the differential distribution of cultural competences and the class-based meaning systems. This distribution, in turn, is anchored and reproduced through class-based differentials in family socialization.

Bourdieu follows orthodox socialization theory in nominating the family as the key agency of cultural transmission. The family hands on what he calls the primary *habitus* which consists of 'a set of generalised schemes of thought, perception, appreciation and action'.[7] These provide the basic conceptual categories and action frames through which people think about and respond to the social world, including the world of culture and leisure. The aesthetics of the different social classes are therefore', Bourdieu argues, 'only one dimension of their ethos.'[8] Consequently, the class distribution of cultural preferences and involvements can only be properly understood as one facet of the general distribution of class-based systems of meaning and competence.

According to Bourdieu then, a person's class location structures their cultural consumption and leisure participation in two main ways. First, and most obviously, it imposes material constraints on access in terms of the amount of money and time they have available. Class is also correlated with factors such as area of residence and car ownership which play an important part in limiting access to facilities. Secondly, he argues, class position imposes invisible constraints by systematically structuring people's access to the necessary cultural competences. It is this hidden, symbolic dimension of class stratification which most interests him. Its operation emerges particularly clearly in cases where cultural goods are easily available at nominal cost. Bourdieu's best known example is attendance at art museums.[9]

Museums are open to everyone, but apart from tourists and people killing time or sheltering from the rain, Bourdieu's research showed that most visitors tended to come from the non-manual strata, and to have received more than the minimum amount of schooling (a point we shall return to presently). They felt entirely at home. They moved with ease and confidence among the exhibits and could talk knowledgeably about them. Working-class visitors on the other hand tended to experience the museum as an alien environment. They felt out of place, uncomfortable. Museums reminded them of churches, and they saw both as mysterious and intimidating.

Television viewing provides another illustration of this hidden dimension of stratification. Television is now the major channel of cultural participation. Most people, for example, hardly ever go out to a theatre, although most watch a good deal of televised drama of one sort of another. Audience research however indicates a strong class stratification in patterns of preference. Whereas the audience for 'classic' drama and 'serious' modern plays is concentrated in the upper middle class, *Coronation Street* and the other 'soap operas' find the bulk of their audience among the working class.[10] Once again, although television makes cultural capital available to all at the flick of a switch, it is an offer most people refuse. According to Bourdieu, they count themselves out primarily because they are culturally incompetent in the sense that they lack the conceptual and aesthetic keys required to unpack and master the cultural codes involved. For Bourdieu, then, the class distribution of television preference and museum attendance reflects the prevailing distribution of cultural competences, a distribution which is reproduced initially through differential patterns of family socialization and later confirmed through differential schooling.

Stratified schooling: reproducing incompetence

Bourdieu has devoted considerable research effort to uncovering the dynamics of the education system and the general thrust of his argument is broadly in line with the position developed independently by Michael F. D. Young and the other 'new' sociologists of education in England.[11] Like them, he sees the curriculum as the crucial mechanism for reproducing and legitimating the culture and competences of the dominant class. It does this, Bourdieu argues, in two ways. Firstly, its structure of selections and exclusions plays a key role in defining what will count as cultural capital and what won't. Cultural capital is in fact more or less coterminous with the contents of the curriculum in the élite sectors of the education system. If you can study it as part of an 'A' level or degree course, then it counts. However, Bourdieu argues, curriculum classifications follow the contours of class power, so that by and large élite educational knowledge is organized around the culture and competences of the dominant class. The curriculum therefore transmits and consecrates the dominant system of cultural classification together with the dominant modes of analysing and using cultural artifacts. As Bourdieu points out, 'any cultural asset, from cookery to dodecaphonic music by way of the Wild West film, can be a subject for apprehension ranging from the simple actual sensation to scholarly appreciation'.[12] Schools formalize dominant competences by systematically inculcating analytical and academic modes of appreciation and response. They 'hand on and demand' not only 'an aristocratic culture' but 'above all, an aristocratic relationship with it'.[13]

Although theoretically offered to all, systematic training in legitimated competences is only really open to those who have already been socialized into the dominant 'habitus' by their family upbringing. Equality of educational opportunity simply offers everyone a chance to compete in a race which is rigged in favour of the already privileged. 'The education system', Bourdieu argues, 'demands of everyone alike that they have what it does not give. This consists mainly of linguistic and cultural competence and that relationship of familiarity with culture which can only be produced by family upbringing when it transmits the dominant culture.'[14]

The success of all school education . . . depends fundamentally on the education previously accomplished in the earliest years of life . . . through the skill-learning processes of everyday life . . . the acquisition of the mother tongue, the manipulation of kinship terms and relationships, logical dispositions are mastered in their practical state. These dispositions, more or less complex, more or less elaborated symbolically, depending on class, predispose children unequally towards mastery of the operations implied in decoding a work of art. . . . Because learning is an irreversible process, the habitus acquired within the family forms the basis of the reception and assimiliation of the classroom message, and the habitus acquired at school conditions the level of reception and degree of assimilation of the messages produced and diffused by the culture industry.[15]

As a result of these structured inequalities in prior access to socially valued competences, pupils from subordinate strata tend to fail academically within the school system. Consequently they are denied access to systematic training in the dominant culture and its competences, relegated to a simpler curriculum and encouraged to internalize the schools' definition of them as culturally incompetent. Schools, Bourdieu argues, 'inculcate the fait accompli of the legitimacy of the dominant culture . . . by making those it relegates to second-order teaching recognise the inferiority of this teaching and its audience' and the 'naturalness' of their exclusion from access to cultural capital.[16] According to Bourdieu, this inequality of provision is justified primarily by what he calls 'the ideology of giftedness'; the notion that academic success is due mainly to the genetic roulette which allocates intelligence and ability on a more or less random basis.

By presenting structured inequalities as *individual* differences the notion of innate giftedness plays an important role in legitimating the prevailing distribution of wealth and power. Unlike the traditional ruling class, élites in modern advanced societies can no longer justify their claims to privilege on the basis of birth. In a nominally meritocratic and open society, entitlement needs to be backed by the aura of ability. The ideology of 'giftedness' enables the educationally successful to present themselves as competent, expert, and knowledgeable, and hence as ideally equipped to take on the key positions of power, and therefore entitled to unequal material rewards. Conversely, the fact that the unsuccessful are tacitly labelled as ignorant and incompetent helps to justify their exclusion from control and their allocation to routine tasks and subordinate positions.

Not that the possession of cultural capital automatically

guarantees access to élite positions. On the contrary, Bourdieu argues, the real dynamics of class reproduction are still firmly rooted in the inheritance of wealth and property and in the privileged entrée to élite positions facilitated by family connections and 'old boy' networks. In the case of the capitalist class, command of cultural capital is more often than not the icing on the cake. It glosses claims to positions and powers which are guaranteed by other means. Indeed, the only sphere where ownership of cultural capital is directly translatable into economic position is within the education system itself. As a consequence, Bourdieu argues (and his empirical research lends him considerable support), teachers and other members of the intelligentsia who owe their class position entirely to their possession and manipulation of symbolic wealth and valued competences, tend to overvalue the importance of élite cultural activities and to be the most involved and committed to participation. Conversely, the capitalist class proper – the heads of industry and commerce – tend to be the least interested and involved of the non-manual groups. At this point Bourdieu's work touches on the deep-seated but often neglected division in the class structure, between the bourgeoisie and the intelligentsia, and the complex and uneven relations between the accumulation of economic capital and the circulation of cultural capital.

In the space available here I have only been able to offer a very bald sketch of some of Bourdieu's basic ideas. But I hope I have done enough to indicate something of the fertility of his work and its relevance to the contemporary sociology of leisure. I want now to go on to outline some of the issues and possibilities his work raises for future research.

Beyond Bourdieu: directions for future research

(1) As several commentators have pointed out, the stockpile of surveys conducted by the major market research organizations offers sociologists of leisure a massive but so far almost untouched source of primary data on the leisure activities and cultural preferences, both of the general population and of specific sub-groups. Bourdieu's work on the stratification of consumption offers a useful starting point for the secondary analysis of this data, and one moreover which poses a number of theoretically pertinent questions. (a) Is the highly stratified pattern revealed by Bourdieu's research peculiar to France (as some critics have argued) or is

it replicated in the British data? If there are significant differences, how best can they be explained? (b) How far are there consistent preference clusters across different spheres of cultural activity? Is theatregoing, for example, necessarily linked with attendance at classical concerts and art exhibitons? Exactly how strong is the dividing line between participation in élite cultural activities and involvement in popular and mass culture? How many people participate in both and are they located in specific segments of the class structure? Are there cultural forms and activities which find a significant audience in all classes? (c) Is class position necessarily always the major stratifying principle underlying cultural consumption? How important are the cross-cutting dimensions of stratification – sex, age and life-cycle stage, and ethnicity?

(2) Bourdieu's explanation of differential consumption in terms of differential cultural competences also raises a series of interesting research questions. How far does cultural competence vary between different class groups? How far are there systematic differences in the ways that people classify, evaluate, and interpret cultural artifacts? How are these patterns of selection, emphasis, and exclusion related to wider ideological configurations? Given two people in the same basic class location, for example, what difference does it make to their patterns of cultural consumption if one is a socialist and the other votes for the National Front?

These kinds of questions are best approached through qualitative research rather than through conventional quantitative techniques. One-off sample surveys offer a convenient way of mapping the general distribution of cultural preferences and involvements. However, in order to uncover the dynamics of these choices and the complex and often contradictory meanings and values underpinning them, accounts of procedures are required. One strategy is offered by the technique of repeated depth-interviews as employed, for example, by Sennett and Cobb in their magnificent excavation of class imagery, *The Hidden Injuries of Class*.[17] In order to maximize the theoretical return on this kind of work however, it is necessary to sample purposively by selecting people in theoretically significant locations within the class structure. Bourdieu's work suggests that as well as taking people from both the manual and non-manual strata, it is also important to compare and contrast different non-manual groups – particularly those such as managers and company directors who are directly involved in organizing productive economic activities, and those such as teachers who are engaged in manipulating and transmitting symbolic wealth. His work also points to the crucial importance of taking account of differences in the duration and type of education received.

(3) Although Bourdieu lays great stress on the family as the primary agency of cultural transmission, apart from his anthropological fieldwork in Algeria he has never studied family socialization empirically. Even so, his work does indicate the importance of understanding how exactly children come to acquire particular cultural competences and attitudes towards the cultural domain. Some of the relevant work is already being undertaken in sociolinguistics. The work of Basil Bernstein and his collaborators offers a particularly relevant precedent, and one whose implications deserve serious consideration from sociologists of leisure. Are there, for example, general equivalents in the cultural field of Bernstein's 'elaborated' and 'restricted' codes? How far is the possession of a particular linguistic code associated with particular patterns of cultural classification and use? To what extent are linguistic and cultural competences and styles of use embedded in specific family structures and interaction styles?

(4) Bourdieu's analysis of the education system suggests a number of possible links between the sociology of leisure and contemporary research and theory in the sociology of education. Once again it is worth asking how far his analysis is specific to the French system and how far it applies to the situation in Britain. How exactly does the English education system operate to reproduce the unequal class distribution of cultural competences? How far do the selections and priorities embedded in curriculum structures legitimate the cultural activities and competences of dominant groups? What are the implications of the growth of 'progressive' as against traditional structures? How far does participation in more 'open' curriculum structures modify pupils' patterns of cultural classification and choice? Once again these sorts of questions deserve serious consideration from sociologists interested in understanding and explaining contemporary patterns of leisure and cultural consumption.

(5) As yet, Bourdieu has not matched his research on educational transmission with a comparable body of work on the other major secondary agencies of cultural transmission and leisure provision – the mass media and the agencies sponsored by national and local government. Here again, however, his work suggests a number of pertinent questions for further investigation. (a) What are these organizations' strategies of surveillance and incorporation? How do they set about deciding what to sponsor and what to exclude, and on

what criteria are these decisions made? (b) What are their classifying practices? How do they package and present material for public consumption? What kind of cultural competences do their presentations presuppose and what modes of appropriation do they encourage? How are these expectations signalled to the potential customer through, for example, location of presentation, accompanying publicity and explication, etc.? (c) How far do these classifying and presentation practices serve to reproduce and legitimate the dominant hierarchy of cultural evaluations and competences, and at what points do they challenge it?

(6) Finally, Bourdieu's work raises very basic issues about the general relationships between the economic and symbolic dimensions of class stratification, and about the part played by leisure and culture in the processes of legitimation and social control. For example, there is a whole series of crucial questions to be asked about the institutional, social, and ideological relations between the groups controlling the culture and leisure industries and other economic and political élites. How far are the areas of culture and leisure 'relatively autonomous'? How far do they operate as agencies of class power and social control? At what points, if any, do they operate or erode or undermine the prevailing class structure?

The brief list I have given here only indicates some of the areas for research that Bourdieu's work opens up and renders problematic. It is by no means exhaustive, but hopefully it is sufficient to suggest the potential of his work in reconnecting the sociology of leisure not only with some of the most fertile growth points in current sociological research, but also with the basic underlying problems of explaining order and change in social and cultural life.

Notes

1 N. Parry and D. Johnson, 'Sociology and leisure: a structural approach and some policy implications', in *Sport and Leisure in Contemporary Society*, Proceedings of the Leisure symposium held at the City of London Polytechnic, January 1975. See chapter 9 below.
2 Pierre Bourdieu, 'Cultural reproduction and social reproduction', in Richard Brown (ed.), *Knowledge, Education and Cultural Change*, London, Tavistock, 1973, pp. 71–112.
3 ibid.
4 Pierre Bourdieu, 'Outline of a sociological theory of art perception', *International Social Science Journal*, vol. 20(4), 1968, pp. 589–612.
5 A. D. Edwards, *Language in Culture and Class*, London, Heinemann, 1976, ch. 1.
6 Bourdieu, 'Outline of a sociological theory of art perception'.

7 Pierre Bourdieu and J. C. Passeron, *Reproduction in Education, Society and Culture*, London, Sage Publications, 1977.

8 Bourdieu, 'Outline of a sociological theory of art perception'.

9 Pierre Bourdieu and Alain Darbel, *L'amour de l'art: les musées d'art Européens et leur public*, Paris, Editions de Minuit, 1968.

10 B. P. Emmett, 'The television and radio audience in Britain', in Denis McQuail (ed.), *Sociology of Mass Communications*, London, Penguin Books, 1972, pp. 195–219.

11 See for example M. F. D. Young (ed.) *Knowledge and Control*, London, Collier-Macmillan, 1971.

12 Bourdieu, 'Outline of a sociological theory of art perception', p. 593.

13 Pierre Bourdieu, 'The school as a conservative force', in John Eggleston (ed.), *Contemporary Research in the Sociology of Education*, London, Methuen, 1974, pp. 32–46.

14 Bourdieu, 'Cultural reproduction and social reproduction', p. 80.

15 Bourdieu and Passeron op. cit., pp. 43–4.

16 ibid.

17 R. Sennett and J. Cobb, *The Hidden Injuries of Class*, New York, Vintage, 1975.

8

The Swedish experience:
life and leisure in an affluent
mixed economy (1980)

HARALD SWEDNER

Introduction

There are probably many who are reluctant to take seriously the social problem suggested in this chapter. They have my sympathy. This problem is rightly overshadowed by our energy problems, by threats of overpopulation, and by threats against peace the world over. The problem treated here concerns only a limited part of the world's population, living in highly industrialized, prosperous areas in Europe and some other countries of the same kind throughout the world. Furthermore, it is hardly possible to carry through any general reasoning about this problem, which will hold true for all or even most of these western societies.

For fairly obvious reasons I will base my arguments on observations on Swedish society and I cannot, with any degree of certainty, claim that my statements and conclusions are valid for such countries as Great Britain or Holland. On the contrary, there is reason to believe that every one of these highly developed nations has its own fairly specific variety of this problem.

A man who speaks on a subject with so many aspects should reasonably be an authority in a number of fields. I must admit that the basis of my authority to discuss this subject is limited, perhaps absurdly limited. Any authority I may have is related to the fact that, as a social scientist, I have for several years been engaged in research aimed at describing and explaining what is usually referred to in Sweden as 'cultural life', and particularly in studies of a limited part of it, which has in recent years frequently been called 'fine culture' – in Swedish *'finkultur'*. In later years I have broadened my views on this problem by being engaged in studies concerning the quality of life for some problem-loaded and under-privileged groups in Swedish society, particularly immigrants and slum-dwellers.

Free time and leisure time in Sweden at the beginning of the 1960s

Let me begin with a distinction that may appear to be trivial: that between *free time* and *leisure time*. By free time, I mean the time a person is free from work, that is work-free time. By leisure time, I mean the time a person is free to do as he pleases, the time when he is unhampered by unavoidable maintenance needs (washing, cooking, eating, etc.). Leisure is yours in those hours when you can choose your activities.

Our leisure time is, of course, much shorter than our work-free time. Most of us must travel to and from our place of work; most of us have unavoidable errands to perform, to the grocery store, to the post office, to the dentist, to the doctor, and so on. We must be punctual for our meals, we must set aside time to rest, to sleep, to renew our ability to work and function as human beings. How much time is left to us to choose our activities from the range of activities we happen to like, in the remaining hours when all these matters have been attended to?

It is well known that we have had a big reduction in working hours for those large groups of the Swedish population who are employed in offices and factories. This, however, does not give an accurate picture of societal change in this area during these years. Longer trips to and from work, increased obligations during work-free time, greater work intensity, and more extra jobs, with subsequent exhaustion and over-fatigue, are minus factors, which in practice mean that very large parts of the population have a more limited amount of free time. The working environments in today's 'free-time society', for those working in offices and factories, are, moreover, much more effectively separated from people's leisure-time milieux than they were and are for agricultural workers and skilled tradesmen where work and leisure are still closely linked. It is only in the distant future that we can expect the realization of the dream, described by Constant Nieuwenhuys in his talks about 'The new Babylon',[1] where people can live a varied, creative life, where work time is no longer separated from leisure time, where work and leisure go together without conflict.

I would like to start my analysis with some factual statements about the ways in which various groups in Sweden use their leisure time.

This question itself has many aspects. One is: which social groups shall we compare with each other in such an analysis? A reasonable answer is that the researcher should compare those groups that people in general usually compare with each other, such as men and women; married and unmarried; the young, adults, and the elderly; those who live in the countryside and those who live in the cities; those with high incomes and those with low; manual workers, office workers, entrepreneurs, and intellectuals; those with a few years of schooling and those with many; the working class, the middle class, and the upper class.

Such comparisons usually demonstrate that people in these various groups use their leisure time in different ways. In most cases it is possible to predict with some confidence the direction of the differences.

But matter-of-fact descriptions of that kind sometimes give rise to critical comments. There exist divisions of people which are frequently considered uncomfortable and irritating to compare. Comparisons between working class, middle class and upper class are such comparisons. When such comparisons were made at the beginning of the 1960s, they were considered – and are sometimes also today – to be irritating both by those who think that ordinary people in our society do not actually distinguish between different social classes, and by those who think that in Swedish society – for political reasons – one ought not compare social classes (although they admit that the members of this society actually locate each other, and themselves, in such categories).

In Sweden large segments of the working class speak of themselves and the bourgeoisie (*borgarna*) as two easily identifiable social strata, but many both among the workers and within the bourgeoisie dislike the idea of dividing people in this way according to their social and economic background.

Reluctance to use these terms in an analysis of the Swedish society – and leisure – derives from several sources. First, many Swedes on principle consider it to be 'undemocratic' to divide people into groups that are looked upon as hierarchically arranged. That reason, I think, was common among conservatives and social democrats. Second, many do not wish to be reminded that there still exist privileged and underprivileged groups in Swedish society. Third, many Swedes do not wish to be reminded that there still

The Swedish experience

Table 8.1 *Participation in leisure activities*

Leisure activity	Percentage who participated at least twelve times a year (on average, at least once a month)
Visits to art exhibitions	2
Visits to concerts	3
Visits to theatres	5
Visits to restaurants	11
Visits to public lectures, etc.	13
Visits to libraries	18
Visits to dances	18
Churchgoing	21
Participation in union meetings, board meetings, etc.	21
Visits to sporting competitions (as spectators)	24
Visits to the cinema	26
Active participation in sports and athletics	35
Book reading	64
Car journeys outside the home district (for recreation)	67
Visits to friends (parties)	68
Listening to the radio in the evening	73
Watching TV in the evening	92

exist reasons for a struggle between privileged and underprivileged groups in our society. The two latter reasons, I think, were – and are – most common among people who know that they themselves are privileged.

The results of a large number of empirical, time-use-oriented leisure studies showed that there were many groups in society whose leisure time is poor with regard to variation. For example, women seem, on the whole, to be less engaged in leisure activities outside the home than men. Countryside people, for easily under-standable reasons, utilize leisure facilities in agglomerations and cities far less than do city dwellers. Facilities for leisure activities outside the home are to a considerable extent directed at younger people. The frequency of most leisure activities outside the home falls rapidly after the age of 25 years.

It is a well-established fact that the use of leisure time is more varied among upper-class and middle-class people than among the working classes. An interview study with a representative sample of the Swedish population, which I carried out in November 1964 (in co-operation with The Swedish Institute of Public Opinion Research) showed that the frequency and the variation in leisure-time activities was lowest among the working class, particularly as regards such leisure activities which I named the *finkultur* of the bourgeoisie.

Table 8.1 shows what percentage of those interviewed said that they devote themselves to specified leisure activities at least twelve times a year, or, if these occasions were distributed fairly evenly over the year, once a month.

A conspicuously small percentage of the population devotes itself with some regularity (at least twelve times a year) to those three leisure activities among those mentioned in the table, which can be referred to as *finkultur*: art exhibition visits, concert visits, and theatre visits. On the other hand, leisure activities related to the home environment and those associated with intercourse with friends are those to which a much larger percentage of those interviewed devote themselves fairly often (at least twelve times a year). This group of activities comprise among others, watching TV, listening to the radio, participating in parties, car journeys, and reading books.

Table 8.2 shows an index of the frequencies for leisure time activities among the upper-class (social group I), the middle-class (social group II), and the workers (social group III). The means obtained for different subgroups, when these point values were used, are shown in Table 8.2. Most of the differences shown in the table were statistically significant.

It is easy to see, in this table, that the frequencies were lowest in the working class for almost all those seventeen leisure activities which were investigated.

Explanations of leisure and culture barriers in Sweden

It is frequently noticed that Swedes live in an unusually monolithic society, and that there exists some kind of uniform Swedish culture. It is a truth that has to be modified. In Sweden at least three separate cultures exist. A *peasant culture* with a thousand-year anchorage in agricultural production; an *upper-class culture* which since the end of the eighteenth century has developed a life-style related to the living conditions of entrepreneurs and civil

Table 8.2

Leisure activity	Men				Women			
	Social group				Social group			
	Total	I	II	III	Total	I	II	III
	(587)	(48)	(255)	(284)	(579)	(40)	(316)	(223)
Visits to concerts	0.27	1.04	0.32	0.10	0.36	0.83	0.44	0.17
Visits to art exhibitions	0.43	1.06	0.51	0.26	0.43	0.98	0.48	0.26
Visits to public lectures, etc.	0.77	1.60	0.95	0.49	0.72	1.35	0.77	0.55
Visits to the theatre	0.78	1.58	0.83	0.60	0.84	1.68	0.91	0.59
Visits to restaurants	0.92	1.83	0.88	0.81	0.59	1.43	0.62	0.40
Visits to libraries	1.07	1.71	1.23	0.85	1.67	1.25	0.69	0.55
Visits to dances	1.15	1.50	1.14	1.10	1.98	0.45	1.05	1.00
Churchgoing	1.22	1.21	1.46	1.02	1.69	1.73	1.87	1.43
Participation in board meetings, etc.	1.56	1.94	1.87	1.24	0.80	1.13	0.84	0.70
Cinema visits	1.56	2.23	1.38	1.60	1.26	1.80	1.31	1.08
Visits to sport competitions	1.91	1.40	1.75	2.12	0.62	0.48	0.63	0.64
Active participation in sports and athletics	2.27	3.42	2.37	2.00	1.50	2.33	1.54	1.29
Visits to friends (parties)	3.00	3.15	3.12	2.87	3.07	3.55	3.21	2.80
Car journeys for recreation	3.43	3.65	3.43	3.39	3.20	3.93	3.28	2.96
Book reading	3.80	5.54	4.02	3.34	3.57	6.03	3.69	2.98
Listening to the radio in the evening	4.69	4.60	4.76	4.64	4.74	4.13	4.82	4.74
Watching television in the evening	6.50	6.45	6.56	6.46	6.32	6.68	6.23	6.39

By giving different points to a number of frequency categories, answers given to questions were transformed to a 'quasi-logarithmic' frequency scale. The number of points given to the different answer categories were as follows:

0 = Never or only rarely
1 = 1–3 days a year
2 = 4–11 days a year
3 = 12–23 days a year
4 = 24–51 days a year
5 = 52–99 days a year
6 = 100–299 days a year
7 = 300–339 days a year
8 = 340 days a year

Note: Lowest frequencies for each activity are underlined.

servants. But there also exists a *working-class culture*, with a history linked to working-class neighbourhoods in large industrial towns and mining districts, for example.

The peasant culture is now rapidly disintegrating because of the industrialization and urbanization of the countryside. The bourgeois way of life gains ground everywhere. Representatives of bourgeois *finkultur* have built up its bastions – they might be called

Trojan horses – both within the countryside and the working-class environments. It also has commando troops operating in the culture departments of newspapers, radio, television, etc. However, there seem to be barriers that, at least temporarily, have checked its progress along some sectors of the front.

These life-styles stand ostentatiously opposed to each other in industrial cities, where the upper classes and the working class to some extent work side by side, but are at the same time socially confined in their own segregated neighbourhoods and districts.

On both sides of the barriers between the bourgeoisie and the workers, different ways of regarding leisure and *finkultur* can be found. Among the bourgeoisie, one frequently comes across an 'élite reasoning', but one may also find a 'proselyte reasoning'.

Élite reasoning

Élite reasoning is found among those who are apt to accept the status quo. For them, *finkultur* is something that the masses can never acquire. It is an element in a way of life that is reserved for a limited élite privileged by their talents, their powers of imagination, their richness of ideas and their intelligence. Because this culture-aristocratic view is strange to me, I am afraid I cannot do it justice with my own words; I will therefore quote Sebastian de Grazia's *Of Time, Work and Leisure*.

> The world is divided into two classes. Not three or five or twenty. Just two. One is the great majority; the other is the leisure kind, not those of wealth or position or birth but those who love ideas and imagination. Of the great mass of mankind there are a few persons who are blessed and tormented with this love. They may work, steal, flirt, fight like all the others, but everything they do is touched with the play of thought. In one century they may be scientists, in another theologians, in some other bards, whatever the going may be that grants them freedom to let their minds play. They invent the stories, they create the cosmos, they discover what truth it is given man to discover and give him the best portion of his truth and error.
>
> It is a select small world of thinkers, artists and musicians – not necessarily in touch with one another – who find their happiness in what they do, who can't do anything their demon won't let them. Their demon doesn't depend on environment. You have it or have not. The pleasures for this handful of persons differ strongly from those of the rest. It cannot be otherwise. The

ordinary person must buy his pleasures with the time and the income of his occupation, while this selected class is actually occupied in its pleasure. That is hardly no matter how much the class is underpaid, it is a luxury class and will always have its select spirits as members. As long as it has leisure.

Its felicity is assured in each act and at the very moment. The others, moreover, need to recreate themselves from their occupation, whereas this class has, if anything, only a need of distraction.[2]

Sebastian de Grazia here eloquently expresses his conviction – and the conviction of many Swedes – that culture must be reserved for the chosen few. His way of regarding the problem may stand as a fitting exposition of 'élite reasoning'.

Proselyte reasoning

There is unquestionably among many members of the upper class and the middle class a wish to 'export' their own culture to other social strata. Many academically trained persons in Sweden have considered it a duty to act as ambassadors or missionaries of *finkultur* in the working-class and countryside environments, to a large extent within the framework of adult education, but also in other ways. There is something almost pathetic about the feverish activity in that direction among many adult education enthusiasts, a naïve innocence which probably often originates from a complete ignorance about the fact that the style and the content of great parts of *finkultur* are actually classbound. They also sometimes demonstrate a dangerous lack of knowledge about the negative attitudes towards this *finkultur* on the other side of the barrier. Disappointment that these proselytizing activities produce so meagre a result is seldom coupled with an insight into the factors which make the work so ineffective.

The élite attitude as well as the proselyte attitude is based on the assumption that *finkultur* is something extraordinarily valuable. Both reasonings also have another debatable assumption as a further premise. The élite argument is often associated with the idea that participation in the exclusive varieties of *finkultur* is genetically determined and that social background factors and environmental factors play a negligible role in the development of an interest in such activities. 'The genius always finds his way to a starting point.' The recruitment attitude is based on another

Freedom and Constraint

Table 8.3

	Type of reasoning	
	Upper and middle classes	Working class
Persons who accept the barrier between middle-class *finkultur* and working-class culture as inevitable	Elite reasoning	Solidarity reasoning
Persons who consider that the barrier between middle-class *finkultur* and working-class culture can be bridged	Proselyte reasoning	Climber reasoning

debatable assumption: 'What I have found to be good for me, is good for other people too.'

In Table 8.3, I have attempted to illustrate the fact that élite reasoning and proselyte reasoning within those sections of the upper and middle classes which have taken *finkultur* on contract, are paralleled by two kinds of reasoning within the working class. These ways of reasoning naturally start from other premises, but in practice they lead to a parallel division of attitudes to *finkultur*.

Climber reasoning

Many workers, who by way of schooling, or later in life by way of social and political activities, have moved from the working class into the middle class, seek frequently during their upward mobility – consciously or unconsciously – to acquire the veneer and the value system associated with *finkultur*. For many, this acquisition is a natural consequence of their social mobility on the basis of other factors. For others, the acceptance of the veneer and values of participants in *finkultur* may function as an anticipation of future advancement or even as one of the vehicles by which they try to reach a higher social stratum.

Solidarity reasoning

There can be no doubt that large groups of workers consciously dissociate themselves from bourgeois *finkultur*. This is common among workers who are aware that there is in their own group a style of living which is a meaningful alternative to the *finkultur* of the bourgeoisie. The manner in which workers spend their leisure is a way of life which has developed outside the chalk circles of bourgeois culture. It is a way of life created through sacrifices during years of hard class struggle in the nineteenth century and the early part of the twentieth century, when the workers built their own amusement parks (*Folkparker*) and meeting halls (*Folkets Hus*) , when they marched enthusiastically on May Day, when they went on strike and protested against bourgeois society.

In mining villages and in working-class areas in large cities, they created during these years their own way of life, characterized by solidarity and *Gemeinschaft* between workmates, neighbours and relatives, a life where the spectacular happenings in bourgeois *finkultur* and the etiquette of their style of living were exchanged for intimacy and shared ideas on essential and vital matters.

Relations between working-class culture and bourgeois finkultur

I have permitted myself to base my thinking about the problems of *finkultur* and leisure on the well-established fact that considerable differences still exist in the use of leisure among the various subcultures in Swedish society. These differences are so conspicuous that I find it quite natural to speak about culture barriers.

The fact that many inhabitants of the cities have accepted aspects of traditional country life has resulted in a renaissance of this way of life: cottage living, farm tools, peasant costumes, folk dances, hunting, fishing, are all highly valued as leisure activities. Actually, peasant culture in Swedish society, with its centuries old traditions and its strong material anchorage in the farming environment and in important economic activities, has in practice now become wedded to the bourgeois *finkultur*.

It is otherwise with the working-class environment in, for example, mining districts and the large industrial cities. The workers here, during a short, hectic period of harsh conflicts and class struggle created their own way of life. However, the short period that this way of life really functioned as an independent subculture was not long enough to permit it to gain strength and to become resistant to attacks from the outside. One of the reasons why the working class was unable to build up an effective alternative to bourgeois *finkultur* was unquestionably the fact that its members – in contrast to a large segment of the people in the countryside – did not own or create their means of production; they had consequently no opportunity for creating a strong economic base for their way of life.

Despite its obvious weakness, working-class culture has, however, not proved an easy prey for the apostles of bourgeois *finkultur*. It seems as if the élite thinking of the bourgeoisie together with the attachment of the workers to the way of life of their own class have effectively prevented the growth of a truly monolithic uniform culture in Sweden.

It seems to me that, providing no new factors are added, we will have to wait a long time for a situation to arise in which the interests and aims of individuals rather than socio-economic factors will have a decisive influence upon the use of leisure time in Sweden. This is true to some extent for all leisure activities but to a particularly marked degree for those leisure activities which are linked to bourgeois *finkultur*.

Attempts to influence leisure life in Sweden

Many attempts to influence the basic features of Swedish leisure life have been made since the beginning of the 1960s, when information regarding the non-egalitarian structure of the Swedish way of life became available to a wide audience and became the target for a broad attack from a number of liberal and radical groups and parties. Let me describe briefly some examples, in which I became involved as a researcher, but also as an active member of those groups which initiated these actions.

The actions were all based upon the idea that it would be possible to influence the use of leisure in a neighbourhood through initiatives taken by activists within such institutions as libraries, free theatre groups, or groups of residents. Ideas similar to those which influenced community work projects in, for example, Great Britain and the Netherlands, were frequently at the root of these attempts.

Attempt to change neighbourhood life through new library archives

I will begin with a description of an attempt to animate the population in five local communities in Sweden via their public libraries, in which I became engaged as a researcher – paid by the state – at the beginning of the 1970s. Heavy stress was laid on studying the effectiveness of the means used by animators (i.e. the librarians). The ultimate goals were not much discussed and analysed. In the planning of this experiment it was almost taken for granted that an increase in activities such as reading books and participation in cultural activities was something good, which should be strived for – as it was supposed to contribute to people's capacity for an active life, for creativity, for communication, for adjustment, for personal development, and meaningful and varied leisure.

The action programmes in the five communities These experiments are interesting because they were combined with an ambitious attempt to measure their effect upon the population. The animation techniques used were chosen by the librarians in the respective communities in close co-operation with a group of experts at the national level. The evaluation study was led by the author of this paper. The experiment as well as the evaluation was financed by the Royal Literary Commission within the Department of Education. The libraries in the five communities obtained some additional money for their activities for one year (1970). The staff of the libraries were permitted to use this money at their own discretion. The animation techniques suggested to the librarians were, for example, to increase the cultural facilities and services which were available for those who lived in the community, through libraries, but also to give more information about the library and to buy books that one would expect to be interesting for their community. It was expected that this would increase the number of books borrowed from the library, the participation in arranged meetings in the libraries, and the number of books read by the inhabitants.

The extra amount of money placed at the disposal of these libraries was actually used in many different ways. Its use was partially influenced by suggestions from those who participated in the overall planning of the study, but to a great extent the activities selected by the staff at each of the libraries took into account local conditions and traditions, the ways the libraries were already functioning, and the knowledge the librarians had of needs and wishes among the inhabitants of the area and the users of the library.

The five areas were rather different in character.

Kirseberg is an old working-class suburb in the city of Malmö, with a century-long history; this area has a low income level per household and has for decades been regarded by the inhabitants of

Malmö as a 'slum area'. The district houses approximately 15,000 inhabitants.

Oxhagen is a 'new suburb' in the city of Örebro with only 4,000 inhabitants. It was built during the last two decades; this area is looked upon as a 'fine suburb' with a population of a rather high socio-economic level (an upper-middle-class area).

Skärholmen is a modern Stockholm suburb with a big shopping centre built during the last decade. It is expected gradually to become a commercial centre for a surrounding 'hinterland' with about 100,000 inhabitants. When we began our studies there, in 1969, the area had a population of about 25,000 persons.

The other two investigation areas lie in Västerbotten, in the northern part of the country. **Skelleftea** is a densely populated small town, which has about 25,000 inhabitants. Differing from the rapidly built-up Stockholm suburb of Skärholmen, it represents a settlement that has existed for centuries.

Jörn is a rural parish, the centre of which has developed during the past century around a railway station, situated thirty-seven miles from Skelleftea. Like most rural parishes in the northern part of Sweden, it is rapidly losing inhabitants. The agglomeration at present has about 1,500 inhabitants, and the entire parish includes a further 700 persons, spread over a large and sparsely populated forest district.

Some of the money placed at the disposal of the libraries was used to buy new types of books for the library shelves and to apply for new means of distribution and for information of these new means. Among the activities implemented by one or more of the libraries studied, the following may be mentioned:

the acquisition of several copies of the same title

the acquisition of paperbacks

the acquisition of easily read literarure

the acquisition of literature for immigrants

the starting of 'mini-libraries' in factories and other places of work

the starting of 'mini-libraries' in social welfare offices, immigrant clubs, etc.

the starting of 'mini-libraries' on the pavements outside the library

the use of book buses

the extension of opening hours (particularly evenings and Sundays) the use of new information techniques (letters sent to households, posters, folders, advertisements, etc.)

However, a large amount of money was also used for cultural and social activities within the premises of the library: activities for children with story-telling and children's theatre shows, author's evenings, films, shows, plays, exhibitions, and musical events. In Oxhagen and Skärholmen ambitious family Sundays were arranged with programmes for all ages. Of particular interest are the programmes presented in one of the villages in the parish of Jörn in co-operation with the library, by Riksteatern (the National Touring Theatre) and Riksutställningar (Swedish Travelling Exhibitions). In Kirseberg, Oxhagen, and Skärholmen the library hosted information meetings and discussions about controversial aspects of the city's planning proposals for the area. The library's social functions were tested primarily in Kirseberg and in Skärholmen, but 'the Family Sundays' in Oxhagen also had a social slant. In most of the five communities (particularly in Kirseberg, Skärholmen, Oxhagen, and Jörn), children and adolescents were given something to keep them occupied in their leisure time (there was a real shortage of leisure facilities in all five communities). For example, in 1970 the library in Jörn functioned, in the words of the librarian, as a 'pure youth centre'.

Specially designed programmes were particularly frequent in Kirseberg, Oxhagen, and Skarholmen. Programmes for immigrants were organized at the libraries in Kirseberg and Skärholmen. Of particular interest were the city planning discussions in Kirseberg. These attracted a large public and led to the formation of a local action group (*byalag*). The positive response of the population in Kirseberg appears to be connected with the fact that the library staff were very involved in arranging the introductory exhibition and the discussion which followed. The fact that special work groups were set up in order to develop guidelines for the exhibition and the programmes, seems to have been just as important. These groups included members of the library staff as well as interested outsiders. A number of similar discussions in Oxhagen and Skärholmen attracted considerably fewer people. In the case of Oxhagen the explanation was probably that the discussions dealt with problems which the inhabitants considered to be of less importance. With regard to Skärholmen, this was probably not the explanation. The decisive factor in favour of Kirseberg was possibly the broader social involvement of the librarians and the fact that many of the inhabitants participated in the planning. In principle it is important to note that by arranging discussions and exhibitions libraries can provide information about important municipal matters.

Among the arranged events, family Sundays were particularly successful. All the libraries in the experiment invited authors to make guest appearances. As a rule these were arranged in the traditional manner for such encounters, but less conventional forms were also attempted.

Exhibitions were arranged at all the libraries studied. In recent years libraries in Sweden have, to an increasing degree, become recipients of exhibitions arranged by Riksutställningar, a national organization financed by the government. One of the reasons for this is that libraries usually have premises large enough to accommodate an exhibition without other activites being hampered. They also have relatively long opening hours and have a staff available to keep an eye on the exhibition. The relatively large number of people visiting the library indicates that many people will see an exhibition arranged there.

The library has the necessary premises for many functions, which are not usually located there. In Kirseberg the library served as a meeting place for immigrants and as a 'warm room' for teenagers. This role may on the surface seem to be a passive one. In fact it requires a considerable effort on the part of the staff to arrange it so that these functions are satisfactorily planned for.

When libraries go beyond the function of distributing books, they have to co-operate with other municipal authorities. Of special interest in connection with this are a couple of experiments carried out in Kirseberg and Skärholmen, involving the co-ordination of personnel at the libraries and employees of other municipal authorities. In Kirseberg close co-operation was developed with the social workers in the poorest housing district. In Skärholmen the library participated in a committee for cultural activities with some fifty people, representatives of various organizations, and individuals.

Attempts were also made to involve the inhabitants of the area in library activities, e.g. by forming consumer councils. The initiative was greeted with interest by the inhabitants, but interest diminished during the course of the experiment. The original aim of approaching associations and organizations with proposals that they should appoint members of library committees with the task of stimulating their members to utilize library services was not realized.

The effects of the action programme   What happened with the inhabitants in these five communities? Did they come to the library in increased numbers? Did they use the facilities and services offered to them by the animators in the libraries?

We tried to measure this by studying the habits of the population before the intensification period (in 1969) and during the intensification period (in 1970).

Two such before/after studies were carried out, one among representative samples from the adult population of 16–19 years of age (the samples consisted of 400 individuals from each community) and one including all schoolchildren in grades 3, 6, and 9 in each community (the number of children varied between 150 and 950 in the five communities).

All data consistently point in the direction of increased use of the facilities of the libraries in 1970. Tables on the number of loans at the libraries studied for the years 1969, 1970, and 1971 (according to the statistics of the libraries) also indicate that the number of loans per inhabitant increased considerably during the year of the experiment. In 1971 the increase rate dropped at three of the experiment libraries and an actual decrease took place (compared with the figures for 1970) at the other two.

A comparison with five 'control libraries' indicated that the libraries where the animation experiments were carried out increased their loans considerably more than their 'control libraries'. During the year following the year of the experiment this was not so. Then at three of the control libraries the number of loans increased more than at the corresponding experiment libraries. These figures – and our analysis of data from the interview studies with adults and schoolchildren – indicate that the animation work led to an increase of library activities in all our five experiment neighbourhoods.

As one can conclude from this, we obtained the result we had hoped for. We were able to prove – beyond any reasonable doubt – that one can increase such activities as the borrowing of books and the participation in library-centred activities by increasing the amount of money placed at the disposal of personnel at the libraries. Giving the library staff an open permit to use their 'extra' money at their own discretion, either for the buying of facilities, for the hiring of personnel, or for buying particular services, they were able to find ways of using this money, which meant that the results aimed at were actually achieved.

The demographic, economic, and political ramifications of the action programme   However, using the technique of participant observation, we noticed many other things. Some of these observations were just as important as, or possibly more important than the above findings from the analysis of available statistics 1969, 1970, and 1971. Much of what happened in the five areas of experimentation could not be found by the analysis of library statistics and answers to questionnaires, distributed to large samples of the population in the five areas. In spite of the fact that many of these observations cannot be substantiated by figures, and were, consequently, not stressed in the detailed research reports from the study.[3] I would like to bring your attention to a few of them.

(1) It seemed comparatively easy to build up a meaningful pro-
    gramme for an intensification of library work in those com-
    munities, where the library staff had a personal commitment to
    their local community. This was particularly the case among
    the librarians in the working-class area of Kirseberg in the city
    of Malmö, and in the depopulated rural parish of Jorn in the
    northern part of the country. It was also obvious that a personal
    adherence to the idea of a multi-functional library was an
    important prerequisite for becoming an effective animator
    within the library framework (many Swedish librarians, prob-
    ably a majority of them, are strongly book-oriented and were
    reluctant to participate in activities which were not book-
    centred).
(2) It was, for many reasons, extremely difficult to build up a
    meaningful animation programme in a newly created library
    unit in a big and rapidly developing high-rise apartment
    suburban area (such as Skärholmen in Stockholm).
(3) It was much easier to develop an effective animation pro-
    gramme in small communities such as the suburb of Oxhagen
    in Örebro and the suburb of Kirseberg in Malmö (small from the
    point of view of the size of the area as well as the size of the
    population); this probably depended upon the fact that the
    library staff in these communities could count upon the
    existence of a rather homogeneous and well-integrated local
    subculture with shared values and similar habits.
(4) An increased coverage of the activities conducted by the

libraries frequently meant that they were counteracted by other municipal authorities and by organizations, which felt that the librarians threatened to take over tasks which they looked upon as their own prerogative and were not inclined to give up. In Kirseberg, where the library is housed in the same building as a youth centre, complications arose from the fact that the youth centre had opening hours other than those of the library and also charged entrance fees – which the library did not. The meagre resources for child and youth care within the premises of the Skärholmen library made effective co-operation between library and the child welfare authorities difficult.

(5) The staff at those libraries which encouraged local associations and groups critical of the policies of the municipal authorities (which in Sweden finance and govern the activities of public libraries), quickly ran into conflicts with the authorities. This was particularly the case in Kirseberg, where the library staff co-operated closely with local citizen groups who raised issues against local government in their public meetings and in the local newspaper.

What has been said here suggests that when studying animation attempts one has to consider the reality behind such concepts as 'animation' and 'animators' from the perspective of history and the tradition of the nations and the municipalities where the attempts are made. It must always be taken into account, when planning an attempt to influence leisure life, that it is conducted within a given demographic, economic, and political framework.

The Gorilla Theatre in Malmö

My own and Göran Arnman's study of the Gorilla Theatre in Malmö was heavily influenced by that perspective on the theatre which derives from ideas about how to achieve social change and the role of theatres in such attempts. In our report we described the circumstances which led to the early death of this small, local theatre in a suburb of Malmö.[4]

We went out to find a theatre which functioned more in accordance with a social change perspective than was usual for well-established theatres. The short, two-year history of the Gorilla Theatre clearly exemplifies that even relatively modest political aims almost inevitably come, sooner or later, into conflict with the established and controlling societal institutions which it is engaged in criticizing. Its history demonstrates that a theatre which functions in accordance with the social change model must always struggle to survive, and if and when it does not adjust to the power-holders, it is doomed, sooner or later, to be killed.

The study was carried out at the end of the 1960s within the framework of an international study of the theatre as a social institution. Behind our choice of topic was the fact that we regarded the theatre as a significant and precious aspect of the cultural life of our society, even though we were tired and somewhat critical of the repertoire we had experienced on the stages of well-established theatres. The starting point was that we had observed that those working in theatres were bad at marketing their products, and that few of them seemed aware of having failed to sell their product to large groups of the population. The theatre de facto, despite all flowery speeches to the contrary, was bourgeois orientated and isolated from the working classes.

We saw it as our task to make those who worked in the theatre, and others, such as politicians and administrators, aware of the extent to which they had failed in this respect. We attempted to achieve this through empirical studies of the means of production in the theatre, its channels of distribution, and the social composition of audiences. Indeed, at the beginning, we unconsciously and uncritically applied to the theatre all the marketing ideas which govern the work of those who deal with commodities in an affluent consumption-orientated society.

Later we departed from this mode of thinking and saw how this way of thought, prevalent in the early 1960s, hindered us from formulating a number of significant problems. We slowly developed alternative conceptions which allowed us to postulate new tasks for theatre research. We found it relevant to analyse critically the effects of marketing thinking in theatre research, and introduced 'therapeutic thinking' and 'social change thinking' as relevant to this field of research.

The marketing perspective

Each generation is struck by thoughts and reasonings which function as strait-jackets for political and scientific thought. With regard to the theatre, it is easy to see in retrospect that much of that which has been written about the theatre in recent decades is governed by the notion that the theatre is something which can and should be effectively placed at the disposal of people in much the same way as other commodities which contribute to our material well-being. Without careful consideration, writers on the problems of theatre seem often to have derived ideas from a marketing model.

There exist basic contradictions between the theoretical pre-requisites of the marketing model and other ways of looking upon culture. This is exemplified by those no longer inclined to perceive culture as a particular sector of society, but as a signficant aspect of all human activities and relations. Culture exists, according to this way of thinking, to the extent that interaction among human beings really means that they communicate feelings, ideas, and values to one another. However, the public sector support to culture which is provided today reaches almost exclusively only those institutions which define their main goals according to the marketing model; that is, which attempt to sell their products as effectively as possible. They are not at all concerned with creating the conditions for that kind of understanding among human beings which the advocates of the therapeutic model have in mind when they speak about culture. Neither do they support the idea that the theatre is one of the means of changing today's society into a better one, which is fundamental to the thinking of those who use the social change model as their point of departure.

There is much in modern marketing techniques which conflicts with the therapeutic model and the social change model. This is true, for example, for the division into 'producers' and 'consumers' implicit in the marketing model. This assumes that it is a good thing to concentrate production into the hands of a few. It may be motivated by the idea that it is good if as many people as possible consume what is produced since the basic and necessary costs of production can be shared among a large number of consumers. Large-scale production for a great number of consumers apparently works in the direction of low costs 'per consumed bit of culture'. The advocates of the marketing model have not realized that this model, in practice, means that reports about experience and perception (that is, what is communicated) can only travel in one direction – from producer to consumer. One consequence of this way of thinking, thus, is its direct opposition to regarding theatre, music, and art as media through which the interplay of individuals and groups may lead to mutual changes in knowledge and understand-ing. The division in the marketing model of human beings as producers and consumers is in direct contradiction to the idea that the fostering through culture involves a lifelong and continuous process of communicating with other people, of talking and listening, of penetrating and identifying with their situation as human beings, of developing mutual understanding and co-operation.

Both the demand for large-scale production benefits, and the corresponding attempts to reduce basic costs in the consumption situation (by having many consumers for each produced 'bit of culture') have created a need for some kind of 'middleman' between the 'producers of culture' and the 'consumers of culture'. Figuratively speaking, their duty consists of the packaging and delivery of pieces of culture in the most attractive possible manner. In practice, these middlemen often function as a screen between the producers and consumers of culture. Their appearance on the scene means that the producers and consumers of culture never come into personal contact. Even when they want to, it may prove very difficult since thereby the middlemen would lose their *raison d'être*.

It is obvious that many of those who have something to do with culture see the division of people into producers and consumers of culture as something which is necessary and even an advantage. Many, indeed, have come to regard the screening function of the middlemen as something inevitable. Of course, it still happens that producers and consumers of culture meet each other in a mutual give and take. It also happens that middlemen do not only function as screeners, but also as creators of contacts, shaping the necessary conditions for personal encounters and immediate communication between human beings. To be fair, they sometimes provide the settings for encounters where none of the actors – the producers, distributors, and consumers – stick to the parts assigned to them in the programme. Such a reservation is a necessary addition to what I have said above. There exist, no doubt, relevant roles in cultural life for interpreters, for conveyors, for middlemen, but there are also role configurations within theatre, based upon this way of thinking, which are to be questioned from the point of view of therapy and social change.

The therapeutic perspective

The reader may, of course, now ask: what are the alternatives to the well established marketing model, with its consequences of dividing people into producers and consumers of culture; of widening the gap between consumers and producers through the screening function of the middlemen; of an increasingly marked division between professional and amateur cultural workers; of setting great actors upon pedestals; and, lastly, of hindering the sharing of knowledge and experience among human beings, and thereby preventing the development of a profound awareness of the conditions and ramifications of human life in our affluent industrialized societies?

My answer will start with an attempt to guide your thoughts to what happens in a market place where producers and consumers meet in person, exchanging knowledge and experience about what they sell and buy, on how the goods have been produced, their nature, and how they might function. It may seem superficially as if, in principle, the difference between the abstract market of the marketing model and this actual market is not very great, but the difference is significant.

The actual market is a meeting place where everybody meets on an equal footing. There you will find no middlemen – nor are there any stages or pedestals. The market place is in principle an open square where just about everything can be said and where anything can happen. The idea of a market place steers our thoughts in the direction of interaction and a particular way of speaking about and defining culture. The essential thing in the market square is not the buying and selling; this is but one aspect of the activities which go on there. The essential thing is that it is a place where people meet each other face to face, where human beings can exchange experiences, where they may show grief and joy, where they can tell each other about hardships and disappointments and about their dreams and hopes.

It is only when those who work in the theatre think and act in the spirit of the market place that the theatre can be what it should be – not a special activity located in some segregated corner of life, but something that accompanies all that we do, something which helps us to a deeper knowledge of the human condition.

This way of thinking became very important in the activities of the Gorilla Theatre. The therapeutic perspective has since then – the end of the 1960s – slowly gained a firm footing among those who work in the Swedish theatre.

This is particularly the case among those who work with children's theatres, youth theatres, in amateur theatre, and with puppet theatres. There are also many people outside the institutional theatre who have realized the significance of role-playing in mental health programmes, particularly among those who work with group therapy, with socio-dramatic techniques, and sensitivity training.

The social change perspective

There are other alternatives to the marketing model apart from the interaction or therapeutic perspective. The limitation of the marketing model which the therapeutic model seeks to overcome concerns its strong connection with the idea that culture is something to be produced and transferred from the few (producers) to as many (consumers) as possible. If one wishes to add poignancy to the actual state of affairs, it can be said that the marketing model has at its foundations a non-egalitarian way of thinking. One of its basic assumptions seems to be that what a very few individuals have to say in our society is so essential that society should spend some considerable part of its resources on making sure that everybody is acquainted with what they have to say. But common to both the marketing perspective and the interaction perspective is that they place the theatre in a static and ahistorical perspective. They begin with the fundamental idea that there is a cultural life in every society of which the theatre is a significant part – and that this cultural life should be modelled in such a way as to make human beings in these societies as happy as possible. The marketing model contains the idea that happiness increases if facilities and opportunities for cultural experiences are created and made available. The interaction model implies the idea that happiness will increase if opportunities for human beings to interact on mutual and equal terms are created.

Neither of these perspectives raises the question of how cultural life is related to societal structure. Cultural life, according to these two models, can fulfil its function irrespective of how society is otherwise equipped: for the marketing model by offering members of our society 'cultural experiences' as efficiently as possible; for the interaction model by increasing opportunities for mutual inter-action and co-operation. One might, however, ask the question whether or not a society really can be equipped with the necessary facilities to provide for entertainment and happiness – for 'a good life'. Do there not exist societies where actions and decisions induced both by the marketing and the therapeutic perspectives can contribute little or nothing to people's happiness? The structure of these societies might be such that interaction on equal terms cannot easily develop and what interaction may occur cannot really contribute to the creation of the 'good life'.

Under these conditions one might ask whether cultural institu-tions such as the theatre should not involve themselves in the work of changing the structure of the surrounding society as a whole towards 'another kind of society' in which the theatre can really fill its entertaining and communicative functions in a meaningful way. This means looking at the theatre as a social institution, which, in collaboration with other social institutions, should participate in changing the structure of society. This is the basis of the 'social change perspective' of the theatre.

Taking as its starting-point the ideas about social change, the analysis of the theatre will, among other things, find it natural to relate what happens in the theatre to what happens outside it. According to the social change model the theatre – in parallel and close co-operation with other societal institutions – fills a function in a wider social system. The aim for the work of the theatre in this perspective consists neither (as in the marketing model) of making sure that productions are completed and distributed as efficiently as possible, nor (as in the interaction therapeutic model) in functioning as a meeting place which creates opportunities for communication and understanding within a given structure of existing society. Both of these may be interpreted as legitimating this defective society, which is under attack by those adhering to the social change perspective.

These were ideas that came to influence the activities of the Gorilla Theatre as time went by, although they were not expressed at that time in a very clear way. But they have later become a well-established ideological cornerstone in the thinking within the Swedish free group theatre movement, of which the Gorilla Theatre was one of the forerunners.

Swedish leisure policy: some limitations

I cannot here go into all aspects of leisure life concerned with the fact that subsidies and grants to leisure activities in Sweden are biased in favour of the established culture. It is without doubt this part of leisure life which is still promoted and supported in today's Swedish society. But I will try to make clear what I am thinking of by discussing some basic failings in Swedish leisure policy of today.

Swedish cultural policy suffers from the fact that those who administrate cultural grants and those who debate our leisure life regard it as a matter of course that we should, primarily, promote a kind of national culture, and by that they usually do not mean a culture based upon the experience of Swedes but a commercialized and easily distributed culture, which is not very well integrated into our Swedish cultural heritage.

The character of this thinking is revealed in our choice of names for those governmentally subsidized organizations that have been given the task of distributing leisure facilities and culture to areas outside our main cultural centres in the big cities – Riksteatern (the National Touring Theatre), Riksutställningar (Swedish Travelling Exhibitions) and Rikskonserter (The Institute for National Concerts). (The English translations do not really carry over the authoritarian connotations of the corresponding Swedish names.)

It is a crucial and debatable fact that leisure life is based upon effective distribution of leisure facilities. This seems to be one of the reasons why distinct regional patterns of culture have had such difficulties in maintaining themselves. Should we not, in this case, have a lot to learn from countries such as the Netherlands and Switzerland, with their much more varied and decentralized cultural life?

Cultural policy-makers in Sweden seem to regard it as a matter of course that it is in the well established cultural institutions in our big cities that culture is created. From these cities it has, according to our established leisure policy, to be portioned out to the rest of the country in suitable parcels. Some time ago, when I read about a photographic exhibition from Malung in Dalarna (Dalecarlia), coming to the Museum of Modern Art in Stockholm, I got proof of people coming to terms with the idea that the provinces can contribute to the national culture. But there are, unfortunately, a lot of mechanisms working in the opposite direction. Those libraries which build up their supply of books by ordering them from the collective lists of the National Library Service (Bibliotekstjänst) in practice often miss books published by small local publishers in their own part of the country. In public libraries around the country I have, time and again, met librarians smiling apologetically when asked to find some book written by a native of the area who is not a member of the established corps of writers. Most people involved with the production of culture in our country seem to be convinced that a certain size of population (not less than our eight million Swedes) is necessary for a literary culture to grow and remain viable. A rapid glance across the borders of Sweden shows us that this is not the case. Iceland with 200,000 inhabitants (fewer than in most of our Swedish counties) enjoys an intense literary life, based on both national and international work.

The fact that the leisure policy-makers in our country mainly think of a culture for an educated élite becomes apparent from the fact that they often imagine that cultural policy problems would more or less solve themselves as soon as everyone is sufficiently educated. But this is in strong contradiction to the fact that even when almost all Swedes have passed through nine-year comprehensive school (this will be the case a few years from now on) there will still be a need for a leisure policy.

The professional cultural workers – those who earn their living by creating and dispersing culture – usually regard it as a matter of course that those leisure facilities which are to be promoted and distributed are the facilities in which they themselves have a professional interest. The professional interest is concealed by ideas such as 'good art', 'serious writers', 'trained actors'. For them the main policy problem seems to be to guarantee themselves and their colleagues opportunities to express themselves and to promote the welfare of their own professions.

I agree to the extent that these are important goals – all people have a right to good opportunities of expressing themselves and to secure welfare. But it is wrong to put these particular problems of professional cultural workers in the foreground in the debate about the basic goals of our leisure and cultural policy.

Closely linked with this professionalism, we find the influence of the strong position maintained by the established genres, such as traditional theatre performances, painting on canvas, symphony concerts, feature films, and fiction writing. Opportunities to express oneself, to get acknowledgement and social approval are too strongly linked with the mastery of these established genres.

Connected with this is the tyranny of form, resulting in the neglect of leisure activities, which do not meet the demands of formal perfection set up by professionals and critics. Professional cultural workers have an irritating inclination to push the demand for social and political action into the background, in favour of purely formal demands on ability and perfection. How else can one explain the lack of interest, among the professional critics, in Swedish working-class poetry and in our local cultural heritage and activities. That which is not authorized in 'the cultural pages' of the main Stockholm dailies is just not taken into account.

Behind all this one can recognize almost everywhere the false notion that culture is something else than and something above what belongs to our everyday life, that it is something with which we should embellish our leisure time. But, of course, this is not the case. Culture is a product of people's attempts to learn to know and understand each other. In this connection there exists no relevant separation of work time from leisure time. One of the most serious problems in today's society is that, for many people, because they accept the idea of such a separation, 'development' has chased culture into that corner of life which we call leisure time. The new cultural policy must break down the barriers which imprison culture in this narrow corner of existence.

Towards a new leisure policy in Sweden

Let us suppose that because we adhere to certain values we regard it as desirable that within the framework of Swedish society there be created rich and varied facilities for leisure life which all citizens should be able to utilize in accordance with their interests and aims.

(1) It is then quite obvious that we must abolish income differentials, working-time differentials, environmental barriers, educational barriers, and other social factors which contribute to an uneven distribution of the life-chances between different population groups – not least regarding the use of leisure time and cultural activities.

(2) Working-class traditions and forms of activity must be made alive, investigated, vitalized, and revived. The forms of leisure to be developed shall incline towards a content closely linked to the working-class environment, and shall not cling to the forms and the content offered by bourgeois culture.

(3) It is necessary to break down the barriers between our work milieux and our leisure milieux. In agrarian society, the work milieu and the leisure milieu were the same, a unity without visible demarcation lines. In industrial society, offices and factories relentlessly slam their doors behind all who enter. Despite talk about creation of satisfying work conditions in offices and factories, the outer and inner environments of our workplaces are all too often dirty, inhospitable, shapeless, drab and monotonous – in unpleasant contrast to the leisure milieux we long for and to some extent have at our disposal.

(4) We must be aware of the fact that a generous leisure policy, which will really be of benefit to underprivileged groups in our society, will always be opposed by those power-holders who fear that such a development will in the short or long run threaten their rights and privileges.

The Swedish experience

Herbert Read, in *To Hell with Culture*, says,[5] in a simple but memorable formulation: 'One cannot sell culture from above. It must rise from below. It grows from the soil, from the people, from their daily life and work. It is a spontaneous expression of their joy in living, of their joy in working; if this joy is not there, we will not have any culture.' It is those people who drag out their lives in our deprived areas, who are the truly wretched in our prosperous and affluent society.

We must resist the tendency to split away our so-called *finkultur* from our daily leisure lives. When I refer to a 'good leisure life' I imply that almost everything can become a work of art and function as a work of art. There is, in my view, no sharp and obvious border between, on the one hand, hard manual labour and, on the other, the serious activities called culture and art. A tool may be experienced as a work of art; a work of art may be used as a tool. Daily leisure may become culture and culture may become a tool for getting our daily bread. There must not be watertight bulkheads between culture and leisure, between art and everyday life. For primitive people, work and art usually are the warp and weft of life. For them it seems meaningless to draw any demarcation line between the daily toil for food and shelter and the playful embroideries that decorate everyday life. That is how life ought to be shaped – as a well-knit unit – our everyday life – our leisure – our fine culture.

Notes

1 Constant Nieuwenhuys, 'The new Babylon', *Louisiana Review*, 1966, no. 1, pp. 37–8.
2 Sebastian de Grazia, *Of Time, Work, and Leisure*, Hartford, Ct, 1962, pp. 377ff.
3 The reports are *Reading Habits and Book Habits in Five Swedish Communities*, Stockholm, 1972, and *Experiments with Libraries*, Stockholm, 1972. Both are in Swedish with English summaries.
4 Göran Arnman and Harald Swedner, 'The Gorilla Theatre', in Harald Swedner and Björn Egeland, *Teatern Som Social Institution*, Köpenhamn, 1972.
5 Herbert Read, *To Hell with Culture*, New York, 1963.

9

Sociology and leisure: a structural approach and some policy implications[1] (1975)

N. C. A. PARRY and D. JOHNSON

M.-F. Lanfant,[2] in her survey of international literature on leisure
and free time, concludes that there is a process of convergence
between the conceptual thinking of Marxist and liberal writers and
between east and west. She demonstrates that the Marxists
originally looked at the question of free time in the context of
economic exploitation based on social class, said to be characteristic
of capitalism. Efforts were made to demonstrate the very small
quantities of genuinely free time available in a developing capitalist system, and the gradual erosion of such freedoms as the
process of 'miserization' of the proletariat proceeded. As a legacy of
this perspective the time-budgeting approach has been strongly
favoured by researchers in eastern Europe. Liberal writers, on the
other hand, have tended to take the optimistic view that industrial
capitalism leads to higher living standards, greater affluence and,
through the application of more advanced automated techniques in
industry, not merely to a reduction in hard physical labour but to a
diminution of the hours of labour. They have sought, through the
use of survey techniques designed to elicit the attitudes and
opinions of the population, to show that there is not merely a
greater quantity of leisure but also that people feel more liberated
and less constrained in their leisure time. They predict that the
liberation of people from grinding toil is not merely a utopian
dream, but a possibility in process of realization. They reject the
Marxist view that we are constrained in our leisure time in modern
industrial societies, by suggesting that sheer economic limitations
on our freedom to choose from a wide range of available leisure
activities have largely been removed, and they suggest that as a

consequence considerations of class differences in leisure are no longer relevant. In addition, they argue that while in the work situation the hierarchy of command may militate against participatory democracy, outside it we are moving into the era of the leisure democracy in which all are equally advantaged.

M.-F. Lanfant concludes that there has been a process of convergence between eastern and western approaches to the study of leisure and free time.[3] In particular, theoretical and conceptual schemes have become somewhat less sharply defined in oppositional terms and there has been a blurring or merging of approaches. In the eastern bloc it is increasingly commonplace to find writings on leisure which have all the characteristics of the obsession with culture which was typical of the American literature in the 1950s. It would not perhaps be overstating Lanfant's findings to suggest that rather than a process of convergence there has been an assimilation by Marxist writers, including those in the eastern bloc, of the liberal democratic thesis on leisure.

Paradoxically, the theoretical sophistication of the liberal position is less well developed than that of the Marxist. There has been a tendency among those seeking to establish a separate identity for leisure studies to seek to free them from the claims to sovereignty which arise from the sociology of work, and also to sidestep what they regard as the economic frame of reference of Marxist writers. In the event, leisure studies have often been reduced to psychological measurement of attitudes and opinions rather than the development of a vigorous sociology of leisure based on a theory operating at the structural level of analysis. Our work is intended as a modest contribution towards a structural approach. Before going on to present the conclusions of our own research, it might be useful to extend Lanfant's overview of the literature by considering two recent books on leisure which have been published in Britain while our research project has been in progress.

The first of these is *The Symmetrical Family* by Michael Young and Peter Willmott.[4] It is a product of the Institute of Community Studies and is a study of work and leisure in the London region. The authors took to heart two criticisms of their earlier community studies, which had been based on the techniques and concepts of social anthropology. The critics had suggested that their community studies were insufficiently grounded in history and that they were unintegrated with sociological theory. In this book there is a considerable discussion of the historical background to the presentation of their survey findings about family life, work, and leisure. In regard to sociological theory, they draw rather heavily on the work of theorists whose conception of society is fundamentally grounded in liberalism. The dominant influence is de Tocqueville's belief which he articulated when looking at the United States, that 'henceforward every new invention, every new want which it occasioned, and every new desire which craved satisfaction were steps towards a general levelling.'[5] Young and Willmott go on to say that 'the endurance with which the distribution of incomes and wealth has resisted change is one of the most striking obstinacies of history. The differences between the classes are not markedly less than they were in the past.'[6] Yet in spite of this they agree with Bell[7] that de Tocqueville was right in suggesting that the notion of advancement and ambition in democratic societies breaks the bonds that once held them fixed and provides the great engine of social change. It is through this mechanism that the promise of equality in America was to reach realization in the achievements of American democracy. This idea becomes the basis for what Young and Willmott call the *Principle of Stratified Diffusion* which suggests that what the few have today the many will demand tomorrow. The principle plays an important part in *The Symmetrical Family*, and is associated with the evolutionary perspective which likens social change to a slow march of progress.

At the centre of Young and Willmott's position, as we understand it, is the liberal view that society is being transformed by the removal of constraints which have hitherto bounded the aspirations and activities of its members. Liberalism suggests that in the area of law, for example, social class position should not give some individuals greater claims than others, but that all should be treated impartially, as citizens. Similarly, an issue very much central to the thesis is the idea that increasingly constraints are being lifted from a disadvantaged group of people, namely women. This is not merely a matter of removal of disabilities before the law, but of increasing employment opportunities and of changing mores within the family itself. Such changes are producing a greater equality between the sexes, and thus a greater thrust towards what they describe as the 'symmetrical' family, in which men and women can now each participate in the activities which were formerly defined as attaching to the male or female role on a segregated basis. 'The modern idea of symmetry is [that] there should be no monopolies for either sex in any sphere. Women should have as much right as men to seek, and to gain, fulfilment out of the home as in it.'[8]

Young and Willmott's argument is very much in line with the trend towards a liberal and social democratic view which we note M.-F. Lanfant had found as a predominant trend in the contemporary literature.

In *Leisure and Society in Britain*[9] it is not so easy to discern an overall thesis in a book to which so many writers have made distinguished contributions. In their general introduction, however, the editors align themselves with a liberal democratic position and tend to underplay the significance of structural factors especially social class. This is made very clear in the following quotation:

> There is a trend, with the growth of a mass-consumer market and a strong youth culture, towards ego-conscious rather than class-conscious symbolism. Status symbols and life-styles are becoming *expressions of individual taste* rather than *reflections of economic position* or social class. The growth of individuated self-awareness underpins the movement towards ego-conscious symbolism. As people become more aware of themselves as separate individuals, the process of choice becomes a conscious one and they are less guided by what is 'appropriate' than what expresses their own self-image and style of life. The result is a loosening of the social fabric in which class consciousness is tied to recognized class symbols and life styles. The growth of mass communication is one of the important factors involved in such a loosening process.
>
> Part of the increasing diversity and variety of leisure values may be due to the declining significance of social class as a basis of people's behaviour. One indication of such a decline may be in the decreasing centrality of work. . . . Another may be found in the break-up of traditional working-class communities brought about by slum clearance and re-housing policy. The break-up of such communities has tended to be associated with a reduction of single-industry areas. It is also possible that there is some truth in the image of the 'affluent worker' aspiring to be middle-class, but the extent of such affluence and aspiration is doubtful. Although different levels of income give access to different styles of life and status symbols, people may be becoming less class-conscious in the way they express themselves and the choices they make. There are some things that only money can buy, but they are becoming fewer and more people are able to buy them.[10]

Although individual contributions to *Leisure and Society in Britain* do not always fit in with this overall perspective,[11] the prevailing impression is of a concern with the 'cultural' level of analysis rather than the 'structural', and this again confirms Lanfant's conclusions from her extensive survey of the literature.

Class divisions

The principle of stratified diffusion suggests that aspirations and artifacts which at one time are the monopoly of the middle and upper classes gradually percolate down to the mass of ordinary people. This process is based upon the extraordinary industrial power and productivity available in modern societies, which have produced conditions of unparalleled affluence. This is in essence a restatement of the *embourgeoisement thesis*, which was so cogently challenged by Goldthorpe and Lockwood on the basis of evidence collected in their study of the affluent worker.[12] They suggest that three conditions have to be satisfied before assimilation of affluent working people into the middle class can be said to have taken place.

First there is the 'economic' factor, relating to income and other emoluments. Their argument is that an equivalence of income and increasing purchases of consumer durables do not in themselves signal the assimilation of working-class people into the middle class. On the contrary, there are additional factors which are currently not favourable to such a development. The second factor is the 'normative', namely that the lack of aspirations for education, for promotion into alternative careers or even to the manual supervisory level does not suggest an identification with the middle-class values of individualism and career advancement. The collective orientation of the working class remains strong, even if no longer based on the traditional community nexus which was once the case. In spite of increasing home-centredness and privatization the orientation of affluent manual workers was found to be what Goldthorpe and Lockwood call 'instrumental collectivism'. The third factor is the 'relational', and this refers to the network of relationships with members of the family and friends. The sharply segregated patterns found by Goldthorpe and Lockwood between the middle classes and the affluent workers were especially marked in the sphere of leisure. The tendency of working people to be less involved in membership of all kinds of voluntary groups and organizations, and their concentration on relationships with family and neighbours, is in sharp contrast to the tendency of middle-class people to belong to organizations, to participate as members, and to invite people, especially those associated with their work, into their homes on a reciprocal basis. The most important element was the re-affirmation of research findings conducted much earlier, that there is little cross-class relational activity.

The overall conclusion was that affluence itself and the spread of consumer durables was not a basis for the erosion of social class boundaries or for the assimilation of affluent workers into the middle class. Young and Willmott offer no evidence which contradicts this view. Indeed, their own evidence tends to support it. Thus there is a confusion evident to readers of *The Symmetrical Family* and sometimes to its authors, between the principle of stratified diffusion and the powerful evidence about continuing class divisions which is reaffirmed by an inspection of Young and Willmott's own data, not to speak of Goldthorpe and Lockwood's, and our own.

Sexual divisions

One matter which is treated much more fully by Young and Willmott than by Goldthorpe and Lockwood is the issue of the changing social position of women – at work and in the family. Young and Willmott underline the significance of feminism as a social movement, but their affirmation of increasing equality in the context of the family tends to underplay the importance of class as a barrier to the achievement of sexual equality. We took the view that a structural analysis of leisure and life-style must include not only an examination of class divisions but also of sexual divisions, which cross-cut the class issue. Young and Willmott's view, which is also shared by other liberal writers concerned with the leisure question,[13] is that there has been a movement from segregated sex-roles, in which the duties and privileges of both men and women are clearly marked out and delimited, to a situation in which desegregation ushers in a period of reciprocity or symmetricality. This is characterized by the opportunity of members of both sexes to choose elements from what formerly was the role of the opposite sex, if they wish to do so. The freedom to negotiate between married partners is held to be completely open, within the limits of human biology. This situation is regarded as an ideal, but one which is already being lived out by, for example, the dual-career families studied by the Rapoports.[14] By contrast, we have suggested[15] that the desegregation of sex roles was likely in the immediate future to expose a hitherto latent contradiction between the values and norms inherent in the familial ideology on the one hand, and those of the market ideology on the other. These contradictions would be experienced by both men and women trying to adhere to the norms of free choice and equality enjoined by the above mentioned liberal writers.

In any case, our evidence suggests that sexual divisions, while profoundly important at every social class level, are currently undergoing the process of desegregation only among some sections of the middle class, especially the more highly educated. The contradictions between the familial and market ideologies are most likely to become apparent among highly educated men and women who both have considerable potential career opportunities.

The influence of life-cycle

Nearly all studies of leisure recognize age as an important factor. Usually it is treated as an empirical category, and efforts are made to 'control' for it. For example, Goldthorpe and Lockwood in their study of affluent workers chose their sample specifically to obviate the dilution of their thesis, by excluding persons from an older age group who had experienced a different epoch of social history. Similiarly, Harris and Parker[16] focus specifically on the problem of leisure in *old* age. Another approach has been to contrast age subgroups, without stating the theoretical rationale for doing so. For example, Sillitoe, who draws the useful conceptual distinction between chronological age and domestic age, contrasts the leisure behaviour of domestic age groups without attempting to link these with a broader theoretical explanation.[17]

One area in which the question of age has been incorporated in leisure studies in a manner which has led to theoretical debate is the issue of 'youth culture'. One thesis suggests that in a period of increasing affluence during which young people have been receiving higher incomes, and at a time when an expanding consumer market has created opportunities for the commercial exploitation or even manipulation of their needs and interests, there has sprung up a youth culture which stands over against the culture of adults. In addition, this thesis proposes that the unification of teenagers on the basis of their own culture is likely to transcend the divisions of class, and to produce a society in which class considerations lose their significance. Graham Murdock has argued, on the basis of empirical studies of 'teenage culture', that in its most important manifestations – for example, in pop music – the market for this 'culture' is divided into different tastes and interests on the basis of class as well as of rapidly shifting age groupings. He finds little evidence for the view that teenage culture is weakening class divisions, and opening up what some writers have called, following the popular usage 'the generation gap'.[18]

Our own evidence suggests that the age factor, particularly domestic age, is of crucial importance in understanding the leisure 'careers' which groups follow as they proceed through the life-cycle. Our central point is that only by treating age, sex, and social class as variables of theoretical significance which are simultaneously related in practice is it possible to provide an adequate structural analysis of leisure patterns. We fully agree with Murdock that young people must not simply be treated from the point of view that they share age in common, but must be seen at the same time in relation to class structure and sexual divisions. Equally, in regard to old age, it has been argued, on the basis of a small research project undertaken in Hertfordshire, that it is misleading to treat retired people as a homogeneous category simply because they are all above a certain age.[19]

Implications of research findings

One object of our research was to explore patterns of participation in community-based activities outside the home. Participation has become a fashionable issue in contemporary politics and our research was designed to elicit some of the constraints which impede or facilitate participation in all kinds of activities by the public. We felt that insufficient attention had been paid by planners to the operation of these constraints. They have tended to assume that in a democracy each adult will have an equal chance to participate and that participation is likely to occur on something approaching a random basis, directed only by the tastes and attitudes of individuals. Our assumption has been that, on the contrary, rates of participation are highly structured, and we feel that sociological investigations such as ours can illuminate the mechanisms underlying such patterns. Our research findings in general confirm those of earlier researchers and suggest that marked differences exist between the social classes in the extent of participation. The lack of participation by working-class people in particular is a continuing phenomenon which has not been markedly eroded by the social changes associated with affluence, full employment, and longer exposure to education, which have been characteristic of British society since 1945. In this sense our findings are consistent with those of Goldthorpe and Lockwood, as well as of Barry Hindess, who was looking particularly at political participation.[20]

Where we have been able to add to the findings of previous researchers is in the matter of differences between the sexes in the *extent* of participation. The most important difference is that women are grossly under-represented in occupational associations but they are also themselves divided by the fact that middle-class women are very active in special interest or charitable associations whereas working-class women scarcely belong to or participate in any associations. This underlines the importance of our stress on the sexual factor as a structural variable, and it is worth reiterating that domestic age also plays an important part in the extent of participation of both sexes, but particularly women.

In spite of this temporary approximation between women from both middle- and working-class backgrounds, there is in general a marked tendency for their leisure patterns and life-styles to remain sharply different throughout the age range. This is illustrated by our data on patterns of companionship. This demonstrates that although there are differences between the sexes and the classes in the extent to which they spend time with friends or family or 'as a couple', generally they demonstrate a balanced pattern between these types of companionship from which only the working-class woman markedly deviates. Half of her main weekend activities are spent with members of the family and only a tiny fraction with friends. Where she is involved in activities outside the home, this is almost invariably with family members rather than with friends.

It seems that the contrast between the manual working-class woman and the rest of the community lies in this fundamental lack of friendship activities, and a more exclusive involvement with members of the family.

Looking at a slightly different facet of the situation of the manual working-class woman, namely the activity patterns as opposed to the companionship patterns which they manifest, we note again that in the use of the pub, club, and restaurant they are sharply different from working-class men and from middle-class men and women. The fact that they scarcely use these facilities at all is in line with their general low levels of involvement outside the home.

Nevertheless, even within the home, the level of activities characteristic of the manual working-class woman is far less than that for women of the middle class. Despite the fact that the middle-class woman typically spends less time at home, when she is there she is much more active in occupying herself with a host of pursuits within the home whereas the working-class woman is very reliant on television.

It would appear that the manual working-class woman is the most 'privatized' of any group in the community, much more so, for example, than the working-class man. According to the thesis offered by Goldthorpe and Lockwood, this should mean that she is among the avant-garde of a new working class. However, it is unlikely that the authors of *The Affluent Worker* would wish to make this claim. The problem seems to focus on the concept of 'home-centredness', which is usually linked with privatization. If one concedes the sexual division as a structural factor, cross-cutting the class issue, the problem may be clarified. Mark Abrams first used the concept of home-centredness,[21] and following him Goldthorpe and Lockwood implied a shift in male attitudes and behaviour under conditions of affluence. It is possible that the home may become a more attractive place in which to spend time, and home decorating, car maintenance, television, and an increased involvement with children may render home life more lively and absorbing.

For the woman, however, the situation is different. Apart from the often researched claim that in new towns or on new estates there is likely to be an attenuation of the neighbourly relations characteristic of the traditional working-class woman, we found no substantial change in her situation of the kind which Goldthorpe and Lockwood would recognize as a major shift in normative or relational patterns as suggested by the home-centredness thesis. In view of the low 'activity-pattern' level of our manual women within the home, we contend that although 'home-located' they are not markedly more 'home-centred' than in the past. We suggest the alternative concept of 'family-centredness' as the key to the manual working-class woman's life-style. As we have indicated already, in comparison with all other sections of the community her companionship patterns indicate that her time is spent overwhelmingly with family members. An additional pointer is that when asked for what reasons her leisure activities might change in the future she was almost exclusively inclined to give an answer relating to the children.

Although Goldthorpe and Lockwood focused their attention in

the affluent worker study on countering the embourgeoisement thesis, they did so by selecting a sample of male affluent workers. They thus tended to underplay the significance of working-class women in relation to that thesis, even though they studied the family life of their respondents. Goldthorpe and Lockwood concluded that embourgeoisement was not taking place but that there had been a degree of convergence, especially in relation to the *instrumental collectivism* which typifies the orientation of workers to their trade unions and political parties. In other words, the instrumentality usually regarded by sociologists as typical of the middle class is now linked with the collectivism regarded as a traditional feature of working-class life. Our evidence suggests that where women are concerned, there is a considerable disparity, not to say a polarity, of orientation and attitudes between middle-class and working-class women. It is middle-class women who appear to experience contradictions between their aspirations in relation to family life and career. In the case of working-class women, such a conflict simply does not exist because it is not seen as a contradiction. Similarly, in regard to patterns of participation, it is the middle-class woman who is typically involved and committed and the working-class woman who is withdrawn and family-centred. On this evidence, if embourgeoisement has not taken place so far as working-class men are concerned how much less does the embourgeoisement thesis apply in the case of the working-class woman, whose life-style might be described as the polar opposite from both the aspirations and the practice of the middle class.

A substantial area of our research findings refers to the work context. The centrality of work has been one of the predominant assumptions of industrial sociology, and a wealth of research material now exists on 'the world of work'. There are few writers who would admit that there is an exclusively one-way causal relationship by which the work situation affects family and leisure patterns, but in practice we contend many writers make this assumption. An important reason for this is that occupation related to class division has been the central structural factor in the debate, and that sexual divisions have either been treated quite separately or ignored. The male worker has been considered to be the 'typical' worker, not merely from the point of view of the industrialist, but also from the point of view of the industrial sociologist. Work has been researched as a possible central life interest for men, but not very often where women are concerned. The male orientation to the occupational world is indicated by our evidence regarding male membership of occupational associations, and the weaker saliency for women of the world of work is indicated by their lack of membership of such associations. The point is, however, that women do work in very large numbers (currently 40 per cent of the labour force), and their orientation to the family significantly affects their relationship to work. Consequently, it is among women workers that one would seek to find efforts, either individually or collectively, to adapt the work situation to the exigencies of family life.

The evidence we have does not refer to collective action by women to adapt the work situation to the family, but does suggest that women, in response to their particular structural situation, adapt to it in typical ways which affect them as individuals. It is they rather than men who are constrained to mediate between the requirements of work and family situation and their patterns of work, such as part-time work, are indicative of their efforts to adapt work considerations to family life. In an age when work seems to be increasingly regarded as a fundamental duty of all capable adult citizens, the role of the housewife who does not go out to work is the ultimate expression of adaptation to the demands of the family. Among employed married women overtime is negligible, whereas among working-class men, especially while they are single and after the birth of children, it is considerable. Women workers seldom if ever bring work home, or work irregular hours. One other possible indication of the greater centrality of family rather than work, for women, is our finding that married women tend to have shorter journey times to work than unmarried women in similar employment. We infer from this (and it would be useful to make a check in any further research) that at the time of marriage women tend to change their jobs and take employment closer to their new home. There is no indication from our data that men do this, and we believe that it may be a pointer to the fact that married couples typically choose a place of residence which enables the husband to remain, without too much inconvenience, in his former job.

One of the most significant ways in which we are able to demonstrate the falsity of the leisure democracy thesis is that it pays no attention to the constraints which arise from family life and which are greatly influenced by domestic age. Thus the thesis neglects the ways in which, as we have indicated, the woman's leisure time is limited by family responsibilities. Neither does it take into account the differences in the man's work situation (for example, in regard to overtime working), which vary considerably not only by class but also by domestic age, and which therefore produce marked disparities in the opportunities and resources available for leisure.

Some implications for social policy

In our view our research findings have implications both for sociological theory and for social policy. Elsewhere we have argued that one of the weaknesses of contemporary sociology was its fragmentation into a number of 'special' sociologies, such as those relating to the family, education, work, and leisure.[22] We felt in particular that the sociology of leisure has tended to become somewhat isolated from the mainstream of sociological thinking, and it is precisely this trend which we have tried to rectify by studying leisure within the context of the constraints arising from social structure. Here we take the opportunity to set out the implications of our research findings for social policy.

There are those sociologists who are deeply committed to the view that sociology, if it is to be true to itself, ought not to have any direct implications for social policy.[23] We have tried to remain aware that the sociologist should not be over-committed to one line of policy, before engaging in research. We have felt, however, that a sociological contribution to social policy in the area of leisure is both possible and useful, and that it ought to be critical. We shall suggest that the constraints arising from social structure profoundly affect people's leisure behaviour, as they do their work and family life, and that these factors are often neglected by policy-makers and planners.

There is a contradiction, not to say a conflict, in our kind of society between the standpoint that leisure ought to be an area in which people make their own arrangements, or at least in which private enterprise should be left to make whatever provision is profitable, and the belief that leisure policy should be actively developed by local and central government, with a view to improving the availability of leisure opportunities, particularly in ways which offer facilities thought to be publicly desirable. The fact is that we currently have a mixture of public and private provision and the question of the extent to which desirable but uneconomic public provision ought to be subsidized is raised in an acute form. In general, private commercial provision has established itself in those areas which are profitable and has retreated from those in which it is difficult to make a profit. We found, in our research on the use of leisure facilities outside the home, that the frequency with which people use them is a good indicator of the likelihood that they will be commercially viable. Even the simple question which we put to our respondents about the frequency with which they engaged in particular leisure pursuits produced a remarkably clear-cut pattern. As might be expected, if large numbers of people answered 'frequently' (rather than 'occasionally' or 'never'), there was a strong probability that the activity concerned was already catered for on a commercial basis.

A conflict appears to be inherent in public provision. On the one hand, local authorities have been active in building swimming pools and sports halls, and have laid it down as a principle of policy that these should be freely or cheaply available. Nevertheless, even if they are not intended to make a profit as such, there is always the incentive within operating constraints to make these facilities as little reliant on subsidy as possible. The criterion of maximum intensity of use is employed as a justification for the investment of public money in the first place. Where facilities are provided but little used, the expenditure is judged unjustifiable. In seeking maximum intensity of use, local authorities and the managers of facilities tend to seek continuity of usage by allowing bookings exclusively to clubs and organizations. This policy shuts out the casual user, and is a sore point with some members of the public. It also clashes with the criterion of 'openness', which, as we saw, is regarded as desirable where public provision is concerned. As working-class people are less likely to belong to clubs, groups, and organizations, they are thus discouraged even from casual use as individuals or families.

There are established and institutionalized forms of leisure amenity – the pub is an important not to say predominant example – which are almost entirely in commercial hands. There are important variations in patterns of use of the pub which is by far the most popular of leisure facilities outside the home. It remains a male-sponsored leisure activity, in the sense that although increasing numbers of women have been going to pubs in recent years it is still very much a 'male club', to which women go normally only by the invitation of men and in their company. It is true that in some respects the image of the pub has been changing, and that the 'men-only' bar or the pub wholly used by men has become rare, especially in the south of England. Nevertheless, even where facilities for meals or snacks are provided, and the old pub image has been moderated by new decor, women apparently find it uncomfortable to go into pubs alone. Even if they do go in the company of others of their own sex, they do so more typically to utilize the restaurant facilities rather than the drinking facilities.

The pub is not a place to which most people simply go to drink. For young people it is a centre of conviviality which requires no formal membership. It functions as a location where young men and women can meet each other, where they can go in groups on an informal basis, and where the process of 'chatting up' and courtship can be conducted. It has the advantage of being away from home, but warm and readily available. In addition, there is often a choice of several establishments so that in most cases no particular pub has a monopoly. This generates an increased sense of freedom and variety. It is perhaps for these reasons that the pub is by far the most important centre for leisure among young single people. However, this must be qualified by the recognition that the sex-segregated life-styles of working-class men and women are manifested in the smaller numbers of working-class girls who use the pub. Even on a Saturday night, which we found to be the principal night in the week when women are found alongside men in the public house, it is the case that far more of these women come from the middle class rather than the working class. In fact middle-class women were present in almost equal proportion with middle-class men. Working-class men were absolutely preponderant among pub users in the age range whereas only a small proportion of working-class women were present.

There is a clear transformation in the importance of the pub and its use after marriage. Among young married people without children, we found that although there was a fall-off in use of the pub overall, this was greater among women than among men. It was particularly marked among working-class women. After parenthood, the trend towards a decline in frequency of pub use was accentuated especially where women were concerned. It should be stressed that the fall-off was in the *frequency* of use for all groups.

Those concerned with social policy have been much exercised by the problems which are seen as side-effects of the popularity of the public house. Alcoholism, 'bad management' of income by some groups, crime including violence, vandalism, and driving offences, have all been connected with the use of alcohol and its wide availability. Efforts have therefore been directed not merely towards limiting pub hours and excluding children and young people, but also to providing alternative facilities which are regarded as more socially desirable. The creation of voluntary

associations and statutory services offering clubs and organizations for children and young people are a case in point. The data
collected in an earlier survey[24] suggested, however, that young
people quickly drop out of associations or organizations of this kind
at the point where they become sexually mature and begin to
establish relationships with the opposite sex. Thus in practice the
limitations on age are often ignored because the public house has
become an important institutionalized locale for conviviality associated with dating and peer-group interaction.

In the sociology of social problems a predominant approach has
been to look at the circumstances under which particular social
phenomena come to be defined as problematic, and are subsequently taken up for remedial action by public or private
agencies. The question of the 'visibility' of groups whose behaviour
is regarded as problematic is central to this approach.[25] One of our
most striking findings has been the extent to which women from the
manual working class are non-participators and although family-
centred are, relatively speaking, inactive within the home. Even
prior to marriage our evidence creates a picture which is fully
consistent. In girlhood, the working-class girl, like her mother, is
less involved outside the home in any sort of organized activity
which is provided either by voluntary or statutory bodies. Even at
school she is very little involved in school-based clubs, groups, and
organizations, outside formal school hours. Girls in general are
paid less pocket money at each class level than boys of the same
class, but among working-class girls, especially those from unskilled manual backgrounds, there are a considerable number who
receive no pocket money at all. Puberty signals an important
transformation which involves for most children a more active
social life with peers of the same age, especially between the sexes,
but there is little evidence of this flowering of social activity among
working-class girls. This was at least the finding of an earlier
research project, based on a sample of Hatfield schoolchildren, up to
the age of 15 years.[26] In our Stage II data, with which we have been
dealing in this paper, we were still looking at a very young age
group, of 17 plus, and this confirms the trend of the earlier finding
that the life-style of working-class girls and women is demon-
strably very restricted. For example, the patterns of companionship of single working-class girls appear to be confined to the
boyfriend and members of the family. In other words, the exclusive
relationship with one other which we designated going out 'as a
couple' occurs so early among working-class girls, and is so soon

followed by marriage or co-habitation, that friendship patterns of the type which are found among middle-class young people and also among working-class boys never become established.

Manual working-class women, considered as a group, have not been regarded as particularly 'visible' or problematic from the point of view of social policy, in the sense that as a group they do not attract the attention of social agencies. This is not to say that broken marriages, wife-battering and other social problem indicators do not arise from this group, but rather that the life-style of the group as a whole is not seen to present a problem. Yet, from the standpoint of the believers in participation and activism, this group, on our evidence, might be defined as seriously deprived, and living a stunted life-style with little contact outside the immediate family.

The question arises – and it is a value question – of whether some action ought to be taken which would constitute an attempt to widen the horizons of this group. On the other hand, should the principle be reaffirmed that in a democratic society people may live out their lives according to styles which may not be especially approved by politicians or activists? One reason which is sometimes adduced to encourage intervention is that the mother is regarded as particularly influential in the shaping of attitudes towards education and in the formation of the aspirations of her children. The evidence suggests that low aspirations on the part of parents, and particularly the mother, tend to be transmitted to the next generation. In particular, for girls, aspirations shared by parents and the girls themselves tend to be lower than for boys. The argument is that if by the time children go to school the basic levels of aspiration, and the fundamental skills which are required in the learning process, have not been attained the chances of educational or occupational success for such children will be small. Logically, therefore, the point of intervention has been pushed back to the relationship between parents and children in the early pre-school years, particularly the relationship with the mother. The question is, would social intervention designed to influence the social behaviour and social attitudes of the mother be the appropriate place at which to break the cycle of low aspiration and low achievement which in its most extreme form has been characterized as 'transmitted deprivation'?

Although sociological research has suggested that the working-class girl is in a situation of restricted opportunity and aspirations, the efforts so far made in the education system, in the youth service, and elsewhere have merely served to confirm her secondary position within the working class. The working-class male has constituted at various times a threat to the social order as seen from the standpoint of the authorities, in his role as trade unionist, striker, unemployed person, or vagrant, as well as delinquent or criminal, and social policies to control trade unionism, strikes, vagrancy, and unemployment have formed a major part of private and public social policy. The working-class woman does not figure in an important way in any of these guises. In this sense she has been far less 'visible' and has not been defined as a social problem.

At the present time, the increasing strength of the movement toward the liberation of women has been primarily a movement by the middle class for the middle class. We have isolated, in terms of our research findings, the narrowly constrained life-style of the working-class woman. Her situation, if change is to be effected, must, however, be put in the context of the general position of her sex in contemporary society. It is from this point that any movement or any policy designed to transform her life-style is most likely to begin.

Notes

1 This chapter is drawn from part of the conclusions of a report to the Social Science Research Council, *Leisure and Social Structure*, August 1974, published by the Hatfield Polytechnic. Thanks are due to the SSRC which funded the project.
2 M.-F. Lanfant, *Théories du Loisir*, Paris, Presses Universitaires de France, 1972.
3 A possible manifestation of such a convergence is examined in a study of International Labour Conferences relating to holidays with pay, D. Johnson, 'The annual holiday – a study in convergence?', unpublished dissertation, University of London, 1972.
4 M. Young and P. Willmott, *The Symmetrical Family*, London, Routledge, 1973.
5 A. de Tocqueville, *Democracy in America*, New York, Vintage Books, 1945, vol. 1, p. 3.
6 Young and Willmott, op. cit.
7 D. Bell, *Towards the Year 2000: Work in Progress*, New York, Beacon Press, 1969.
8 Young and Willmott, op. cit., p. 275.
9 M. Smith, S. Parker, and C. Smith (eds), *Leisure and Society in Britain*, London, Allen Lane, 1973.
10 ibid., pp. 7–8.
11 See for example A. Harris and S. Parker, 'Leisure and the elderly', in ibid., pp. 171–80.

12 J. H. Goldthorpe, D. Lockwood, F. Bechhofer, and J. Platt, *The Affluent Worker in the Class Structure*, Cambridge, Cambridge University Press, 1969.

13 M. P. Fogarty, R. Rapoport, and R. Rapoport, *Sex, Career and Family*, London, Allen & Unwin for PEP, 1971.

14 R. and R. Rapoport, *The Dual Career Family*, London, Penguin Books, 1971.

15 N. C. A. Parry and D. Johnson, 'Sexual divisions in lifestyle and leisure', paper given at the BSA Conference, Aberdeen, 1974.

16 Harris and Parker, op. cit.

17 K. K. Sillitoe, *Planning for Leisure*, London, HMSO, 1969.

18 G. Murdock, 'Culture and classlessness: the making and unmaking of a myth', paper presented to Symposium on Leisure, Salford University, 1973.

19 J. Flowers and N. C. A. Parry, 'Old age in Hertfordshire', Herts County Council, Social Services Department, 1974.

20 B. Hindess, The Decline of Working Class Politics, London, MacGibbon & Kee, 1971.

21 M. Abrams and R. Rose, *Must Labour Lose?* London, Penguin Books, 1960.

22 Parry and Johnson, op. cit., pp. 3–8.

23 This position has been passionately argued by J. Rex, *The Demystification of Sociology*, London, Routledge, 1974.

24 N. C. A. Parry and J. Flowers, 'The Hatfield Survey, Stage I: A study of the leisure patterns of children and young people in the 7–15 age group,' Report for the Hatfield RDC, 1971.

25 R. K. Merton, 'Social problems and sociological theory', in R. K. Merton and R. A. Nisbet (eds), *Contemporary Social Problems*, New York, Harcourt Brace Jovanovich, 1961.

26 Parry and Flowers, op. cit.

10

Boys muscle in where angels fear to tread: the relationship between physical education and young women's subcultures (1984)

SHEILA SCRATON

Introduction

This paper considers the relationship between PE[1] in secondary schools and young women's subcultures. For many years PE teachers have been concerned with the apparent loss of interest and 'dropping out' of many adolescent young women from the PE lesson. This paper attempts to relate PE teaching to the subcultural experiences and resistances of young women and thus move beyond a biologically determined position which traditionally has explained young women's responses to PE as 'natural' and inevitable.

The paper provides (1) a brief critical introduction to youth subcultural analysis, (2) a more detailed examination of recent work on young women's subcultures and their school-based resistances, and (3) a consideration of the relationship of PE to this work on young women's subcultures. The analysis in this third section draws on eight years' teaching experience in secondary school PE and qualitative research carried out in Liverpool secondary schools during the 1983–84 school year. In conclusion the paper looks forward to possible initiatives which could help move towards a more positive and challenging approach to PE for adolescent young women.

Youth subcultures

Analyses of youth culture and subcultures can be summarized by dividing them into generational and structural explanations. The first analysis is concerned with the continuity/discontinuity of inter-generational values, and the second with the relationship

149

to social class, the mode of production and its consequent social relations.[2]

This summary of the main analyses of youth subcultures which developed during the 1970s emphasized two main categories – age and class. Almost without exception 'youth' was presented as being white, working-class, and male and studies of 'the lads' dominated the literature.[3] Throughout this work young women rarely were visible, appearing only in relation to 'the lads' and their experiences. Young women were defined either as extensions of the experiences of 'the lads' or as direct inhibitions on these experiences. Either way the judgements passed on young women focused on their sexuality and its objectification:

> Ellen was very popular among the girls – she was always surrounded by her mates; but she was less often seen with a boy. The boys had, of course, classified all the girls into the two familiar categories: the slags who'd go with anyone and everyone (they were alright for a quick screw, but you'd never get serious about it) and the drags who didn't but whom you might one day think about going steady with.[4]

> So the conversation went on, with Joey suggesting that the girlfriends should be kept in their place and not allowed to interfere with 'the boys' who if they were real mates would see to it. At this time Joey practised what he preached. He had been 'going with his tart' for six months and although he obviously liked her he would not allow his affection to change his relationship with the Boys. . . . Basically the girls are divided into three categories: 'somebody's tart', 'dirty tickets' and the 'not having anys'.[5]

In these typical examples, young women's experiences were viewed through the eyes of the lads and this vision was sharpened by the assumptions of male researchers.[6] It was a vision which condemned young women's lives to the periphery of youth culture, leaving the centre-stage to 'the lads'. As McRobbie and Garber point out, however, the position of young working-class women is structurally different to that of young working-class men. The commonsense assumptions, upon which much of the interaction between young men and young women is apparently founded, demarcate clear boundaries for 'acceptable' masculine and feminine behaviour and responses. The boundaries, however, are not derived simply from the shared assumptions of everyday life. They

150

are structural in the sense that images of sexuality become institutionalized and legitimated within the policy responses of agencies such as schools, youth clubs, and sports centres. It is here that images translate into ideologies and form part of the political management of sexuality. It is at these levels – ideological and political – that the experiences of young women and men are structured differently and provide an institutionalized process of reinforcement to assumptions which are commonly held. McRobbie and Garber argue that the position of young women cannot be explained simply by a social marginality within subcultures but has to be located with reference to the structural location of women in a patriarchal society. Thus young women are not appendages to male subcultures (although to a large extent their presence within dominant male subcultures remains undocumented)[7] but inhabit their own specific subcultures. If an analysis of youth subcultures is to include both young women and young men then there should be generational and class considerations and, furthermore, an understanding of patriarchal power relations.[8]

An understanding of the experiences of young women requires class, race, age, and gender considerations. Brake states:

> women have reality mediated not just by class location interpretations, but also by patriarchy, the system of surbordination in a world which is male dominated in sexuality and procreative potential; a system where women's labour is organised economically, ideologically and politically by males. It is a world where sexism is the articulated, as well as the taken for granted unquestioned superiority of men. In this sense women inhabit two locations: their role in their specific social class and their position in patriarchy.[9]

Furthermore race produces significant differences, for patriarchy is not experienced in the same way in all cultures. In British society black women and women of colour face different opportunities and restrictions in relation to school, family, work, and leisure. They are often subjected to the patriarchy of different cultures while also experiencing the patriarchal oppression of white racist society. This duality of oppression is further intensified by class so that working-class black women have their reality mediated by the complexity of race, gender, and class relations.

It is not 'just in order to tell us something about the position of women that we should make such an analysis'.[10] Any analysis of male youth subcultures much acknowledge similar complexities. Brake (1980) moves beyond the traditional concern of male cultural analysis – class and generation – by stressing that male subcultures are primarily an 'exploration' of masculinity. In working-class male subcultures the 'macho', aggressive image of masculinity, which strongly reinforces gender identity, is presented as a resistance to a collectively experienced sense of failure or rejection. However, some men through choice, physique, or temperament, are not involved in this aspect of masculinity and the 'culture of masculinity' with its aggressive, competitive, 'macho' image. Male subcultures, for example the 'bikers' in Willis (1978), demonstrate a culture of masculinity which reinforces their male identity.[11] Those who fail to meet this expectation are excluded from the groups which stress other kinds of 'masculinity'. Similarly, while cultures of masculinity cut across class locations there are differences *between* classes. The physically aggressive, 'macho' form of masculinity in some working-class male youth subcultures[12] is expressed in a similar way (although more socially legitimated) in the rugby playing 'macho' competitive culture of the male middle class.[13] However, 'masculinity' does not have to be physically aggressive in order to be oppressive both to women and to men outside the culture. Sexist comment and the intellectual/verbal aggression of male middle-class culture presents a powerfully oppressive 'masculine' image. An understanding of patriarchy, therefore, is not only necessary to an understanding of the position of women; it is also central to an analysis of male subcultures.

For young women, as McRobbie explains:

> The culture of adolescent working class girls can be seen as a response to the material limitations imposed on them as a result of their class position, but also an index of and response to their sexual oppression as women.[14]

Middle-class young women, while benefiting from a more privileged material position, experience sexual oppression as women. However, this oppression may take on different forms which can produce differing responses from these young women. The next section will look more closely at young women's cultures and the responses that young women make to their class and/or position and role as young women.

Young women's subcultures and school-based resistances

Within the work on youth subcultures the invisibility of young women's lives and experiences does not reflect a simple marginalization to the main action of 'the lads'. Rather it represents an absence informed directly by patriarchal power relations. Recent work has attempted to redress the balance by providing a feminist perspective on subcultures which starts from the experiences of young women.[15] An initial consideration in the analysis of young women's experiences is that collectivity (that is, the 'gang' or group), which is integral to the definition of male subcultures,[16] cannot be taken for granted for young women.[17] McRobbie (1978) and Griffin (1981), in two separate projects with white working-class women, found that they tend to form small but intense friendship groups with a 'best friend' central to their experiences. However, as young women begin relationships with boys, feminine cultures based on supportive friendships begin a gradual process of breaking up.[18] This does not occur to the same extent for 'the lads' who usually retain their male group membership. The earlier quote from Parker (1974) confirms the significance of male group membership even when girlfriends have arrived on the scene. Before heterosexual relationships begin to fragment the supportive feminine cultures, various constraints work to discourage or to restrict the possibilities for young women to form large groups or gangs. (These constraints also inhibit alternative expressions of women's sexuality.) It is in this way that young women's sexuality becomes regulated and controlled.

First, women, especially young working-class women, have little access to 'space'. Social and sporting facilities are dominated by men and male groups with the pub, working-men's clubs, snooker halls, rugby/cricket clubs all clearly male domains. Often the street corner where 'the lads' can be found is unsafe territory for young women as they regularly face harassment ranging from verbal abuse or put-downs to actual physical violence. This does not mean that young women are totally excluded from the street. Research by Cowie and Lees (1981) suggests that young working-class women can be found in groups hanging around shopping centres or street corners. They acknowledge, however, that 'the extent of girls' participation or exclusion on the street would seem to be less than boys', but remains to be fully investigated'.[19] They conclude that the appearance of 'girls' on the street is always constrained by their subordination. It would seem that for many young women the answer is, as McRobbie suggests, to retreat to a 'home base' where best friends can meet, chat, and negotiate their existence.[20]

Working-class young women also experience material constraints which, together with a lack of access to private transport, further inhibits their movements. Middle-class young women have greater opportunity for participation in social and sporting activities. Not only do they have economic support,[21] but also parental help to transport them to the gym club, swimming pool, youth centre, etc. Despite increased access, however, the very real threat of violence on the streets exists for all women. Facilities remain dominated by men and within families 'free time' is defined differently for young women than for young men. This raises the issue of domestic and child-care responsibilities which many young women, unlike young men, experience from an early age. Young women are expected to help with housework and the care of younger siblings.[22] The strength of the ideology of domesticity emphasizes women's 'natural' domestic and child-care role. Young women also have a realistic view of their future which they see as involving domestic/child-care responsibilities. They recognize this as preparation for their future roles as wives and mothers, and although not always accepting it unquestioningly, it is regarded generally as inevitable. The extent of expectations of domestic/child-care responsibility is also related to class. Working-class young women are expected to take on these responsibilities to a greater extent[23] although middle-class young women often still have their share of washing up and cleaning to do!

Young women's subcultures, then, do not correspond to male subcultures in any simplistic way and an understanding of gender, class, race, and age constraints is important. Indeed the term 'subculture' takes on 'masculine' connotations. It is more useful perhaps to consider young women's 'cultures' which are structurally separate and distinct from those of male youth. McRobbie identifies 'romance' and the 'culture of femininity' to be central to the daily lives of adolescent young women.[24] Her research highlights the importance for young women of talking and planning around fashions, make-up and boyfriends. The culture revolves around the intense task of 'getting a man' but always within the constraints of 'keeping a good reputation' which is by no means easy or unambiguous.[25] Young women are well aware of the inevitable future, influenced by political, economic, and ideological constraints, in which a heterosexual relationship leading to marriage, home, and family is the expected outcome. Within this 'culture of femininity' there are obvious class and race differences. Just as 'masculinity' cannot be viewed as a static, universal concept so 'femininity' demonstrates marked variation across class and ethnicity. As Griffin rightly asserts:

> There *are* some parallels with the position of young black and middle class women, but it is crucial to understand the ways in which young white women benefit from cultural, ideological and institutional racisms; how race and racism affect and are affected by the experiences of young black women; and how young middle class women negotiate their relatively privileged position in education and waged work.[26]

Turning now to schooling it is important to examine its relationship to the 'culture of femininity'. There is clear evidence that young women and men experience schooling differently, and this leads to distinct outcomes.[27] Young women and young men are prepared for their future roles in society, which for young women is expected to involve becoming a wife and mother as well as being involved in the world of work. Within the curriculum this need not take the overt form of differential option choices (for example domestic science for girls; woodwork for boys) but as Stanworth recognizes it can involve 'a myriad of subtle ways in which the educational process brings to life and sustains sexual divisions – the process of, quite literally, teaching girls to be women and boys to be men'.[28] Again this cuts across class boundaries and is experienced to some degree whether in a local comprehensive school or a privileged public school.[29] Griffin confirms this in her discussions with white middle-class girls in school:

> Whilst some of these young women clearly realised the extent of their privileges as white and middle class, as women they will always have to play second fiddle to men, denied full access to the spheres of power in which they have apparently been granted 'equal opportunities'.[30]

Within school there are clearly female counter-school cultures just as there have been shown to be male counter-school cultures.[31] Whereas the *class* significance of male counter-school culture has been stressed, female counter-school cultures are seen to involve negotiation around age, race, class, and *gender* relations. Resistances to schooling for young women are not solely about gender or class but are bound up with the complex development towards adulthood. Indeed age-based resistances have been a part of struggles by young women and young men within schooling since formal schooling began. It is likely that this has been further intensified with the raising of the school-leaving age which leaves young adults in a system geared to childhood and based on a clear age-related authority structure.[32]

Young women's resistances within school, however, do take on a specifically female form and cannot simply be equated to those of male youth. Young women who are considered 'non-academic' are in conflict with a school system geared to examination results. However as research into girls' schooling has shown, schools are concerned also with producing young women who will fit into our society as wives and mothers. Resistance here is gender-based and cuts across class considerations for it is challenging the school definition of a 'nice' girl which is seen to emphasize neatness, passivity, hard work, politeness, etc., which will result in a 'good', 'suitable' job, for example nursery nurse, nurse, infant teacher. It is important here to see resistance not necessarily as a 'problem' (as viewed by the school) but perhaps a 'legitimate source of pressure'.[33] Young women in this situation could be seen to be challenging the 'culture of femininity' and reasserting their right to define their own existence. This becomes dependent on the form of resistance taken. McRobbie stresses the importance of 'appearance' as a form of resistance for adolescent young women.[34] By wearing make-up, jewellery, altering the school uniform, young women often use overtly sexual modes of expression which demonstrate quite clearly that they are overstepping the boundaries of girlhood (as demanded by the school) into womanhood. As young women constantly are judged by their sexuality, be it by the 'lads' in Willis's study or the teachers in their classrooms, it is a powerful means of challenging 'the system'. However, McRobbie argues that young women's own culture then becomes the most efficient agent of social control for, by resisting, they reaffirm and reinforce patriarchal power relations – 'they are both saved by and locked within the culture of femininity'.[35]

Clearly by asserting a more sexually orientated appearance young women run the risk of being labelled as a 'slag' or a 'tart'. However, by rejecting the image of the 'nice' acquiescent girl, a more positive assertion of femininity is possible such that resistances can be used to challenge the dominant culture of femininity. Griffin discusses this positive assertion of femininity, which

> partly rejects the idealised notions of the 'nice' girl in a very direct manner, undermines images of the passive asexual young woman waiting for her 'fella' found in teenage magazines and romantic fiction; and serves as a partial attempt to re-appropriate femininity by young women, and for young women.[36]

Young women's resistances are not restricted to those involving appearance. Griffin discusses a further strategy that young women use to negotiate their existence in schools. Most teachers would recognize her description of young women's silence and the 'sullen stare'. For many young women this is a more subtle and acceptable challenge which does not rely on the more extrovert use of appearance. This, too, cuts across class and cannot be seen only as a working-class resistance to schooling.

What becomes clear is that young women's cultures exist in specific structural forms and cannot be equated simplistically with those of young men. Within school young women's counter-school culture is complex and again cannot be viewed only in relation to issues around class location. Certainly forms of 'femininity' are used by working-class young women as class-based resistances. However, as in middle-class schools, notions of 'ideal' femininity (that is the 'nice' girl) are also challenged and can be seen not as 'locking' them within the 'culture of femininity' but indeed forming a challenge to that culture in an attempt to redefine 'femininity' for themselves. The complexities are such that counter-school resistances by young women serve to reinforce, negotiate, and challenge the 'culture of femininity'. There is no clear-cut line that can differentiate between these outcomes. Cultural analysis which recognizes these complexities and acknowledges the importance of gender, class, race, and age considerations remains at an innovatory stage.

The final section of this chapter relates the teaching of physical education in secondary schools to young women's cultures and especially their resistances. PE is a subject which receives little attention in the considerations of young women's schooling.[37] However, it is an area which experiences resistances from young women particularly around adolescence. The centrality of the 'physical' makes it an interesting confrontation, for a biologically deterministic position is attractive when dealing with physical issues.[38] This final section stresses the importance of a cultural analysis and considers the implication of this for the future teaching of PE.

Physical education – what is on offer?

PE in the majority of secondary schools is taught to single-sex groups even when part of a co-educational school system. My own research in Liverpool schools[39] demonstrates the existence of a core curriculum in the first three years of secondary schools consisting of team games, gymnastics, athletics, with some schools including swimming and/or dance. Within this core component half of the total PE time is taken up by competitive team games, with the other activities sharing the remaining time. A programme of 'options' including more individually based activities (for example badminton, trampolining) or less competitive situations (keep fit) is offered, in most instances from the fourth year upwards. The extra-curricular programme offers team games in specific age groupings, gym, swimming, and/or dance clubs for the younger girls with a badminton club a usual addition from the age of 15 years. PE is theoretically compulsory up to the school-leaving age and is taught in mixed ability groups apart from extra-curricular representative year team practices.

The notion of 'good practice' and 'standards' in PE has been at the forefront of PE teaching throughout its history and development. 'Good practice' centres around discipline, neatness, good behaviour, appearance, and so on. It is stressed by PE teachers today as one of the most important features of their work. In 1905 the magazine of the Anstey College of Physical Training[40] reported that the main aims of physical training included:

Regular attendance, good behaviour throughout the year, and general improvement in all respects.

Smart personal appearance shown by general care of the body as regards hair, teeth, skin, nails, clothing and good health.

Good posture when standing and sitting and good carriage in walking.

Attention to word of command, absence of mistakes and vigorous work in the gymnasium.

General forms and style of movement, sense of time, self control and power of relaxation.[41]

Good behaviour and discipline whilst very much part of the general school ethos have a particular association with PE. Margaret Stansfield, the first principal of Bedford PE College (founded in 1903), believed that 'the discipline of the school emanates from the gymnasium'.[42] The content of PE for girls has long been associated with 'discipline'. The rules and regulations of team games combined with the discipline of Swedish gymnastics[43] made girls' PE every bit as regulated as the more formal, regimented military drill associated with boys' PE. Although Swedish gymnastics tended to be associated with a freer type of movement that was less restricted than that offered to the boys, Hargreaves notes that in the Ling system, 'the potential for natural, spontaneous movement was denied by the exact parameters of behaviour laid down and by the very nature of the system, which was remarkably similar to drill.'[44]

Today PE continues to stress discipline. Lining up in the changing rooms in silence, entering the gym quietly and responding without question to rules and regulations of games, are an essential part of contemporary PE lessons. In many schools the 'success' of PE is still measured by the achievements on the sports field or netball court. PE often provides the 'public face' of the school when it represents them at tournaments, inter-school matches, swimming galas and gym displays. Even the discipline and behaviour of the girls when outside, playing hockey or tennis, are on view to the rest of the school in their classrooms and the local residents as they walk past. In many respects what occurs in PE is under far closer scrutiny than teaching in the classroom where doors and walls can provide a useful barrier to observation and comment!

Similarly appearance in relation to dress, neatness, and posture can be identified as having been important in PE throughout each decade of its history. In the training of PE teachers it remains an obsession and the continuing emphasis on appearance for teaching practice in schools today demonstrates its importance for teachers of PE and subsequently the transmission of such values to the pupils. The wearing of PE uniform remains throughout Liverpool schools. In most instances the uniform is regulated to a specific skirt/shorts/top of a defined colour. Even where this has been relaxed, which was only evident in three situations, there is an insistence on 'suitable' clothing as defined by the PE teacher.[45] A considerable amount of time it taken up in the PE lesson by the enforcement of correct PE uniform and neatness of appearance.

While 'good practice' and 'standards' inform the teaching of PE, the primary aims and objectives are dependent also on economic, social, and political forces. Kane's (1974) survey of secondary school PE for the Schools' Council found that women teachers ranked leisure as their fourth most important objective in PE teaching out of a table of nine major objectives.[46] In my own research in Liverpool schools I found that in 1984 every girls' PE department placed leisure as their main or second objective for the teaching of PE especially from the third year upwards. The emphasis was on enjoyment and preparation for participation in post-school leisure time. Most teachers recognized this as a changed emphasis throughout the 1970s and early 1980s due to economic changes identified as producing increased leisure time both in terms of shorter working hours and most importantly through the reality of probable unemployment or part-time work. The validity of these points will be discussed later.

The PE on offer to adolescent girls, therefore, is influenced both structurally and ideologically by a number of interrelated factors. In considering the relationship of PE to young women's subcultures, it is important now to turn to the influences which impinge on the young women's responses to the PE experience.

Young women's responses

It is obvious that young women experience certain biological changes during puberty, which occurs on average between the ages of nine and thirteen. These changes are often dramatic, with changed body shape, related to the onset of menstruation, happening over a short period of time. How far these biological changes influence young women's responses to PE remains questionable. Whereas menstruation was regarded in the past as an inhibition to young women's physical movement and thus a direct restriction on her participation in most physical activity, in recent times research had debunked this myth[47] and it is now widely accepted that in most situations menstruation does not negatively affect women's ability to participate in physical activity. What would seem more important is the social construction of young women's biology – the ideology of biology, that is the expectations placed on young women as to how they *should* be reacting to these physical changes. It is reasonable to assume that for some young women the changes of puberty produce such distinct changes in body shape that they find it awkward to move physically in the same way as in the past, for example in gymnastics or athletics. It is, however, the social and

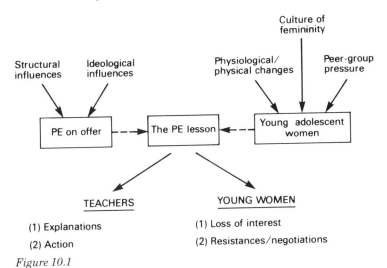

Figure 10.1

ideological pressures linked to sexuality and body physique that produce the inhibition rather than a biologically determined restriction on movement. As discussed in a previous section of this paper young women's experiences at adolescence centre around the culture of femininity. In terms of the 'physical' the expectation is one of inactivity, passivity, neatness (reinforced through socialization, media, schooling). Young women are not expected to run around, get dirty, or indeed sweat. The old adage that 'young ladies glow' as opposed to sweat remains firm in today's thinking.

Peer-group pressure intensifies the culture of femininity. Whereas an individual may still be interested in playing netball or swimming in the team, it is often pressure from friends which encourages her to 'drop out' or certainly diminishes her enthusiasm. Option lists in the PE department often show names erased because the 'best friend' does not want to take part in that particular activity. Certainly many potential senior team members are lost, not necessarily through a loss of interest by the individual but more often because of the subcultural influences that surround her.

So, what happens when the PE on offer encounters the young women it is intended for? The meeting place is the lesson and it is here that the relationship between secondary school PE and young women's subcultures becomes either the 'problem' for the teacher or the negotiation and resistance of the student.

Teacher and student: the meeting of PE and adolescent young women

Figure 10.1 (p. 161) shows the centrality of the PE lesson and the resultant effects for both PE teacher and student.

First, PE teachers attempt to explain why young women tend to lose interest in physical activity during and immediately after puberty. This 'loss of interest' of adolescent young women is confirmed by the majority of heads of PE interviewed during my research.

> Girls at this stage are going through . . . they're changing fairly rapidly. They get embarrassed very easily. They change shape more and feel more self-conscious than lads do. They just lose all interest in physical activity at this time – it's just natural.

> I've talked to my girls and they always say 'we're just beginning to be interested in outside'. They lose interest in PE at school. If they go to a disco they expend more energy than they ever would in a PE lesson.

The explanation is given as 'natural' – an inevitable problem inherent to adolescent young women. In general they see young women at this time as less interested in physical activity, lethargic, and inactive. My own research indicates that this gender expectation cuts across class and ethnic divisions, and PE teachers tend to generalize for all young women. Whereas this may indeed reflect the reality of the experience, the explanation must involve more than a simplistic biological determinism. However, for many PE teachers the problems faced with 3E or 4X on a Thursday afternoon are real and in general result in one or two coping strategies.

First, many teachers, identifying the 'problem' as biologically constructed and/or individually based, tackle the solution by reiterating the belief in the value and ideals of the PE on offer, and attempt to enforce participation through disciplinary means. Obviously this has minimal 'success', for even if the young women involved continue to participate in theory, in practice they remain uninterested and unmotivated. The value of 'enjoyment' placed so high by all PE teachers on their list of aims and objectives cannot be achieved by the use of hierarchical disciplinarian methods. Secondly, teachers have attempted to alleviate the difficulties by adapting the curriculum and making it more relevant to young women's needs and requirements. During the past decade and a half this has included the introduction of a scheme of options for the upper school age group. These 'option' activities, whilst retaining the compulsory element of PE, allow more choice of content. The options offered tend to be individually based which is recognized as being more 'appropriate' for older girls. The emphasis is on indoor activities 'which won't mess up their hair or make them too sweaty' (interview, PE teacher). In some situations activities relating directly to appearance are encouraged, with stress on the development of an 'attractive' figure and body shape. This can be through keep fit/aerobic classes or the development of specialist health and beauty courses which cover a wide range of issues including care of the hair, nails, diet, make-up, and clothes.

The difficulty with these latter developments in PE is that they reinforce the cultural expectations of femininity and in many ways fall into the 'double bind' described previously. Once more, as McRobbie suggests, young women become 'both saved by and locked in the culture of femininity'.[48] The message being reinforced in these situations is that young women should not be interested and involved in physical activity in order to develop strength and fitness, but should be concerned in enhancing their appearance – in making themselves more 'attractive', particularly to the opposite sex.

The response from young women to the PE lesson can involve resistance to the activities and teaching of PE. These resistances take on similar forms to those described in relation to schooling in general. Resistances based on appearance take an intensified form when related to PE. As has been discussed, appearance in relation to 'standards' and 'good practice' is an integral part of the ethos of PE teaching. Young women who use their appearance to challenge their school experiences confront PE by contesting its central ideological tenet. Young women refuse to wear the required PE uniform, they wear make-up and jewellery and will not consent to the 'golden rule' of tying their hair back. These challenges to authority are more obvious in the changing room than elsewhere in the school, and indeed produce a confrontation which often can be avoided by many other school staff. Whereas other teachers can choose to ignore the wearing of a ring or earrings which contravene school regulations, PE teachers not only have their own standards and values around appearance to uphold, but have the added concern of safety during physical activity. Rings, earrings, necklaces, badges, and long hair can be exceedingly dangerous in some physical situations.

The 'sullen stare' takes on particular significance in PE. A sullen, silent 'participant' on the hockey pitch or in the gymnasium is inordinately difficult to manage. In the classroom a young woman using the 'sullen stare' often simply encourages less attention from the teacher. In a mixed group situation, where boys have been shown to dominate the lesson and receive more attention from the teacher,[49] a silent, sullen member of the group provides little overt challenge to the successful continuation of the lesson. Indeed it provides a reinforced view of the stereotypical female pupil as passive, quiet, less articulate, and so on. In PE, however, where lively, active behaviour is demanded, a silent sullen participant produces far more conflict and can affect the participation of the whole group. It is a particularly successful resistance to PE for adolescent young women.

Towards a cultural explanation

A biological explanation for young women's loss of interest in PE and their resistances within the PE lesson is not sufficient. Whilst acknowledging the physiological changes of puberty I would argue that an understanding of cultural expectations is vital if young women's experiences, attitudes, and behaviours are to be fully understood. It is necessary to analyse from a cultural perspective why many young women 'drop out' or lose interest in PE during the period of adolescence. The PE on offer to young women conflicts with their interests and attitudes, not simply because they are undergoing the biological changes of puberty, but because the cultural expectations of gender-specific attitudes, behaviour and role are at odds both with what is on offer in PE and with the values, ideals, and ethos underpinning the subject.

PE for girls in most secondary schools remains dominated by team games. Team games are synonymous with sport, which in our society is problematic for female participants. The relationship of sport to masculinity is well documented.[50] Sport celebrates a certain kind of masculinity with its sporting heroes dominating the headlines on the sports page. Young women are immersed in a culture of femininity and romance, reinforced through the magazines they read, the television they watch, and their everyday experiences. PE appears incompatible with their expected lifestyle. Sport is seen primarily as a male pursuit bound up with masculine values. Young women spectate, support and admire, but they do not expect to participate.

Furthermore sport, in the form of team games, is problematic not only in definition but also in form. Young women's cultures which emphasize the 'best friend' or small groupings do not relate easily to the collective team situation. PE stresses the collective through team sports, gym clubs, dance groups, athletic teams. Young women often reject these situations as incompatible with the expectations of adult femininity.[51] Young, fit, virile men are expected to revel in group camaraderie and team spirit. It is less acceptable for their adolescent sisters.

'Preparation for leisure' was stated as a primary aim of PE teaching by every secondary school in my current research. This confirms Kane's findings in the only major survey of secondary school PE undertaken for the Schools' Council.[52] This, however, is problematic for adolescent young women. Recent work on women's leisure has emphasized the problem of defining leisure for women. Women's leisure is constrained by many factors including class, race, age, and not least 'men, collectively and as individuals'.[53] The very existence of 'leisure' for women as traditionally defined has been questioned by Deem (1984) and Griffin (1982). They insist that in order to explain women's leisure, or lack of it, both the public and the private spheres of women's experiences must be understood. As Griffin states: 'women's position in waged and unwaged work in relation to the family means that the existence of 'leisure' as a pure category for women is questionable'.[54]

Preparation for leisure creates problems of relevance for all women especially in the realm of physical leisure activities. Deem's research confirms this, for in her study of 168 women drawn at random from five areas of a new town, she found 'scarcely any adult women who continued with any sport or physical activity done at school once they had left, with swimming the only widespread exception to this'.[55] Therefore 'preparation for leisure' is a dubious objective for young women's PE. Not only does leisure not exist for many women but where women have opportunities for leisure the most frequently pursued activity is swimming. My research suggests that swimming is offered to adolescent young women as an option in schools only where the school has a swimming pool on site. This is restricted further by staffing problems, as most departments cannot release a member of staff to cover the numbers opting for swimming. In most schools there is no choice, as access to swimming facilities is not available.[56]

The emphasis on leisure as a realistic objective for young women seems particularly illogical given that many PE teachers recognize their own personal limitations on time and opportunities at a private level. Many PE teachers described the problems they had around family and domestic responsibilities which affect their ability to spend more time on extra-curricular activities or personal leisure pursuits. This failure to recognize the problems of using leisure as a relevant and useful concept for women produces a contradictory and, in many ways, an unachievable aim for PE teaching. PE teachers need to look more critically at both the structural limitations and the reality of everyday experiences for women in physical leisure activities in order to provide a more realistic link between school and future physical participation. The recognition of a sexual division of leisure as well as a sexual division of labour is an important aspect of the teaching of girls in schools. Furthermore young women themselves often recognize the constraints put on their 'leisure' time. Even where they succeed in challenging their lack of access to time and space (more easily achieved by middle-class young women) they face unequal provision of facilities and opportunities to participate. Their present reality confirms their future 'leisure' participation. When they attend youth groups or clubs they know only too well who dominates the snooker tables, gymnasium, or table-tennis.[57]

The resistance of young women to the discipline and control of PE, described previously as being central to the ideology of PE, is a response similar to the responses of young women to schooling in general. The actual resistance is class- and age-based, although within a particularly gendered form.[58] Although these problems are faced throughout the curriculum, the importance of discipline and control, which is so much a part of both the content and teaching of PE, creates an often intensified conflict between PE teaching staff and students.

Equally, resistances to school uniform by adolescent young women are resistances to the style, restriction, and enforced uniformity of the dress. As Whylde states: 'Collar, tie and jacket for boys and skirt and blouse (or twin set!) for girls imitate the conventional dress of the middle aged and middle class, a group which few pupils will identify with, and against which most will rebel.'[59]

Once more the issue of uniform is intensified during PE. PE uniform is one of the major areas of conflict between young women and PE teachers. To many young women the wearing of a standard tee-shirt, regulation navy shorts/skirt plus ankle socks is one of the greatest indignities and embarrassments placed on them. Whilst they react to school uniform for the reasons suggested by Whylde, their reactions to PE kit are enhanced as their developing sexuality and their desire to achieve adult femininity meet head-on a PE kit which denies not only their individuality but also any hint of a developing sexual person. At a time when fashion, jewellery, and make-up are central to their concern with appearance, the uniform, asexual PE kit is an anathema.

Anxiety around PE for adolescent young women is caused also by showering after a lesson and indeed changing in large, group changing rooms. This relates to the fact that girls reach puberty and mature physically at different rates. Again, while this is experienced throughout the school, the 'physical' nature of PE intensifies the problems. Measor found in her research a great reluctance of young women to take showers as a group:

Pat: I don't like showers. On the first day we were ever so shy. Everyone has got things different . . . some people have got hairs and some haven't.
Carol: There is one big girl in our group . . . she is big chested, and that and she walks through the shower all covered up. It's best to be in between, we all giggle and throw our towels down. She finally went into the shower with her towel. There is one really little girl, who sits there making faces, she looks at everyone, she makes you feel embarrassed.[60]

The explanations for the problems faced by young women in coping with this situation are clearly grounded in physiology and the physical changes of puberty. However it is the interaction of physical development and cultural expectation that is important. It is not the actual physical changes of the young women's bodies which cause the anxiety, but the culturally determined responses to these changes. Those who are 'in-between' or average in their development can cope with the situation. They meet the expectations for desired body shape and development. Those who deviate from the norm face acute embarrassment and often unkind comment. When society emphasizes a desired physique for adult femininity, those who become aware of their differences during adolescence are caused anxiety and often retreat or 'hide' from the situation. PE provides the platform where physical differences are unmasked. Adult women are not expected to expose their bodies and are encouraged to dislike their body shape unless it conforms to the 'ideal' feminine stereotype. During adolescence the PE changing room or shower area is an exposed situation where young women's developing bodies are put 'on view'. The problem is not the physical appearance as such, but the desire of young women to achieve the 'acceptable', sexually attractive physique of womanhood. This body shape is culturally determined and strongly informed by ideologies of woman as a sexual object to be admired, viewed, and used by men.

The way forward

The 'culture of femininity' is based on the social construction of women's roles and behaviour. The ideology of biology emphasizes women as passive and submissive and presents them in appearance, dress, and style in terms of their sexuality. This influences not only women's work opportunities but also their use of leisure, domestic, and family commitments. These images of women cut across class, race, and age although at each of the levels (work, leisure, family, sexuality) there are differences dependent on women's individual location in society. The media reinforce this imagery even when dealing with women involved in sporting activities.[61] Women athletes are presented positively as conforming to the desired image: Zola Budd – 'the waif'; Donna Hartley – 'the golden girl'; Joyce Smith 'mother of two', or alternatively negatively as having overstepped the boundaries of femininity: Martina Navratilova – 'the machine'; Jarmila Kratchvilova – 'the man'.

School PE fails to provide 'meaningful experiences' for many young adolescent women because it appears at odds with the culture of femininity. Their resistances which are complex and not always consistent, relate to what they perceive as on offer from PE – the development of muscle; sweat; communal showers/changing facilities; 'childish' asexual PE kit; low-status activities. It is acceptable for the 'tomboy' in junior or lower secondary school to participate in and enjoy these activities but not so acceptable to adult femininity.

Therefore, PE remains trapped within possibilities which will 'appeal' to young women but will consequently reinforce the culture of femininity. This is intensified by the training and ideological constraints of women PE teachers. Even so-called 'progressive' moves, such as mixed PE, provide superficial challenges to the ideologies of femininity.[62] Any suggestion of substantive change to give young women positive experiences in PE tends to be met with scepticism because it is assumed that young women are so steeped in the deterministic 'Jackie' mentality that they will reject more positive physical values of assertiveness, strength, and control.

There is not necessarily real substance to this argument. Adult women's experiences are not totally determined and the past decade and a half has seen a substantive shift through the development of new directions in the reconstruction of women's sexuality and consciousness. These include the development of self-help groups in medical care/mental health, the emergence of well-woman clinics and other all-women projects geared to giving women more control over their own health and bodies. Women's groups have developed, resisting male violence with rape crisis centres and women's refuges. Education has seen the introduction of 'NOW' courses, 'outreach' projects, and women's writing groups, where women are encouraged to gain confidence and assertiveness in intellectual situations. Women's physical control over their own bodies can be seen further in the development of self-defence/assertiveness training[63] and women's fitness programmes which are geared to developing health, strength, and physical well-being rather than the traditional construction of 'womanhood' around appearance and body physique.

These latter developments indicate a qualitative shift in definitions of 'the physical'. Women in these programmes are reclaiming the right to physical development and appearance on their own terms rather than on the terms laid down in the traditions of 'feminine culture', learned and reinforced in youth. As Lenskyj describes from her own experience, after years of upbringing women are:

> alienated from our bodies not knowing the extent of our physical strength and endurance and not daring to find out. Those of us who have dared have found a new avenue for self-realisation as women and as feminists – joyful at the discovery that our bodies are strong and resilient, capable of hard work and hard play.[64]

It is with these developments in adult women's projects that women's PE should be concerned, rather than a concentration on equal access to male-based sports. For these are part of the same institutional relations of patriarchy (that is, cults of masculinity) which produce young women's subcultures and define/constrict young women's opportunities. By contrast, women's PE needs to develop a new programme geared to assertiveness, confidence, health, fitness and the capacity to challenge patriarchal definitions of submissiveness, passivity, and dependence. It is by no means an easy task but none the less a direction towards which we must at least begin to move.

The unifying feature of all the adult women's projects mentioned, is the emphasis on collective support.[65] PE is in the perfect situation to offer young women opportunities for collective support through co-operative and enjoyable physical activity. Whilst the relationship between teacher and student will retain an age-related power structure, young women can be encouraged to work together through such activities as dance, outdoor pursuits, and self-defence. Indeed Willis suggests:

> sport could be presented as a form of activity which emphasizes human similarity and not dissimilarity, a form of activity which expresses values which are indeed immeasurable, a form of activity which is concerned with individual well-being and satisfaction rather than with comparison.[66]

Many young men thrive on their collective 'rugby club' experiences. Young women too, need the space for collective physical experience whilst rejecting and challenging the competitive, 'macho' values of the male sporting ethos. Adolescence is a time to develop group and collective experiences rather than the channelling of young women into individually based activities, which deny the opportunities to develop group confidence and identity.

Young women also need the space to develop confidence and interests. This is especially true in mixed schools. The evidence clearly indicates that in all social situations men dominate space – physically and verbally.[67] In co-educational schools the primary female-only space is in the toilets, cloakrooms, and changing rooms. These are the areas where young women 'hang out', where they spend time together away from 'the lads' and the teachers.[68] It would be a positive contribution if women PE teachers could recognize the need of young women to have their own space in which to chat, plan, or simply 'have a laugh'. This is clearly problematic given school organization and the enforcement of school rules and regulations. However it would be a positive move to open up changing rooms and facilities during breaks, lunchtime, and after school and encourage young women to use the space available for their 'leisure' whether it be netball, table-tennis, or chatting with a friend. Too often young women are allowed into the PE wing only if they are taking part in organized, formal PE activities. It would be an encouraging move to give young women more control over their extra-curricular PE activities and to provide the space for meeting and chatting together.

Just as adult women are beginning to reclaim the right to control and develop their own bodies for intrinsic satisfaction rather than sexual exploitation, so PE must emphasize these values for young adolescent women. They must be encouraged to enjoy physical movement; to develop strength and muscular potential; to work together to discover body awareness and confidence. It will be only when young women collectively become confident and assertive with control, both physically and mentally, over their own bodies that they will move towards redefining their position. PE has an important contribution to make towards the denial of ideologies of 'femininity'. For this to occur it requires a critical self-appraisal and a more sensitive understanding of young women's position in our schooling system and in wider society.

Acknowledgements

Many thanks to Pat Craddock, Rosemary Deem, and Phil Scraton for their help, support, and critical comments. Also personal thanks to Sally Channon.

Notes

1 For the purpose of this paper PE will denote young women's physical education.
2 M. Brake, *The Sociology of Youth Culture and Youth Subcultures*, London, Routledge & Kegan Paul, 1980.
3 This point is noted across a wide range of literature. For example 'juvenile delinquency' invariably has focused on boys' criminal or deviant activities – see A. Campbell, *Girl Delinquents*, Oxford, Blackwell, 1980.
4 D. Robins and P. Cohen, *Knuckle Sandwich*, Harmondsworth, Penguin, 1978, p. 58.
5 H. Parker, *View from the Boys*, Newton Abbott, David & Charles, 1974, p. 95.
6 A. McRobbie and J. Garber, 'Girls and subcultures' in S. Hall and T. Jefferson (eds), *Resistance through Rituals*, London, Hutchinson, 1976.
7 See L. Shacklady-Smith, 'Sexist assumptions and female delinquency – an empirical investigation' in C. Smart and B. Smart (eds), *Women, Sexuality and Social Control*, London, Routledge & Kegan Paul, 1978, for a further discussion of this point.
8 In this paper 'patriarchy' represents male domination of women. See V. Beechey, 'On patriarchy', *Feminist Review*, 3, 1979, pp. 66–82, for a detailed consideration of the complexity of this concept.

9 Brake, op. cit.
10 C. Cockburn, *Brothers*, London, Athlone Press, 1983.
11 P. Willis, *Profane Culture*, London, Routledge & Kegan Paul, 1978.
12 Parker, op. cit.; Willis, op. cit.
13 K. Sheard and E Dunning, 'The rugby football club', *International Review of Sport*, vol. 8, 1973, pp. 5–24.
14 A. McRobbie, 'Working class girls and the culture of femininity' in Centre for Contemporary Cultural Studies (CCCS), *Women Take Issue*, London, Hutchinson, 1978.
15 A. McRobbie, *Jackie: an Ideology of Adolescent Femininity*, CCCS stencilled paper, 1978; C. Griffin, *Cultures of Femininity: Romance Revisited*, CCCS, 1981; A. McRobbie and T. McCabe, *Feminism for Girls*, London, Routledge & Kegan Paul, 1981; M. Nava and A. McRobbie (eds), *Gender and Generation*, London, Macmillan, 1984.
16 For example see M. Brake, 'The skinheads – an English working class subculture', *Youth and Society*, vol. 6 (2), December 1974; D. Hebdige, 'The meaning of Mod' in Hall and Jefferson, op. cit.; and Willis, op. cit.
17 Griffin, op. cit.
18 McRobbie, 'Working class girls and the culture of femininity'; Griffin, op. cit.
19 C. Cowie and S. Lees, 'Slags or drags', *Feminist Review*, 9, Autumn 1981.
20 McRobbie, op. cit.
21 However many working-class teenage women do have paid jobs outside school hours – see, for example the Low Pay Unit report on children and work.
22 My research in Liverpool schools indicates that young women have considerable domestic and child-care responsibilities which restrict their ability to take up extra-curricular PE opportunities. See also N. Dorn, *Class, Youth and Drink: Historical Analysis of Policy and Contemporary Ethnology of Youth*, London, Croom Helm, 1983.
23 Dorn, op. cit.
24 McRobbie, op. cit.
25 Cowie and Lees, op. cit.
26 Griffin, op. cit.
27 R. Deem (ed.), *Schooling for Women's Work*, London, Routledge & Kegan Paul, 1980; M. Stanworth, *Gender and Schooling*, London, Writers and Readers Co-operative, 1981.
28 Stanworth, op. cit.
29 J. Okeley, 'Privileged, schooled and finished: boarding education for girls', in S. Ardener (ed.), *Defining Females*, London, Croom Helm, 1978.
30 Griffin, op. cit.
31 P. Willis, *Learning to Labour*, Farnborough, Saxon House, 1977.
32 R. Johnson, *Education and Popular Politics*, E353 Block 1, Unit 1, Milton Keynes, Open University Press, 1981.
33 Johnson, op. cit.
34 McRobbie, op. cit.
35 ibid.
36 Griffin, op. cit.

37 ILEA, *Providing Equal Opportunities for Girls and Boys in Physical Education*, London, ILEA, 1984, and O. Leaman, *Sit on the Sidelines and Watch the Boys Play: Sex Differentiation in PE*, London, Longman for Schools' Council, 1984, provide specific work.

38 Physical sex differences have been taken for granted until recently. See E. Ferris, 'Sportswomen and medicine', Report of the 1st International Conference on Women and Sport, 1978; A. Mees, 'Women in sport: a review of physiological factors', *Physical Education Review*, vol. 2 (1), 1979, pp. 44–9; K. Dyer, *Catching up the Men*, London, Junction, 1982, for evidence that challenges many of the 'myths' surrounding physical sex differences.

39 This research examines how images of 'femininity' and the construction of gender-appropriate behaviour are reinforced or challenged by the structure, content, and teaching of girls' PE in secondary schools. The qualitative methodology has involved extensive interviews with Heads of girls' PE departments in Liverpool state secondary schools, periods of close observation in selected schools, and structured interviews with PE advisers, lecturers in the specialist teacher-training college, and education committee members involved in reorganization.

40 One of the original PE teacher-training colleges founded in 1897.

41 Quoted in C. Crunden, *A History of Anstey College of Physical Education: 1897–1972*, Anstey CPE, 1974, p. 19.

42 S. Fletcher, *Women First – the Female Tradition in English Physical Education 1880–1980*, London, Athlone Press, 1984.

43 Swedish gymnastics originated from the work of Per Henrik Ling. The gymnastics was based on scientific principles of anatomy and physiology and was introduced into the English school system primarily by the work of Madame Bergman-Osterberg.

44 J. Hargreaves, 'Playing like gentlemen while behaving like ladies', MA thesis submitted to University of London Institute of Education, 1979.

45 The definition of 'suitable' PE clothing consists of plain tee-shirt and shorts or games skirt. It varies from a formal uniform only in so far as colours are not specified.

46 J. E. Kane, *Physical Education in Secondary Schools*, London, Macmillan, 1974.

47 See Ferris, op. cit.

48 McRobbie, op. cit.

49 D. Spender, *Invisible Women: the Schooling Scandal*, London, Writers and Readers Co-operative, 1982; Stanworth, *Gender and Schooling*.

50 I. M. Young, 'Throwing like a girl: a phenomenology of feminine body comportment, mobility and spatiality', *Human Studies*, vol. 3, 1980; J. Hargreaves (ed.), *Sport, Culture and Ideology*, London, Routledge & Kegan Paul, 1982.

51 Leaman, op. cit.

52 Kane, op. cit.

53 R. Deem, 'Paid work, leisure and non-employment: shifting boundaries and gender differences', unpublished paper presented to BSA conference on 'Work, Employment, Unemployment', April 1984.

54 C. Griffin, D. Hobson, S. MacIntosh, and T. M. McCabe, 'Women and leisure' in Hargreaves (ed.), op. cit.; Deem, op. cit.

55 ibid.

56 The issue here rests on political and economic decisions.

57 Nava and McRobbie, *Gender and Generation*.

58 McRobbie, 'Working class girls and the culture of femininity'.

59 J. Whylde (ed.), *Sexism in the Secondary Curriculum*, London, Harper & Row, 1983.

60 L. Measor, 'Sex education and adolescent sexuality', unpublished paper, 1984.

61 J. Graydon, ' "But it's more than a game. It's an institution." Feminist perspectives on sport', *Feminist Review*, 13, Spring 1983.

62 See S. Scraton, 'Losing ground: the implications for girls of mixed physical education', unpublished paper.

63 For a discussion of the redefining of women's strength and power and the development of self-defence techniques, see K. Quinn, *Stand Your Ground*, London, Orbis, 1983.

64 H. Lenskyj, 'I am Strong', in *The Women's News Magazine*, University of Toronto, March/April 1982.

65 See R. Dixey and M. Talbot, *Women, Leisure and Bingo*, Leeds, Trinity and All Saints College, 1982, pp. 78–9, for a discussion of the importance of contact and support for women during their leisure.

66 P. Willis, 'Women in sport in ideology' in J. Hargreaves (ed.), *Sport, Culture and Ideology*.

67 Spender, op. cit.; Young, op. cit.

68 Griffin *et al.*, 'Women and leisure'.

11

One-parent families and leisure (1979)

JANE STREATHER

Introduction

There is a growing knowledge of the circumstances of one-parent families, for example, their poverty; their relatively poor housing conditions; limited opportunities to work; social isolation; their public and private image; and their responsibilities in single-handed parenthood. All are factors relevant to their leisure experience and opportunities or, rather, lack of them.

In addition to this knowledge, I draw here on three sources of information:

(1) The National Council for One Parent Families, as well as being a pressure group, advises approximately 10,000 enquirers a year – lone parents and professional advisers – mainly on finance, accommodation, and matrimonial law. A large number of lone parents who contact the Council say that they are isolated and lonely and wish to be put in touch with other lone parents in their area, or with self-help groups. Last year, 559 parents specifically asked for a local contact. Contact with lone parents through advice and information services enables the Council to have a good understanding of their needs, their difficulties, their hopes, their fears and aspirations.

(2) A student placed with the Council carried out a small number of interviews (25) with lone parents in London about their views on leisure. It was not a random selection. Rather, some lone parents who had been in touch with the Council in recent months, were contacted and asked to agree to an interview about leisure: others were approached through one-parent family self-help groups in

North London. These interviews have given pointers to some of the constraints on the leisure activities of one-parent families.

(3) My third source of information comes from a brief questionnaire about holiday opportunities of one-parent families. In 1977, the National Council for One Parent Families prepared a guide to cheap holidays for one-parent families – approximately 2,000 were distributed. In order to assess its value, we sent a questionnaire to 200 (1 in 10) of the recipients. 106 were returned completed, providing us with some useful, if limited, information.

Although these sources should be treated as illustrative, the information we have corresponds closely with other research findings about one-parent families in this country and in the United States.

Demographic and other characteristics

Before focusing on the question of leisure and one-parent families it is necessary to consider, albeit briefly, some demographic, environmental, and social characteristics of one-parent families. Such factors are associated with expectations and opportunities with regard to leisure.

Numbers

One in nine of all families with dependent children are one-parent families. In 1976 in this country, the numbers had risen to ¾ million (with 1¼ million children).[1] One-parent families are currently increasing at the rate of 6 per cent per year, mainly as a result of marriage breakdown.

The numbers may be large and growing, but statistically the two-parent family is still the norm, some would say 'normal'. One-parent family comparisons with the 'ideal' and often 'idealized' two-parent family, identify the one-parent family as different, abnormal, deviant, or problematic. Nothing could be further from the truth – one-parent families are real and normal families. But how often do we hear about the growing problem of one-parent families? Problem? The very definition of where the problem lies structures society's response in terms of policies and services. Too frequently there is a preoccupation with form rather than function when discussion about 'The Family' takes place. Both researchers and professionals have a disagreeable habit of projecting a pathological view of the one-parent family. Yet most lone parents cope as well as other parents, sometimes better, and their children are no better or worse than children of two-parent families.

Sadly, many one-parent families internalize the public image and label themselves as different and abnormal, which adds weight to their sense of personal failure and self-doubt. Hence parenthood in itself is not problematic but being a lone parent means encountering special difficulties – some of which I detail below. Those problems may be more readily dealt with if we understand them to be problems of essentially normal families – particularly problems faced by women arising out of the sexual division of role and labour.

Women

Eighty-eight per cent of one-parent families are headed by women. This is most significant with regard to their difficulties, their needs, and to policy implications. The past and present legal, economic, and social position of women is a major factor in determining the disadvantages and restricted opportunities with one-parent families.

We are all aware that the status of women has changed considerably throughout this century. Nevertheless, it has to be recognized that the 'normal' and primary role for women in our society is 'married motherhood'. Husbandless mothers are still regarded with pity, embarrassment, contempt, and are often threatening to those who wish to stay married. The constant pressures on them are to 'normalize' their situation by remarrying.[2] Many lone parents feel failures for not succeeding in their marriages, and guilty because their children bear the brunt of their reduced financial circumstances. It is not surprising that many women heading one-parent families have low self-esteem.

Such feelings could be temporary, but too frequently they are reinforced by their low status in the community – as women, and as one-parent families. They experience an immediate drop in living standards, often resulting in acute poverty, a major factor in bringing about social isolation, but as 'unattached' women they are frequently excluded from social gatherings in a couple-oriented society. Their poverty and their single-parent status bring them up against state bureaucracies such as Social Security, Social Services Departments, Public Housing Departments, whose personnel frequently treat them with insensitivity and, at times, in a discriminatory manner. As female employees, they are frequently treated on a

par with immigrant workers who suffer low wages, discrimination, and limited opportunities for education, training, and promotion.

Lone mothers, because of inadequate state support in the form
of benefits or day nurseries, are frequently dependent upon
ex-spouses who are either unable or unwilling to provide financial support. They are therefore dependent upon meagre state
benefits, still based on Poor Law principles such as means-
testing.

The female lone parent who works faces other difficulties. Lone
mothers who work do share some of the problems of other working
mothers, for example the marginality, low status, low pay and
insecurity of women's work. Working reduces time for domestic
(and indeed leisure) activities, working creates a strain for house-
keeping and parenting. Not working creates other strains which I
will discuss in a moment. But although there are problems in
common between lone mothers and married mothers, lone mothers
have special difficulties.

(i) Many prefer to work part-time, but have to work full-time in
order to escape dependence on Supplementary Benefit. The
economic needs of one-parent families mean that the
employment rate of lone mothers is much higher than of
mothers in two-parent families. Separated, widowed,
divorced, and single mothers are three times more likely to
be working full-time than married women living with their
husbands.[3]

(ii) Institutions and businesses still operate on the assumption
that there are two parents, with one of them free to carry on
transactions during the day.

(iii) Lone mothers have the double responsibility of combining
wage-earning with single-handed parenthood.

(iv) In order to work, the mother faces acute difficulties in
securing adequate day care for her children. There are three
problem areas: lack of provision; inappropriate services;
cost.

(v) Her family has to rely on one woman's wage, whereas
two-parent families frequently have two wages coming in.
Most women workers do unskilled manual jobs at significantly less than the men's rate of pay; women's earnings are
approximately 65 per cent of men's. The low earnings of the

lone mother thus put her at a considerable disadvantage even when compared with the lone father.

Poverty

The most significant factor about one-parent families in this country is that they are poor, and that their poverty is both acute and chronic.

The Finer Committee drew our attention to the fact that one-parent families had, in 1974, on average only half the income of two-parent families.[4] More recent figures from the 1977 Family Expenditure Survey show that this inequality persists. A family with two parents and two children has a gross normal weekly household income of £108, whereas the comparable figure for a one-parent family is £52.76. Large numbers of one-parent families are dependent on Supplementary Benefit. Sixty per cent of all families with children receiving Supplementary Benefit are one-parent families, and some live at that level for many years.

Taking Supplementary Benefit as the poverty line, of all the families living at that level or below, one-parent families are the largest group in poverty. Moreover, the worst poverty, that is the shortfall of income in relation to the poverty level, is experienced by one-parent families.[5]

Family Expenditure Survey data also shows that one-parent families, compared with two-parent families, are less likely to have incomes derived from wages and are more likely to be dependent upon Social Security benefits.

The Survey data shows the percentage of households with durable goods. Car ownership is a reflection of income (and provides opportunities for mobility and leisure). Only 25 per cent of one-parent families have a car compared with 79 per cent of two-parent, two-child families. One-parent families are less likely to have central heating, washing-machines, and telephones. But they are just as likely to have a television set as a two-parent family with children. Television watching is a major leisure activity for one-parent families. According to the data one-parent families spend a higher proportion of their incomes on essentials, such as food, fuel and housing, but much less on alcoholic drink, household goods, transport, and vehicles.

A little thought about what those figures represent will reveal much about the life-style and restricted opportunities of one-parent families.

What are the leisure needs of one-parent families?

I will consider this question from the parents' point of view. The leisure needs of one-parent families are not very different from those of other parents. Our experience suggests that they wish to be able to relax within their own homes and to have the opportunity to meet other adults and participate, outside the home and either with or without children, in activities which differ from their normal routines and responsibilities.

But, for the majority, the likelihood of experiencing such leisure is severely limited. Nearly every lone parent interviewed, described how, on receiving our letter requesting their co-operation, they had found the concept of leisure for single parents rather amusing. They felt that the National Council's contribution to the debate could be summed up by the question 'What leisure?' However, what they told us about their lives and restricted opportunities proved to be anything but amusing.

In almost every case, the impression given was of a situation of poverty. 'The children are called "paupers" at school because they can't participate in activities' said one mother. Parents tend to bear a heavy load of responsibility, particularly in relation to children. A teacher and mother of four admitted that her life was spent totally surrounded by children – at work and at home – and she said that there were occasions when things got on top of her and she lost her temper with the children. 'There's too much to do and too little time to do it – the slightest problem sets up a chain reaction' said another.

They experience emotional strain and have little opportunity for release. 'The fact that I can never properly relax, makes me flare up at the slightest frustration', said a mother. The constant demands of children and the lack of adult company are reasons for not relaxing. One lone parent said 'One of the hardest things, is not having any adults to talk to. It gets you down when you're with children all day and every day.' Some of the comments were truly sad and pathetic, such as that by a woman who said 'I only relax when I'm ill.'

Leisure activities

Nevertheless, almost all parents reported that they did have leisure activities. However their leisure pastimes reflected low expectations. Most of it was home-based and inexpensive, such as watching television or reading. Although the British public spends a great many hours watching television (twenty hours a week in winter, sixteen in summer), most would consider it a trivial part of everyday life.[6] For lone parents the television is the focus of their leisure.

Constraints

There are then many constraints on the leisure opportunities of one-parent families.

Poverty

Low incomes, often resulting in debt (particularly to the fuel boards), are a major constraint to activities outside the home. Travel, entertainment, and relaxing with friends in pubs all cost money.

Housing conditions

I have not discussed the housing difficulties of one-parent families. But often they are limiting to leisure and relaxation at home. Overcrowding, lack of privacy, poor conditions and environment are all factors that restrict leisure.

Constraint of working

I have mentioned some of the difficulties associated with working – the 'too much to do' syndrome combining working with parental and domestic responsibilities. But the lack of work can be as great if not a greater constraint. Lone parents who do not work tend to be poorer, have lower self-esteem and little social contact with other adults. All these factors militate against leisure activities and all are associated with depression and low motivation.

All the parents we interviewed complained of a lack of adult company, feeling continually on call, and all seemed to be suffering from worrying degrees of depression. Many of the interviewees stated that they were never able to get out without their children, and most only go out occasionally with them. This highlighted their sense of isolation and exacerbated their depression. Work, on the other hand, notwithstanding the difficulties for single parents, can offer a validatory role and do much for self-esteem and enable participation in activities outside home and work.

Depression as a constraint

A number of studies, for example that by A. Hunt, point to a high risk of mental stress amongst lone mothers.[7] In this study of one- and two-parent families in five local authorities, they found that a much higher proportion of 'non-married' mothers reported poor health, mainly due to mental disorder. Brown and Harris, in their study of the social origins of depression, showed that one-parent families were 50 per cent more likely to suffer from severe depression than either two-parent families or all working-class women with children.[8] It is worth bearing in mind that although one-parent families seem more likely to suffer stress, the incidence is also high among working-class women caring for children. Perhaps the similarities of their situation are more significant than their differences.

In his study Brown found that employment is one of the factors protecting against the onset of depression, and Moss has suggested that freedom of choice whether to work or not for mothers may be related to mental health and participation in the community.[9]

Lack of knowledge of leisure opportunities

Even where lone parents have both the time and motivation, they often lack knowledge of facilities. Many, for example, have little idea what low-cost public sector leisure facilities exist in their neighbourhood or local authority area. The providers of services need to address themselves to the question of communication, and relevance to one-parent families of the services they provide.

Day-care for children, or rather the lack of it, is a further constraint. Good day-care services could liberate many lone parents from constant parenting and allow them to explore their own interests and activities outside the home. Crèches in leisure centres and shopping centres may well be one of the best ways to increase the opportunity and enjoyment of leisure of single parents.

Holidays

For most people, holidays are the biggest chunk of leisure they experience – and usually annually. Generally they are of short-term benefit, but necessary to 'recharge the batteries'. One-parent families, perhaps more than most, need holidays, but few have them. In 1973, the Office of Population and Census Surveys reported that in the Borough of Haringey (North London) 71 per cent of motherless families and 61 per cent of fatherless families had not had a holiday (defined as four nights away from home for the purpose of pleasure) the previous year.

The holiday survey (106 respondents) carried out by the National Council for One-Parent Families showed that only 23 managed to get away in the previous year. Of these only 7 had managed to pay for the holiday themselves, the rest had been subsidized to varying degrees by Social Services Departments or charitable organizations such as the Council. Of the 16 who had been subsidized, 8 had only managed to stay with relatives – many people would not regard that as a holiday.

The number of children involved in the 106 replies was 236. Of these 184 (78 per cent) had not had a holiday the previous year, and we asked for the main reason.

43 stated the cost of the holiday was too high.
15 said that cost of transport was too expensive.
17 said that the cheapest holidays were fully booked by the time they enquired.
5 said that the off-peak reductions did not coincide with the school holidays.

Low income was thus the main factor preventing most single parents from taking a holiday.

Although the questionnaire did not specifically request the information, 17 of the 106 respondents mentioned that they had never had a holiday. We asked: 'How do you think your family would benefit from a holiday?' The responses included these comments:

My family and I have never had a holiday and therefore I can't answer the question.

My son who is 7 just doesn't know what a holiday is. He asks: 'What is a holiday, why do people want a holiday?' My son would benefit, as then I could answer his questions. But being a one-parent I just don't have the money to take him.

A change of scenery – but I don't really know, as they have never had one.

They have never had a holiday. It would be one of the three wishes I would make if I have that choice.

Of the 23 who were able to take a holiday, many stated that their holiday had proved invaluable in helping them to 'recharge their batteries'. But a number felt that the holiday was marred for them because they didn't really have enough money to spend on the children, or else the holidays were self-catering and they still had to cook and look after the children alone. Nevertheless, almost all of them felt it had been a relief just to have a change of scenery, and there were a number of stories of how gratifying it had been for parents to see their children enjoying themselves.

Value of holiday

It is difficult to assess the value of a holiday for one-parent families. But it is clear that a holiday acts as a pressure valve for a parent who is under continuous stress the remainder of the year. The beneficial effects on the children are likely to be greater than for the parents who may still have to cope alone even on holiday.

One of the most profound effects of a holiday is psychological, and this is clearly linked to a feeling of self-esteem. Most lone parents, although very much aware of the deprivation they suffer themselves, are upset more by their inability to provide their children with the same standard of living as their friends. A constantly recurring theme during the interviews with lone parents was the distress they suffered when their children asked why they didn't go on holiday like other children. One woman related how her daughter had fabricated a series of stories about non-existent holidays in an attempt to cover up her embarrassment at not having been away.

For many of us, a cheap off-peak week at Butlin's shared with other members of deprived minorities, would be an undesirable experience. For the single-parent family, particularly those living in the inner cities, the prospect is rather appealing. Moreover, it provides a focus of expectations for a family which frequently finds even its limited aspirations unmet. Perhaps, most importantly, it enables children to feel that they are not so unlike all other children whose material environment is immeasurably better than their own.

One-parent families and leisure

What needs to be done?

I have not considered particular leisure and recreational services appropriate for one-parent families. I am in fact somewhat sceptical of the value of leisure services for this group of families, and indeed for many low-income two-parent families, while some of the constraints on leisure, such as I have mentioned, persist.

In short, what is needed is:

(1) The acceptance of one-parent families as normal rather than different and deviant. This in itself will do much to improve their self-image and their motivation to pursue leisure activities.

(2) An adequate income to enable them to choose their leisure activities in the same way as do better-off families.

(3) Good housing in better environments, particularly for lone parents in the inner cities to give them self-respect and privacy.

(4) Expansion of day-care facilities for the under-fives and school-age children is essential if lone parents are to participate more fully in work and the community. Services for children can do much to benefit them and to enhance the leisure opportunities of their parents. We need more play schemes; after-school clubs; crèches in community centres, shopping centres, and leisure centres are essential.

(5) Local authorities, through the urban programme, could do much more to support self-help groups of lone parents. Family or one-parent family centres – such as Gingerbread Corner in Croydon or HOPE House in Haringey – would provide a place of their own, but open to the neighbourhood, where children could play, and parents could meet and relax with other adults.

(6) Telephones for the housebound, elderly, and disabled are accepted as desirable but what about one-parent families? A telephone could be a necessary link with friends for lone parents. Social Services Departments should consider expanding their eligibility criteria.

There are doubtless many possibilities for particular recreational services and ways they can be delivered effectively, but leisure centres and palaces of fun will offer one-parent families little if the pressure of poverty, low status, social isolation, and unrelieved parenting go unaltered.

185

Notes

1 Office of Population Censuses and Surveys, 1976.
2 W. J. Goode, *Women in Divorce*, New York and London, Free Press/Macmillan Company, 1965.
3 Peter Moss, 'Jobs for lone parents', 'Forward from Finer' series, no. 1, March 1977, National Council for One Parent Families.
4 *Report of the Committee on One Parent Families*, London, HMSO, 1974.
5 David Piachaud, 'Who are the poor, and what is the best way to help them?' *New Society*, 15 March 1979.
6 *Social Trends*, London, HMSO, 1979.
7 A. Hunt, *Families and their Needs*, London, HMSO, 1973.
8 G. Brown and T. Harris *The Social Origins of Depression*, London, Tavistock, 1978.
9 Moss, op. cit.

PART THREE

Leisure and work: problems and possibilities

Introduction

The papers in this section all stress that social and economic changes are necessitating the redefinition of the meaning and significance of a range of social institutions – work, education, youth, retirement, and leisure.

The first two papers, by Corrigan and Roberts, address the issues surrounding the changing social condition of youth, especially those affected by unemployment and both reject any simplistic idea of a 'leisure solution'.

The apparent paradox expressed in the title of Corrigan's paper serves to emphasize that unemployment, with its material experiences of poverty, isolation, and powerlessness is the antithesis of leisure, with its elements of choice, autonomy, and self-development.

Roberts expresses scepticism about the proposed 'education' solutions of Stonier (see Part One) and 'alternative economies' and job sharing. Like Corrigan he expresses the strongest doubts about the leisure option. All evidence suggests that within the present organization of society 'leisure' cannot provide unemployed youth with psychological or emotional substitutes for work. Although he sees few real alternatives to work, Roberts suggests that some progress could be made if we devised new ways to value young people other than as consumers, and attribute a meaning and significance to leisure which would permit it to be a sphere in which real personal and social legitimacy could be achieved and adult identities obtained. Roberts suggests that such solutions raise questions of distribution of the social product and as such confront not just technical obstacles but raise important issues of political will.

For Hargreaves the solutions are more specifically about political power. The issue of how to live a full life in the absence of full employment is not simply a problem of leisure but of social, political, economic, and educational reform. He questions the simple nostrums of 'education as leisure' or 'education for leisure' and suggests that the education solution lies within a restructuring of its social role and a redistribution of power within the education system. Like Swedner (Part One) he proposes a solution based on 'humanistic communitarianism' and the restructuring of the content and process of education.' The present hierarchical, individualistic, and instrumental forms of education would be replaced by a 'productive orientation' in which individuals and communities take responsibility for defining and creating their own lives. However Hargreaves is not proposing that we 'ghettoize' solutions within the education system. He suggests that in confronting the future, educational reform is not a substitute for, and in fact depends on, political action.

Following a critique of the Dutch education system for failing to take seriously the issue of education for leisure, de Vink presents evidence from experiments with primary school children which support Hargreaves' arguments for an open, collaborative, and innovative education system. Although the experiments were of a relatively limited nature, being concerned to provide knowledge of local leisure opportunities, the information was used as the basis for pupil self-organization and self-evaluation. De Vink suggests that the key to successful education for leisure (independence?) lies in the process and that it is an integral part of the curriculum – education should become 'tuned in to leisure'.

Whereas Corrigan, Hargreaves, and de Vink are concerned with the problems of young people in gaining entry to the labour market, McGoldrick examines the opportunities presented by early exit from paid employment. Drawing on a research project on early retirees she stresses that 'the retired' (like the young) are not a homogeneous group and illustrates this via an analysis of a wide variety of life-style adaptations to retirement. Those who adapted most successfully were those who came closest to the 'leisure ideal' of freedom, choice, and self-development. Where the (voluntary) escape from the negative aspects of work combined with the financial resources to develop positive opportunities, retirement was regarded as a prize. Although adaptation was not universally successful McGoldrick's study argues for greater flexibility in working lives and an increase in choice regarding exit from the labour market. It would seem that, in certain circumstances, the social problems associated with ending a working life are less than those associated with exclusion from the opportunity to begin one.

The final paper, by Veal, brings us back to issues of prediction and choices about the future. Like Miles, Veal emphasizes the prescriptive nature of forecasting and the necessity to assess critically the assumptions on which such prognoses are based. Providing a summary of the predictions, portents, and paradigms discussed in this volume he outlines three categories of prediction – the need for attitudinal change, the restructuring of working lives, and alternative economic structures based on ideas of an 'information economy' (Stonier) or the 'self-service economy' (Gershuny).

Veal finds some merit in all or a combination of these scenarios but suggests that some of the required changes are so fundamental that the pace of progress will be slow and the direction uncertain. Although we may have increases in leisure it is far from certain that we are entering a 'society of leisure'.

12

'The trouble with being unemployed is that you never get a day off' (1982)

PAUL CORRIGAN

The irony in the title of this paper gains its power from two central theoretical issues contained within the theory and practice of leisure. The quotation itself is an example of vicious, self-ironic, working-class humour from the General and Municipal Workers Union newspaper. Although the G & M is not an organization primarily concerned with 'days off' it does see 'work' and 'unemployment' as of primary importance. As such, it views leisure through the experience and reality of work – a theoretical position that I myself espouse, and one which must highlight the two major problems of unemployment and leisure.

Firstly, the notion of 'choice' is an idea central to most theories and policies of leisure. I believe choice to be a concept toally within the ideology of a capitalist society, rather than one which has any major grounding in reality. Yet within the reality of 3 million officially unemployed, the leisure industry turns to all this 'new spare time' as an opportunity to provide greater demand for its services. If there cannot be 'work' then the opportunity for the choice of leisure must organically increase.

What I shall argue is that 'choice' and the 'experience of unemployment' are opposite, not compatible. Unemployment cannot be viewed simply as more 'free time', as an increased amount of choice. The second point is about the relationship between the 'normal' material activities of school, domestic labour, or work, and 'spare time' or leisure. Under these circumstances commonsense says that the distinction between leisure and work is obvious. It can be easily recognized where work or domestic labour ends and where leisure begins. However, under unemployment the simple empirical, commonsense distinction is not possible since the notion of free time is obscure: the simple movement between the 'constraints' of work and the 'choice' of free time.

Therefore, unemployment creates a situation where the commonsense definition of the relationship between work and non-work poses us enormous experiential and theoretical problems, which can only be met by rejecting commonsense. I feel that the only way we will begin to come to terms with this is to uncover the dialectic between the major material activities within a capitalist society and the experience of leisure.

I will attempt this within three sections, each of which will build a single line of argument. To be really dialectic I will explain the final line of each section here, and then construct the argument for each.

First, it is only possible to understand any aspect of leisure as a result of the major material themes contained within work, domestic labour, or school.

Secondly, the major material experiences of unemployment are humiliation, poverty, isolation, and a feeling of uselessness.

Thirdly, the leisure activities of unemployed people will inevitably be affected by the above and not by the progressive elements of 'choice'.

Youth, schools and spare time

I will illustrate what I mean by a 'materialist approach to leisure' by reference to the sociological work in the area of youth and deviance. During the late 1960s the social scientists who were studying youth behaviour realized that they could not simply divorce the specific activity that they were interested in from its social and experiential context. Thus those of us committed to studying crime, vandalism, or delinquency realized that all such categories of behaviour only had meaning when they were studied as part of a wider context. For example, it was absurd to try to understand the smashing up of telephone boxes unless we fully explored ways in which Saturday evening led up to, and possibly included, the destruction of a phone box or some other public artifact. But the *aim* of the evening had not been to smash up something; rather, the context had assisted in the construction of this act.

However, this limited contextualization of an activity such as vandalism proved ineffective. It is true we stopped trying to isolate one group of actors, 'vandals', from those who simply 'hang about' in

Freedom and Constraint

their leisure, but, we still had no clear idea of why this limited context of 'spare time' should be so directed with a wider experience of 'doing nothing'.[1] To uncover this we had to go beyond looking at the experience of leisure to an understanding of the wider experiences of these schoolboys. We viewed 'school' as being a major defining characteristic of their lives and found it necessary to study this experience to reveal those aspects of it which served to define 'leisure'.

For this analysis, the period of time spent at school is not simply defined as a 'different' period of time in the week, but as one which helps to define and construct the rest of the week. In simple terms what went on at school mattered a great deal through the rest of the week, so much so, that it structured a lot of the lesser experiences of spare time.

As I outline in *Schooling the Smash Street Kids*[2] the most important experience of schooling for the kids whom I studied was the centrality of compulsion. In their own phrase, 'school would be OK as long as you didn't have to go.' The simple concomitant of this experience of compulsion was the fact that they had a feeling of formal powerlessness. Therefore in order to understand other, non-school, activities one had to understand the formative material base experience which structured an input into the rest of their time – the experience of *compulsion* and *powerlessness*.

This overall experience of powerlessness can be seen most clearly when we look at the way in which young boys use the provision of youth clubs. In every youth club in the country there are in fact two different institutions; one inside playing ping-pong, listening to the disco, and chatting to the youth worker; and one outside around the door, causing trouble as people come in, running in and pulling out the fuses, in other words a group that refuses to give legitimacy to the people who run the youth club and therefore try to run them. In my research in Sunderland the boys had a very simple phrase for youth leaders. It was a phrase that I first heard when they were discussing teachers, and this is that they were a group of people who 'wants to rule you'. It is in this way that the specific experience of powerlessness in schools, and the movement into spare-time activities, where they have some autonomy, are so importantly linked.

In terms of young people's spare-time activity, as a result of the rejection of institutions controlled by adults, they are often left literally with 'nothing' to do. My research, and most others on young people, has discovered that their main activity is 'doing nothing'. Doing nothing is at one and the same time both incredibly boring and incredibly important. Contained within the whole experience of doing nothing is a wide selection of important activities, activities which contain some form of interest, some form of excitement. This excitement, this construction of something quite literally remarkable, that is something they can talk about for the rest of the week, is an essential part of doing nothing. In fact contained within the experience of doing nothing there has to be a set of autonomous, interesting activities which will last them for the rest of a week that is bounded by an institution which 'tries to rule them'.

Therefore, in order to understand the activity of young people it is necessary to analyse the themes which run through the material bases of their lives. In the example just discussed, it is essential to understand young people's completely subordinate relationship to power in the school and how this negatively affects their spare-time activity. However, this necessity to understand the material and ideological themes which run through people's lives, and therefore construct their leisure, is not confined to school children or males. For example, for many girls, leisure and leisure activity is a totally different experience.

For most working-class women, a major material experience around which their future lives will be built is marriage and the preparation for it. However much we wish to construct a society where women and men have an equal experience of the world, have an equal set of opportunities, the existing structure of capitalist society constructs material futures for young working-class women which are totally bounded by the importance of marriage. Given this, there are many ways in which young girls do not actually have 'spare time' since their leisure is the equivalent to the preparation for work (that is marriage). In terms of their experience of spare-time activity they are well aware of the importance of marriage in their future, and how mistakes, failures, and stigmas gained in spare-time activity can ruin their prospects for promotion for a steady job, that is a good marriage, as surely as any form of educational failure. Quite simply, if they get a bad reputation as a young girl, they are no longer in such a direct way as good a marriageable property. This emphasis upon the importance of examining the material themes that run through young people's lives and how they construct the very texture of their spare-time activity brings us to the issue of youth and unemployment.

Youth and unemployment

I want to characterize the experience of unemployment as containing the following central themes.

Poverty

Poverty is a major qualitative part of the material experience of unemployment. This is inevitably so, an inevitability which has been constructed in great detail by social security policy since 1834. This construction of poverty, this linking of poverty with the nature of unemployment is made all the more real, and indeed is exacerbated by, the fact that unemployed people exist within the culture of a society which is continually bombarding them with consumption-based values. The whole of advertising has been consistently aimed at trying to create more and more materialistic values in society as a whole, and among young people in particular. Young people exist within a specific form of consumer democracy in British capitalism. They are fully fledged voters only in so far as they have the financial resources to buy goods and services on offer. Unemployment, by withdrawing the capacity to purchase is a direct form of disenfranchisement within our society. Unemployment then is irrevocably linked with poverty.

Humiliation

Not only has social security policy been dedicated to ensuring that unemployment equals poverty for people, but it also plays an important role constructing the experience of humiliation for the unemployed. Thus aspects of social security policy, such as the means test, ensure that people who claim supplementary benefit or national assistance or indeed now National Insurance benefits themselves, have to go through a gamut of stigmatizing experiences. Social security underlines the fact that to be unemployed is to be a failure. This experience is sustained by the mass media and a whole range of cultural relationships to those people who are on the dole. A wide range of images of 'scroungers' and 'layabouts' are labels which are hung round anybody who is not in employment in our society.

196

Externality

Unemployed people are seen as external, that is outside all the major institutions and correct experiences of our society. This is especially underlined in most secondary schools. For nearly all secondary schools in the late 1970s the major contemporary problem is one of order. One of the most consistent ways in which secondary school teachers impose order is to underline the relationship between school behaviour and the future chances in the labour market. There is, then, a very simple link constructed between good behaviour at school – hard work, good marks in examinations, good qualifications – and a successful career. Therefore, a teacher can threaten a person in school with a failed life if they fail to work well and behave themselves. This situation depends totally upon the existence of a fairly structured labour market outside the school. However, in the present situation of permanently high levels of youth unemployment, teachers can no longer utilize this so simply. They themselves are increasingly experiencing a feeling of uselessness, since they are continuing to attempt to define the future of school leavers through work even though they know this work does not exist.

Not only has this had a bad effect on the morale of teachers but, in recent years, its effect on schoolchildren has been catastrophic. In terms of their consciousness the children are prepared by institutions which place essential emphasis on work and career; there is a constant belief that getting on, ambition, a good place in the occupational structure, is what life is all about. Yet these children take their place in the increasing pool of unemployed. By the very definition of all of their experiences in school, their position outside the normal labour market has constructed an experience of being an outsider, someone who is external to those experiences that are centrally stressed at school.

Isolation

Unemployment is linked irrevocably with isolation. Although many people did see school in terms of compulsion, a compulsion enforced by law, they also saw it as an experience of sociability and solidarity. At the end of every school holiday one of the things that school pupils look forward to most clearly is meeting their friends again. The nature of work also exhibits this dual characteristic in that, although it is frequently an alienating experience for most working people, it also enforces a collective relationship, lifting people out of their isolation. This major aspect of the role of work in any society has been recognized by Marxists as one of the bases of political and social experience. Consequently unemployment hits at the very basis of any collective sociability in a society; it constructs an overwhelming, powerless isolation from social relationships. Indeed one of the most successful contemporary social movements has underlined this by their continuing fight for the importance of wage labour for working women.

Powerlessness

Underlining the other four experiences of unemployment is the fact of powerlessness. Although unemployed working-class young people have only their labour power to sell in terms of economic power in a capitalist society, they are denied their right even to do this by unemployment. They experience therefore an inability to intervene in the social world. When people are denied economic power, in this case the right to sell their labour power, any attempt to suggest that they have political, social, or community power is a nonsense.

If we accept that the above five factors construct the major thematic experiences of unemployment then this raises fundamental questions concerning the role of social policy intervention in the area of leisure for unemployed people. Much of social policy provision in a capitalist society is based on the ideology of individualized choice-makers; that is, people who are provided with a powerful ideology which allows them to choose between this or that option. Yet if we compare the notion of these powerful choice-makers with the experiences of unemployment, then there is a direct contradiction between the day-to-day experiences of powerlessness, humiliation, poverty, isolation, and being an outsider with the notion of being able to simply choose between, for example, squash and swimming. For those who formulate leisure policy to see large numbers of unemployed people as an opportunity for an extended series of leisure choices is a nonsense when we look at the thematic experiences of the unemployed. In fact any increase in the existing provision for leisure activities is not going to be taken by the vast mass of unemployed youth since that provision is based upon a culture and a belief that people taking it up are in some way fulfilled in the rest of their lives. For people on the dole leisure will not replace work in a simple hour-for-hour capacity, since work can only be replaced in fact by getting a job.

There are those writers who have suggested that young working-class men and women have become so acclimatized to their present and future experience of unemployment that they have entered a subculture of unemployed youth. Thus most of my analysis, most of the way in which these themes of unemployment are about a lack of something, would be undermined by this perspective. This perspective on subcultural analysis, underlining as it does the power of a very small part of a society to extrude itself from the major material dimensions of that society, gravely overestimates the power of any one group to live outside society. It is true that young people can construct their own groups; it is true that they can have values which are specific to the group; they can construct their own hierarchy within these groups. It is, however, absurd to suggest that these cultures can in some way be outside the major minute-by-minute, day-by-day themes of a capitalist society. Young unemployed people are as affected by the material elements of a capitalist society as any stockbroker, business manager, or car worker.

Throughout this chapter I have underlined the way in which those interested in the theory or the practice of leisure can only construct their understanding or further their practice by an appreciation of the main material element of any social experience, and to trace through the way in which those material elements construct the possibilities of leisure. We have underlined the fact that it is not simply a matter of time, spare time, or unemployed time. In fact, all of those aspects of time are constructed by whether or not people are in work or how they experience school or domestic labour.

None of this is to say, however, that what goes on in people's spare time, in their leisure activity, is unimportant. Indeed there has been a consistent strand of materialist thought which underlines the fact that, in a capitalist society, it is only outside these major alienated experiences of work or school that working-class people have the time and energy to organize, educate, and find out about their world, in a more working-class dominated way. Within this strand of thought stretching through such individuals as William Morris, there has been an emphasis upon the protected and important experience of non-work, of 'education through leisure'. The tradition of working-class adult education is one which sees a wide range of leisure activities in the educational sphere as being important for working-class people. However, while there has been an important stress upon these activities, they have never been stressed or underlined as leisure activities to be constructed and moved forward in their own right, separated off from the major material experiences of work or school. Instead, this particular theme of leisure activity has been constructed around a better understanding of what it means to be at work, or what it means to be unemployed.

Within this perspective, and within this empirical area of young unemployed people, we are not then saying that nothing can be achieved because of the unremitting and inevitably awful experiences of unemployment. What we are saying is that any leisure activity which is to be truly progressive and is really to advance young people's lives, must have contained within it some way of acting on the experience and the practice of unemployment in order to change.

Leisure activities for young unemployed people must not simply be time-fillers. In the end they must also be aimed at the reconstruction of the whole set of material themes outlined in this essay on unemployment.

Notes

1 P. Corrigan 'The dialectics of doing nothing', *New Society*, 19 July 1979.
2 P. Corrigan, *Schooling the Smash Street Kids*, London, Macmillan, 1969.

13

Unemployment, youth, and leisure in the 1980s (1985)

KENNETH ROBERTS

Tolerating the intolerable

In 1983 the Organization for Economic Co-operation and Development calculated that member countries needed to create 20,000 jobs every day until the end of the decade to return unemployment to its 1979 level. In 1984 only the USA and Japan were on target, and the latter was expected to fall behind. In Europe employment had actually declined and further rises in unemployment were forecast.[1] For the western world as a whole, the 1980s are likely to prove worse than the 1930s in terms of average levels of apparently intractable unemployment.

Youth unemployment has risen even more spectacularly than adult joblessness. In 1979 the twelve major OECD countries contained seven million unemployed 15–24 year olds. By 1982 there were over ten million, an average unemployment rate of 17.7 per cent, with no sustained fall in prospect. Virtually every western government has launched new measures to reduce the volume or to mitigate the potential damage of youth unemployment. Despite this, young people's difficulties are undiminished.

In Autumn 1979, when Britain's Manpower Services Commission unveiled its latest manpower forecast, that by 1981 a half of school-leavers would be without jobs, the prediction was greeted with a mixture of alarm, scepticism, and hilarity. Even youth employment researchers found the forecast difficult to treat seriously. It assumed that other things would remain equal. Mass unemployment was supposed to have become an historical issue. Keynes had taught how the malaise could be avoided. Postwar governments had verified his theory. The availability of a cure had made unemployment intolerable, so we believed. Any government that allowed unemployment to rise and persist was supposed to incite a backlash that would force a U-turn or replace the politicians. In the 1960s a million unemployed was often quoted as a ceiling that would never again be breached. By the mid-1970s the threshold had been revised. Redundancy payments and earnings-related benefits had allegedly raised the baseline of frictional unemployment. Even then, few believed that unemployment could rise and settle above three million without undermining the social fabric, destabilizing the economy and polity.

In 1979 unemployment for the majority of school-leavers was a coming crisis that had to be averted. The government was warned that young people who were apparently rejected and unwanted would, in turn, reject and turn upon society.[2] The 1981 street riots appeared to confirm these warnings.[3] Former consolations for educational failure had included an early entry into employment, rapid progress to adult earnings, and immersion in youth cultures. Few 'failures' had resisted their futures. The majority had 'applauded their damnation'.[4] They had celebrated 'being out' of school and childhood. Immediate gratifications had seemed preferable to the examination treadmill. The lure of the brief flowering period had completed the reproduction of the relations of production. Who knew what might happen when the consolation for educational failure, a sugared entry into a lifetime of wage-slavery, was withdrawn?

Postwar youth cultures and the flamboyance of affluent young workers had aroused concern, but unemployment seemed likely to prove more radicalizing. By the 1970s we had a theory to explain how the leisure of industrial capitalism locked participants into 'the system'. Individuals were able to use free time and money to experiment with disparate values, identities, and styles, but even rebellious fads and fashions were channelled into leisure time and activities, institutionalized in consumer roles and thereby neutralized. School-leavers with surplus time, no visible prospects, and limited spending power appeared a more volatile combination.[5]

Today, in 1985, confidence that mass unemployment cannot persist indefinitely is as tattered as school-leavers' transitions to work. It is persisting without becoming a crisis. Unemployment has become yet another problem, like crime, that politicians deplore and others tolerate while the victims cope. Joblessness is not expected to decline. Despite this, business confidence has not ebbed. Output has risen steadily since 1981. A government that presided over an unprecedented rise in unemployment has been re-elected not replaced, forced to U-turn, or even promise a solution. The monthly unemployment figures have become a routine embarrassment, nothing more. Inflation has fallen. Profits have risen. Stock markets have hit record heights. The economy is healthy in most respects save the massive unemployment.

The absence of an effective backlash has now joined the explanation of unemployment itself, the identification of wider social implications and the search for solutions as leading issues of the 1980s. Leisure scholars have made two types of intervention in these debates, and reached diametrically opposed conclusions. The first contributions follow the well-worn residual route and dismiss other remedies before reaching leisure as one of the few plausible solutions to contemporary unemployment. The second arguments derive from empirical evidence rather than theoretical analysis, and explain how the unemployed find little consolation, let alone any sign of a solution, in leisure. The following passages review these arguments, then attempt to bridge the apparent impasse.

Jobless growth

The causes of contemporary youth unemployment are neither new nor mysterious.[6] General unemployment rose steeply as jobs were shed during the 1979–81 recession. School-leavers and other newcomers to the labour market felt the full impact of the brake on recruitment and fierce competition for any remaining vacancies.

These effects of recession have been superimposed on a longer-term decline in entry jobs, especially for less-qualified school-leavers. This decline is a product of mechanization, sector- and occupation-shifts which upgrade workforces, and the disappearance of many small family businesses which once welcomed school-leavers. In recent years, in the advanced industrial societies, the decline in demand for unskilled labour has accelerated with the internationalization of production and distribution. Multinational companies can export unskilled jobs from advanced to less-developed lands where labour is cheap, abundant, and non-unionized. In some countries, the import of unskilled migrant labour has intensified competition for the remaining unskilled jobs.

Sustained economic growth is more likely to accelerate than reverse these trends. This is one reason why reflation, the classic

Keynesian remedy, is unlikely to cure the current youth unemployment. Another is that future economic growth may be jobless. The latest labour-saving technologies are neither in-dustry- nor occupation-specific, and appear to have broken relationships between levels of investment, consumer demand and employment. The growth of output in the British economy from 1981 to 1985 has not been accompanied by any fall in unem-ployment. There may be no technological barriers to creating more public service jobs, but there are formidable political obstacles. Throughout the western world electorates have grown reluctant to vote for still heavier taxes, government spending, and state bureaucracies.

Free market economists, the new radical right, argue that downward flexibility in youth wage rates should lead to more jobs.[7] The British government has acted accordingly and proved the economists wrong. The Young Workers Scheme plus the allowances fixed for youth trainees are intended to hold young people's wages and expectations at 'realistic' levels. Since 1979 the gap between youth and adult earnings has widened, but youth unemployment has risen dramatically.

National civic or community service have been proposed to occupy young people.[8] There need be no unemployment if only young people would work for pocket money! No-wage and low-wage answers are rightly seen as further problems, not solutions, by the intended beneficiaries. As standards of living and expectations rise, so does the threshold beneath which individuals refuse to offer their labour.

Demand for well-qualified recruits remains relatively buoyant. Simultaneously, demand for unqualified and poorly-qualified school-leavers has collapsed. These are the underlying trends that are polarizing labour markets and workforces. In times of full employment, firms had to offer decent wages and reasonable security to attract any labour. Employers protected their own long-term interests by hoarding labour when necessary and encouraging even unskilled staff to develop company loyalty. Those were the days when, according to some sociologists, the population was being drawn into a middle mass and the occupational structure was being reshaped from a pyramid to a diamond. Labour market conditions in the 1980s mean that companies retain a vested interest in cultivating loyalty among skilled workers. Others are dispensable. They can be hired and fired alongside workflows. The new trends are centrifugal.

Less-qualified school-leavers' prospects have deteriorated quantitatively and qualitatively, and conventional economic prescriptions offer no cure.

Education

The decline of youth employment is a long-term trend but not a long-standing problem. It was welcomed throughout the decades when job losses were compensated by educational expansion. Releasing young people from the workforce used to be considered an opportunity to expand education, to invest in human capital and prepare young people for a later entry into upgraded jobs.

Since the Second World War virtually every country's education system has been enlarged and democratized, especially at the upper- and post-secondary levels. In 1945 80 per cent of Europe's 14-year-olds left school. Today, in most western countries, 80–90 per cent of 14 to 17-year-olds are in full-time education.

Educational systems have been swollen by a variety of pressures. At certain times schools and colleges have been used as warehouses, as alternatives to unemployment. However, from the 1930s until the 1970s this use of education was exceptional. Young people did not need to be restrained from leaving. Parents and young people sought prolonged education to qualify for better jobs. It did not seem to matter if educational expansion ran ahead of demand for qualified manpower, which was the rule rather than the exception.[9] Employers simply raised entry requirements, which fuelled demand for qualifications to still higher levels. Economists argued that, in the long term, the investment in human capital could only benefit the recipients and their wider societies.

The intervening expansion of education is one reason why youth unemployment in the 1980s cannot be exactly the same problem faced in the 1930s. Present-day victims are better educated. They have higher qualifications, aspirations, and expectations.

Educational solutions to youth unemployment have not been discarded. Indeed, one body of opinion argues that virtually all the time released from employment by labour-saving technologies must be reinvested in education and training. Stonier envisages a not-too-distant future when education will occupy 50 per cent of the workforce, as teachers and students.[10] British government's responses to youth unemployment in the 1980s seek to apply this traditional remedy. They address an alleged mismatch between school-leavers' capabilities and occupational requirements in the service and high-technology sectors which, it is claimed, contain the best hopes for future job creation. Unless the quality of the workforce is improved, the argument runs, economic growth will be retarded, youth unemployment will remain high, and many victims will face jobless adulthoods. Hence the case for Britain's Technical and Vocational Education Initiative, and the Youth Training Scheme.

However, educational solutions to the disappearance of entry jobs are yielding diminishing returns.[11] Young people in Britain are now being given more vocational advice, work experience, and generic skills than ever. They are being prepared more thoroughly than ever before for employment that has become scarcer than ever. New wine is being poured into old bottles. Traditional academic syllabuses are being replaced by up-to-date technical and vocational courses. These attempts to tighten the bonds between schooling and job requirements, to strengthen young people's vocational orientations and to make them more competitive, lead only to frustration and disillusion when labour markets cannot deliver deferred rewards.

The new technologies that are displacing labour may require more highly educated and trained designers, technicians, and managers. But the pace at which workers can be discarded seems to be running well-ahead of the need for longer vocational preparation. Moreover, there are signs that beyond a critical point, which most western countries are now passing or have already passed, education ceases to increase the value of students' labour power and may have a negative effect. Some employers who insist on well-qualified recruits complain that schools do not instil sound work habits. They criticize students who learn to shirk rather than how to work, and complain that beginning workers expect unrealistic rewards for their qualifications – that too many leave school with inflated self-concepts and aspirations, unwilling to start at the bottom and prove their worth.[12] These complaints may help to explain why, in some countries, youth unemployment has risen while immigrant workers still find jobs.

Another problem with educational responses is that the returns to students gradually diminish. More young people than ever are remaining in education beyond the statutory leaving age. They are not all enthusiastic students. Many 'volunteer' to continue under duress. They feel obliged to stick it out in order to earn the qualifications that lead to jobs, even though the pursuit of credentials strips education of intrinsic satisfactions.[13] Students become knocked-out, school-weary, and book-tired. Only the fear of dropping out keeps them in the system, however tenuously. Truancy rates are an embarrassment to many education authorities. The long-term rewards for attendance seem insufficient compensation. When virtually all young people prolong their education, the extra years of schooling become virtually useless in career terms. Education is a 'positional good'; the more people have, the lower its value to everyone.[14] This is why the near-certainty of unemployment is insufficient to deter all those at risk from leaving.

Relying on educational remedies to contemporary youth unemployment does not equalize opportunities. Indeed, one of the actual results is the creation of severely disadvantaged under-classes. Earlier élitist educational regimes distinguished successful minorities from the mass of young people. Today's enlarged and democratized school systems allow majorities to succeed. The minorities separated from the mainstream are tail-ends of dropouts and failures. No educational system that retains the majority beyond age 16 has avoided the creation of an under-class. However attractive the opportunities, however diverse the curricula and whatever the teaching methods, some young people refuse to take advantage and become a stigmatized minority. They are heavily implicated in most youth problems – delinquency, unplanned pregnancies, and unemployment. Youth workers often describe them as the 'real problem group'. Employers avoid them. Employment agencies label them as 'hardcore cases'.

Alternative economies

The inadequacy of familiar economic and educational remedies has inspired more radical intellectual responses to unemployment, including a broader concept of work. It is pointed out that work need not be in employment. People can work on their own accounts. The rewards may be intrinsic satisfactions or self-provisioning rather than cash. Industrialization involved the commercialization of commodity production and services. It withdrew the population from domestic and community arts and crafts into employment. According to one school of thought, these earlier trends are now being reversed and work returned to informal economies in response to rising labour costs, the amount of capital equipment requiring maintenance now contained in most homes, plus the intrinsic satisfactions of self-provisioning rather than the rat-race.[15]

It may have become difficult to generate more employment. Nevertheless, it can be argued that there remains plenty of work to be done. Instead of educating young people to expect employment, therefore, it is proposed to orient them towards self-employment, and to encourage youth co-operatives, voluntary service, and community projects.[16] These responses to unemployment would restore work to local communities wherein, it is anticipated, the inhabitants will develop life-styles superior to consumerism.[17] Instead of employment, young people are to be offered pioneer roles in alternative, self-provisioning, small-is-beautiful economies.

An obvious problem with this thinking is its distance from the current predicaments of the young and older unemployed. Individuals in conventional full-time employment are the more likely to hold spare-time jobs, and to engage in domestic and community self-provisioning.[18] Employment supplies the skills, social relationships, tools, and, in many instances, other materials that facilitate informal enterprise.

Most of the young unemployed are interested in earning 'a bit on the side'.[19] In high unemployment areas there is fierce competition for such work, and as in the formal labour market, the young unemployed tend to be squeezed out. When obtained, the work is usually slave labour *par excellence* – chronically insecure and low-paid. It is also risky. Envious friends can report dole-fiddlers. The young unemployed know that, at the moment, informal enterprise is no real long-term alternative to conventional employment.

Another 'alternative economy' solution would develop within rather than alongside existing businesses. Persistent unemployment, it is argued, is a symptom of adherence to out-dated values. Is it rational, even in purely economic terms, for advanced countries to continue acting as if they were still industrializing societies where labour was scarce and urgently required in a variety of growth industries? In such conditions it made sense to organize production so that maximum output was ground from each unit of labour power. Does this remain as rational today? Or has it become dysfunctional to strive to manufacture twice the pins in half the time? Labour is becoming abundant. So why continue pressuring enterprises to shed unnecessary hands? Their wider societies cannot discard and must continue to support personnel declared redundant as producers. Why not reorganize work so as to maximize intrinisic job satisfactions by extending professional control to a wider range of occupations, and making work organizations sufficiently flexible to allow individuals greater choice over task design and working hours?[20]

This agenda is easily criticized. It appears incompatible with survival in the western economy, as currently organized. It does not explain how to persuade workers to opt for satisfying rather than better-paid jobs. If the former was already the stronger demand, it would pay capitalist employers to act accordingly. In practice, workers will vote with their feet for monotonous assembly lines, provided the pay is sufficient. However, the apostles of alternative economies do not claim that their visions can be easily realized; only that, in principle, such solutions are now more practical than conventional cures for unemployment.

The leisure option

A different radical solution would convert time released from the formal economy into leisure. In the 1980s armies of young people and adults are not required as producers. Not is it technically necessary for these same individuals to be preparing for future employment. The jobs that many eventually enter do not require lengthy preparation. The individuals' time and energies are literally surplus to economic requirements. So why not encourage unemployment's victims to adopt proactive responses[21] and pioneer leisure-based life-styles?

No one pretends that simply relabelling joblessness as leisure will make the predicament acceptable. Advocates of leisure solutions propose two responses to the decline of employment.[22] Firstly, they urge greater investment in recreational services – for sport, enjoyment of the countryside, and the arts. Secondly, they recommend an appropriate education in which individuals would be weaned from the work ethic and encouraged to engage in activities for intrinsic, aesthetic satisfactions.[23]

If such measures were accompanied by an adequate guaranteed minimum income, it is envisaged that periods outside employment would be seized as opportunities rather than experienced as deprivation. Advocates of leisure solutions envisage more individuals opting for earlier retirement, that some made redundant in mid-career would welcome sabbaticals, and some young people would prove equally appreciative of time out. In addition, it is anticipated that persons in employment would demand shorter hours, thereby spreading the available work around, in order to indulge their leisure interests and benefit from the facilities.

No one believes that this leisure solution is actually taking shape – yet. It is utopian, but not necessarily impractical. The unemployed are severely disadvantaged in economic terms. For many workers, higher earnings still take precedence over increased leisure time. However, none of this evidence undermines claims that a growth of leisure is a potentially practical solution to unemployment, or the attractiveness of the vision. The British government has introduced Job Release and Job-Splitting schemes. Why not strengthen this medicine? Some supporters of the leisure option believe that the material conditions for an Athens without slaves already exist, and that the sole missing ingredients are political will and vision.[24]

The young unemployed at leisure

Reeling off other possible solutions leaves leisure as one of the few apparently viable alternatives to persistent unemployment. In contrast, head-on confrontation with the facts of leisure for the unemployed forces different conclusions. The research evidence is unambiguous: neither the adult nor the young unemployed find leisure a compensation for lack of work. Public leisure services in most parts of Britain have attempted to harness their off-peak capacity to a desire to 'do something' about unemployment.[28] The providers can take credit for alleviating the boredom and reducing the socio-psychological damage of joblessness.[26] Nevertheless, leisure is rarely more than a palliative. Suspicions that the unemployed are work-shy, a new leisure class, cushioned by a too-generous welfare state, are not supported by any research findings.

Unemployment curtails normal leisure activities. Adults' leisure is scaled down. It becomes cheaper, less commercial, and the victims' range of social contacts is reduced. The spare time conferred by unemployment is spent mainly in bed, watching television, and listening to the radio. No age group finds this experience liberating.[27] For many adults, employment is a lynch-pin in their social networks. Out-of-work individuals' social contacts are sometimes cut back to close kin and neighbours. Public opinion, according to pollsters, now accepts that the general level of unemployment is due to economic conditions and government policies. Nevertheless, a combination of pressures leaves many victims feeling that their unemployment is their own fault. They blame themselves for failing to search hard enough, or for their inability to impress employers.[28] Some find all social contact painful. It exposes the stigma of unemployment. One reason why illness rises among the unemployed is that the sick role is a more acceptable status.[29] However, reduced income is the main reason why unemployment depresses leisure activity. Researchers have stressed that it is difficult, probably impossible, to separate the effects of unemployment and poverty.[30]

Like adults, unemployed teenagers curtail their leisure activities.[31] If they continue to visit pubs and cafés they spend less. They are less likely to reduce their frequency of activity than their expenditure. When they 'go out' they usually remain close to their homes. Local discos replace city-centre nightspots. Even travelling costs are prohibitive.[32]

However, unemployed young people appear better able than adults to protect their leisure. Their peer groups are more resilient. Out-of-work youth spend more, not less time with peers than when in employment.[33] The fact that youth unemployment has become so widespread softens the stigma. Furthermore, unlike displaced adults, the young employed have no established occupational identities to shatter, and although they have less cash to spend than working contemporaries, those graduating from school to unemployment experience a rise in personal income. Some of the young unemployed have sympathetic and generous parents.[34] As among students, there are wide variations in spending power among the young unemployed, often reflecting their families' circumstances. Whether unemployed young people *feel* deprived depends on their reference groups, and the more widespread youth unemployment becomes, the more likely are the victims to compare their situations with others who are out-of-work, in education, or on schemes for the unemployed.

This is not to say that anyone actually enjoys unemployment. Even short spells out of work can be traumatic. The research evidence is clear: young people resent the restrictions. Compared with teenagers in jobs, the young unemployed worry more about their dress and appearance. They are more prone to loneliness, anxiety, and self-doubt.[35] According to one inquiry, the long-term young unemployed are also the more likely to have contemplated suicide.[36]

Unemployment can be acutely depressing. However, it is worth recalling the research from the 1950s and 1960s that condemned hollow and trivial commercial youth cultures.[37] With former jobs and affluence gone, it is easy to forget the drabness, monotony, and boredom in surveys of youth at leisure throughout the years of full employment. 'Finding things to do' was a problem for affluent young workers.

Denying that the unemployed are a new leisure class is uncontroversial. Claiming that leisure is not even a potential solution involves a combination of additional arguments. It can be argued that unemployment is too debilitating for the victims to pioneer such solutions, and that the economic deprivations are unlikely to be removed. Whatever minimum income is guaranteed, it is scarcely conceivable that incentives to work will disappear. Moreover, it can be argued that, being voluntary and pursued for personal satisfactions, leisure activities will never replace the non-economic functions of employment – structuring time, supplying social status and personal identity.[38] Young people in some of the world's wealthiest communities whose career prospects and economic security are guaranteed, and whose parents can lavish material comforts, do not glory in their freedom. Nothing to live for but 'kicks' means restlessness, not ecstasy or contentment, intermittent pleasure but no lasting joy.[39]

All the evidence indicates that leisure is low down the unemployed's own priorities. Many reject the concept as inapplicable to their ways of life. They want decent jobs, or the education and training that will open such prospects, plus higher income. Few of the young unemployed are interested in radical solutions. Quite the reverse; the majority idolize normality.[40] Their first response to unemployment is usually to convince themselves that the predicament is abnormal and, they hope, temporary. Most parents, if they retain any influence, discourage adaptation and reconciliation to joblessness.[41] The young unemployed do not abandon conventional aspirations. They daydream about employment in secure jobs, earning the wages to enable them to go out with cash in their pockets and enjoy conventional leisure. These are among the ways in which the young unemployed 'police themselves'.[42]

The definition of youth

There is an impeccable logic in residual arguments that leave leisure among the few plausible solutions to contemporary unemployment. The empirical evidence of unemployment depressing if not eliminating genuine leisure is equally impressive. Can the analyses be reconciled?

Each is manifestly correct, as far as it goes, but both have limitations. They fail to take full account of the manner in which all the changes, not just unemployment, that are restructuring young people's situations, are making youth a different type of life phase. Moreover, neither approach pays sufficient attention to young people's own ways of coping.

Some writers have portrayed unemployment as prolonging youth and trapping the victims in adolescence. However, talk of delays probably understates the significance of the changes in process and misrepresents the age group's predicaments. Youth is not being extended so much as becoming a qualitatively different life phase. Youth cultures in the 1950s and 1960s involved teenagers who acquired adult spending power prior to other adult rights and responsibilities. In the 1980s most young people are making other steps in the transition to adulthood prior to establishing themselves in jobs that confer economic independence. This condition is not unprecedented. Economic independence has a long history as the last stage in the transition for students in higher education. The novelties in the 1980s are, firstly, the spread of the life stage as a mass rather than an élite phenomenon. Secondly, the condition is now compulsory. Thirdly, there may be no deferred gratifications in prospect.

However, the major changes redefining the situations of young people are in adulthood. The normal adulthood of the past is receding as a realistic objective. Adult life-styles have become more fluid. Rates of geographical and occupational mobility have risen. Returning to education or training is becoming a normal career requirement. Young people can no longer expect end-on models to work. The chances are that youth education and training will not provide qualifications and skills that last throughout adult life.

Circulation rates among adult sexual, domestic, and marital partners have also risen. One result is the spread of 'adolescent' life-styles among the middle-aged. Divisions between life phases are more blurred than formerly. There is more backsliding. Pre-adult life-styles are placed in abeyance rather than abandoned for ever.

Changes in the character of adulthood automatically revise young people's situations. Finding an occupation in which to settle used to be treated as a sign of vocational maturity. Today's young people who do not regard their current employment as lifelong, and who are equipping themselves to cope with economic, technological, and occupational turbulence, are probably the better attuned to their futures. Nowadays, young people who are learning to live with impermanence, in temporary relationships, may have stronger claims to maturity than those seeking occupations in which to remain for life, and settling in hopefully lifelong liaisons with opposite-sexed partners.

Emergent ways of living

There are many reasons why persistent unemployment in the 1980s has not become a social, political, or economic crisis. The employed population is better-off than ever, relatively and absolutely. Many victims are demoralized and marginalized. Others have devised effective coping strategies. The most common strategies are individualistic and involve seeking personal escapes. These tactics usually work, which is why the majority out of work at any time have little inclination or reason to identify with the rest of the army. They are more anxious to leave than to seek collective solutions to the predicament. Many of those currently in work have recent experience of unemployment, which does not always foster sympathy for later victims. People who regain work may expect others to do likewise. One of the painful features of being young and unemployed in the 1980s is listening to countless tales, culminating in success, from relatives and so-called friends who once had to struggle. Nevertheless, the numerically dominant response, even among the young unemployed, is to retain orthodox aspirations and to strive to preserve conventional trajectories.

However, some ways of coping involve pioneering novel lifestyles. At present these responses are confined to minorities of young people, but the latter have history and time on their side in so far as the conditions on which familiar adolescent and adult careers were based are disappearing. It is impossible to offer a definitive list of these emergent ways of living, still less the numbers involved in each. However, at this stage quantification is less important than discerning trends, and several clear responses to the problems and opportunities now surrounding young people can be distinguished.

(1) Increasing numbers of young adults are devising their own forms of 'alternation', using low-paid, often temporary and part-time jobs for economic survival and some independence while earning the qualifications that eventually unlock more attractive opportunities.

2) Other young people are opting for *sub-employment*. They drop

out from education but refuse to commit themselves psychologically to low-status jobs, and decline continuous wage-slavery. They work for a bit in order to earn breaks.[43] Neither employment nor unemployment are considered tolerable for long unbroken periods. Intermittent employment is preferred. Breaks are not planned by work organizations' schedules. Some are instigated by dismissals and redundancies. Others occur when the young employees grow fed up. It can be elating and a source of status in the eyes of peers to tell employers to keep their 'shit work', and to prove one's willingness to risk and cope with unemployment rather than tolerate any job, however dismal the tasks and however low the pay.

(3) Some young people are building *medium-term careers* from recently-introduced projects, courses, and training schemes. The stated aim is usually to assist the unemployed towards conventional jobs. However, individuals sometimes move from scheme to scheme and achieve upward mobility in the process, eventually obtaining instructor, supervisor or management positions. Unemployment projects have become an important economic sector, sometimes the sole growth sector, the real alternative economy in high unemployment areas.

(4) Soon after completing compulsory education, other young people are deciding that the most secure and rewarding careers on offer are as *welfare claimants*. Welfare, especially when supplemented by unofficial earnings, often appears a better deal than permanent dependence on secondary labour markets. In the longer term, however, the claimant role invariably leads into a poverty trap – an unattractive lifetime condition for the individuals directly involved, and expensive for their wider societies.

In 1984 the British government announced its intention to remove the under-18s' right to remain unemployed and draw social security instead of actively seeking jobs or volunteering for youth training. The government was alarmed at the numbers settling into long-term unemployment, or opting for the sub-employed life-style.

(5) In some countries, including Britain and Australia, the trend towards *staying on* in full-time education instead of facing a choice between unemployment and low-status jobs has been particularly strong among females. More are delaying their entry into the labour market, earning higher qualifications then obtaining 'good jobs'. A growing proportion of these young women are studying for and acquiring post-entry professional qualifications.[44] Many are

reluctant to desert their attractive and promising careers, even temporarily. Some firms have noted a trend towards such women taking maternity leave instead of terminating employment. The women fear being unable to regain their positions in the occupational structure. Some appear to be opting to have no children. The opportunity costs of child-production and rearing are judged unacceptable. As a result, many are delaying childbearing, maybe indefinitely.

(6) There are trends towards *pre-marital cohabitational relationships*, and towards the formation of temporary households by groups of young adults who may not be sexually related. These developments are explicable in terms of broader trends in family patterns and young adults' economic insecurity, although some cohabiting partners hold attractive jobs. In most countries, the proportions of households containing two or more employed adults have risen alongside unemployment. The partners in these relationships are not dependent on each other for income or domestic services, which is why nothing need be 'for keeps', except their occupational careers.

(7) For women without the prospect of rewarding occupational careers, marriage and parenthood have been traditional escapes. High unemployment makes the escapes appear more attractive than ever. Girls' first reactions to employment difficulties often include more strenuous efforts to '*get a man*'.[45] Unemployment does not undermine but, to begin with, reinforces traditional feminine aspirations.[46] Unfortunately for young women whose feminine hopes are reinforced, high youth unemployment makes male breadwinners difficult to locate. The traditional male role is undermined by employment.

For girls' 'respectable' escapes to economic security and adult status may still be available with older men. If so, another traditional pattern is consolidated – younger women marry older partners. However, some young women in high unemployment areas are deciding that the claimant role is more accessible. They know that the quickest route to independent accommodation is to 'get in a mess' – pregnant.[47] Single parenthood and welfare will not tempt well-qualified career women, but may be no greater economic disaster than dependence on a low-paid or unemployed male. Welfare payments can offer the greater security and, sometimes, higher standards of living, especially when supplemented by casual earnings and gifts from boyfriends. Welfare authorities' cohabitation rules threaten these arrangements. Whoever wins this battle, the quick route to adult status via parenthood usually means a new generation of children being reared in poverty.

A case for leisure

Residual arguments are most impressive in eliminating a restoration of the past as a plausible alternative to youth unemployment. Solutions may be sought in cherished utopias of communal work or a society of leisure, but are more likely to be found within young people's own coping behaviour. Policy-makers are entitled to take a discriminating view of young people's emergent ways of living. Nevertheless, in my view, leisure provisions must feature prominently in any comprehensive strategy to ensure that young people, and society in general, benefit from the changes that are currently consigning many to unemployment. Leisure scholars invite ridicule when offering recreation as a replacement for work. Simultaneously, they are far too modest if and when they imagine that only a disadvantaged minority of school-leavers require improved services.

Youth unemployment in Britain has long ceased to be the minority problem that the well-publicized percentages out of work might suggest. Before youth unemployment in local labour markets reaches 20 per cent, conventionally measured, the majority of school-leavers face spells out of work at some time or another.[48] Official unemployment figures do not include the numbers on government schemes because they are unable to find jobs. Nor do they include those prolonging education for fear of the labour market without any guarantee and, in some cases, little hope of deferred rewards. Not do they measure the extent to which the threat and fear of unemployment have spread even to young people whose careers display no external effects.

During the 1970s, unemployment in Britain rose sharply among 16 to 18-year-olds. Successive government schemes were targeted at this group. These measures are part of the explanation for the 1980s' youth unemployment problem shifting to the 19–25s, a reversion to the interwar situation. During the 1920s and 1930s there were sufficient juvenile jobs and apprenticeships to occupy most 14 to 18-year-olds. Risks of unemployment peaked when juvenile careers reached dead ends, when apprenticeships terminated, and individuals outgrew boy- and girl-wages.[49] This situation is being re-created in the 1980s as young people pass through new educational programmes and training schemes then return to unemployment. Government measures have not helped most trainees into permanent jobs or led up the occupational structure.[50] Success usually means keeping young people 'in circulation', out of long-term unemployment, though, in an increasing number of cases, these descents are delayed rather than avoided.

Bramham and Henry[51] suggest that a consensual approach to leisure is surviving the ideological polarization in British politics since the early 1970s. They argue that the new consensus rejects universalism in favour of concentrating public resources on the disadvantaged; just the opposite to what young people now require. Virtually all are affected by the changes reviewed in the above passages.

It is not difficult to discover what young people want. Priorities vary according to whether individuals are striving to preserve hitherto conventional trajectories or developing more novel lifestyles, but the main pleas are always for jobs, or education and training leading to jobs, housing, and adequate income. Leisure is low down young people's own priority scales. The connotations of leisure in industrial societies – time free from, but earned by, obligatory work, during which individuals can enjoy the fruits of their labour – are inconsistent with the predicaments of the unemployed and insecurely employed. Leisure scholars should have no difficulty in understanding why young people who are denied firm footholds in the workforce often find the concept virtually meaningless, which does not mean that they find leisure provisions useless. It means simply that young people have more basic needs, including a need to be needed. A main challenge facing contemporary societies is to devise ways of valuing young people, other than as consumers. Leisure theory is not at loggerheads with, but can explain young people's priorities.

Loss of producer roles, and the inability of education and training to guarantee lifetime vocations, make young people more dependent on ascribed statuses, sometimes derived from gender and ethnicity, in establishing adult identities and independence. Current trends make young people more dependent on leisure activities and environments to sustain these identities, and to establish and maintain the relationships that allow other aspects of the transition to adulthood to proceed despite the impossibility of stepping directly from full-time education to stable employment. Leisure is likely to grow in importance as a source of stability in adults' and young people's lives in societies where most other things change rapidly, beyond individuals' control. Leisure is likely to become one sphere where people are assured of returns on their investments. Youth is a critical life phase for acquiring leisure interests and skills, and today's young people have a greater need for leisure services than ever.

Many recreational initiatives aimed at young people in high unemployment areas have built impressive track records in attracting then retaining their clientele.[52] Whether the initial appeal is to sporting, musical, or political interests, access to conventional leisure can assist young people who wish to preserve conventional life-styles and trajectories. Simultaneously, young adults who are pioneering less familiar ways of living as claimants, in marriage, cohabitational relationships, or other households, benefit from leisure environments in which to interact and display preferred identities.

Successful leisure provisions tend to become multi-functional. They can be educative. User-participation in management is a common feature. It can enable individuals to develop transferable skills. Leisure provisions can also become a source of work whether producing music, selling sports equipment, or simply assisting with catering and cleaning.

Once the evidence is assembled and systematically analysed, young people's wants and needs are relatively easy to identify. The key choices for policy makers are not *what* so much as *how* to provide for young adults. How are the resources they require – jobs, useful education and training, income, housing, and recreation facilities, to be distributed to and among young people? Should public provisions be concentrated where the need is greatest, as a safety net for the severely disadvantaged?

Financial responsibility for young adults is still unresolved in most countries. Individuals depend on a variety of sources that were never designed to support such a life phase. One state response to current changes, favoured by governments, as in Britain, whose priority is the control of public spending, is to demand that parents accept responsibility for children who are continuing in education, training, confined to low-paid jobs, or unemployed. Such policies are sometimes justified as 'supporting the family'. In Britain state support for young adults in full-time education has become less generous. Training allowances are set at levels that will not permit recipients to live independently. Welfare regulations are being rewritten to deny unemployed young people lodging allowances, thereby forcing them to remain with parents. As previously indicated, it is intended to deny the under-18s all welfare payments, except through their families.

In the short term these measures shift the costs of current changes on to families and thereby protect economic and political structures. In some communities the policies are likely to succeed, especially where unemployment is reviving the traditional values of 'looking after one's own'.[53] However, less secure neighbourhoods' and families' living standards are forced even lower. The economic deprivations of multi-generation households increase. There is a growing problem of homeless teenagers. Young people resent burdening their parents. The latter do not always sympathize with young people's predicaments. Education and training opportunities become more dependent on parents' ability and willingness to pay. Young people complain that income inequalities are unfair and anomalous, as when education and training are less rewarding than idleness.

Private provisioning works, in a fashion. Some young adults receive the support necessary to continue along educational and training routes leading to good jobs. Others are left on the margins of the economy, in impoverished and unstable domestic circumstances. Despite general economic growth, the principle of 'less eligibility' requires claimants to be ground deeper into poverty to force them to seek low-paid and insecure, even non-existent jobs. Neither the privileged nor the impoverished are necessarily sentenced for life. The former could spend the greater part of adulthood fighting to cling on, while the rest fought to get in. Life in a divided society can be exhilarating and fatiguing.

Public provisioning permits a different distribution of resources among young people. It can be organized to encourage all young people to use low-paid, insecure jobs to support themselves in semi-independence while continuing in education and training – the alternation strategy. The jobs will be done, but not as life sentences for anyone. Simultaneously, all young adults can be given access to housing and recreational services to support their peer relationships and preferred patterns of domesticity. There are precedents for such provision. In the past this support has been considered desirable, even necessary for the minorities proceeding through higher education. Current trends make the case for extending these services to the entire age group, and only public provisioning will deliver.

The current obstacles to such provisions are political, not economic. The problems faced and the life-styles currently being pioneered by young adults are not products of economic failure. There is no crisis of production in the western economy. The world's wealthiest societies are growing richer than ever. Their problems arise from industrial success, and the choices to be made are questions of distribution. Western countries cannot avoid, but can well afford to give young people aspirations and expectations which remain beyond immediate reach when they first outgrow emotional and social dependence on parents. The young people would be unimpressed by the quality even if the available jobs were sufficient in quantity. None of these problems arose when the majority of 14 and 15-year-olds could be given no choice but an immediate entry into employment.

Notes

1 Organization for Economic Co-operation and Development, *Employment Outlook*, Paris, OECD, September 1984.
2 F. F. Ridley, 'View from a disaster area: unemployed youth in Merseyside', *Political Quarterly*, 52, 1981, pp. 16–27.
3 Lord Scarman, *The Brixton Disorders, 10–12 April 1981*, Cmnd 8427, London, HMSO, 1981.
4 P. Willis, *Learning to Labour*, Farnborough, Saxon House, 1977.
5 D. A. Chambers, 'Symbolic equipment and the objects of leisure images', *Leisure studies*, 2, 1983, pp. 301–15.
6 K. Roberts, *School-leavers and their Prospects*, Milton Keynes, Open University Press, 1984.
7 P. Minford, *Unemployment: Cause and Cure*, Oxford, Martin Robertson, 1983.
8 D. Marsland, *Work to be Done*, Maidstone, Youth Call, 1984.
9 R. Collins, 'Functional and conflict theories of educational stratification', *American Sociological Review*, 36, 1971, pp. 1002–11.
10 T. Stonier, *The Wealth of Information*, London, Methuen, 1983.
11 I. Bates, J. Clarke, P. Cohen, D. Finn, R. Moore, and P. Willis, *Schooling for the Dole*, London, Macmillan, 1984.
12 I. Berg, *Education and Jobs*, Harmondsworth, Penguin, 1973.
13 R. Dore, *The Diploma Disease*, London, Allen & Unwin, 1976.
14 F. Hirsch, *The Social Limits to Growth*, London, Routledge, 1977.
15 J. Gershuny, *After Industrial Society? The Emerging Self-Service Economy*, London, Macmillan, 1978.
16 A. G. Watts, *Education, Unemployment and the Future of Work*, Milton Keynes, Open University Press, 1983.
17 B. Henriksson, *Not For Sale*, Aberdeen University Press, 1983.
18 R. Pahl, *Divisions of Labour*, Oxford, Blackwell, 1984.
19 K. Roberts, J. Duggan, and M. Noble, *Unregistered Youth Unemployment and Outreach Careers Work, Part 1, Non-registration*, Department of Employment Research Paper 31, London, 1981.
20 S. Parker, *Leisure and Work*, London, Allen & Unwin, 1983; J. T. Haworth, 'Leisure, work and profession', *Leisure Studies*, 3, 1984, pp. 319–34.

21 D. Fryer and R. Payne, 'Proactive behaviour in unemployment: findings and implications', *Leisure Studies*, 3, 1984, pp. 273–95.

22 C. Jenkins and B. Sherman, *The Leisure Shock*, London, Methuen, 1981.

23 D. Hargreaves, *The Challenge for the Comprehensive School*, London, Routledge & Kegan Paul, 1982.

24 W. Bacon (ed.), *Leisure and Learning in the 1980s*, Sheffield, Leisure Studies Association, 1983.

25 S. Glyptis, 'Business as usual: leisure provision for the unemployed', *Leisure Studies*, 2, 1983, pp. 287–300.

26 G. Stokes, 'Work, leisure and unemployment', *Leisure Studies*, 2, 1983, pp. 269–86; P. Warr, 'Work, jobs and unemployment', *Bulletin of the British Psychological Society*, 36, 1983, pp. 305–11.

27 R. Martin, 'Women and unemployment: activities and social contact', paper presented to SSRC Labour Markets Workshop, Manchester, 1983; G. Breakwell, 'Young people in and out of work', paper presented to SSRC Labour Markets Workshop, Manchester, 1983; P. Kelvin, C. Dewberry, and N. Morley-Bunker, *Leisure and Unemployment*, London, University College, 1984.

28 Breakwell, op. cit.

29 L. Fagin and M. Little, *The Forsaken Families*, Harmondsworth, Penguin, 1984.

30 Kelvin, Dewberry, and Morley-Bunker, op. cit.

31 M. Willis, *Youth Unemployment and Leisure Opportunities*, London, Department of Education and Science, 1979.

32 R. Sandhu, 'Young and unemployed in Wolverhampton: provisions and facilities', paper presented at Conference on Unemployment, Wolverhampton Polytechnic, 1984.

33 Kelvin, Dewberry, and Morley-Bunker, op. cit.

34 C. Wallace, 'School, work and unemployment: social and cultural reproduction on the Isle of Sheppey', PhD thesis, University of Kent, Canterbury, 1984.

35 Department of Education and Science, *Young People in the 1980s: a Survey*, London, HMSO, 1983.

36 L. Francis, *Young and Unemployed*, London, Costello, 1984.

37 K. Roberts, *Youth and Leisure*, London, Allen & Unwin, 1983.

38 P. Kelvin, 'Work as a source of identity: the implications of unemployment', *British Journal of Guidance and Counselling*, 9, 1981, pp. 2–11; M. Jahoda, *Employment and Unemployment: a Social-Psychological Analysis*, Cambridge, Cambridge University Press, 1982.

39 R. W. Larkin, *Surburban Youth in Cultural Crisis*, New York, Oxford University Press, 1979.

40 D. Walsgrove, 'Policing yourself: youth unemployment, individualism and the amplification of normality', paper presented to the British Sociological Association, Bradford.

41 Wallace, op. cit.

42 Walsgrove, op. cit.

43 K. Roberts, M. Noble, and J. Duggan, 'Youth unemployment: an old problem or a new life-style?' *Leisure Studies*, 1, 1982, pp. 171–82.

44 R. Crompton and G. Jones, *White-Collar Proletariat*, London, Macmillan, 1984.

45 C. Griffin, 'Birmingham girls – from school to work?' *Careers Bulletin*, Spring 1984, pp. 15–18.

46 Wallace, op. cit.

47 B. Ineichen, 'The housing decisions of young people', *British Journal of Sociology*, 32, 1981, pp. 252–8.

48 Roberts, Duggan, and Noble, *Unregistered Youth Unemployment and Outreach Careers Work*.

49 J. Tomlinson, 'Unemployment and policy in the 1930s and 1980s', *The Three Banks Review*, 135, 1982, pp. 17–33.

50 K. Roberts, *School-leavers and their Prospects*, Milton Keynes, Open University Press, 1984.

51 P. Bramham and I. P. Henry, 'Political ideology and leisure policy in the United Kingdom', *Leisure Studies*, 4, 1985, pp. 1–19.

52 C. Ball, P. Kuenstler, and R. Stares, *Transition to Adulthood: Institutional Innovations*, Paris, CERI/TA/84 01, 1984.

53 P. Allat and S. M. Yeandle, 'Family structure and youth unemployment', paper presented to British Sociological Association, Bradford.

14

Unemployment, leisure, and education (1981)

DAVID H. HARGREAVES

In Western industrialised countries, the hours which must necessarily be spent in earning a living are likely to be markedly reduced during the working lifetime of children now in school. The responsibility for ensuring that new leisure is the source of enjoyment and benefit it ought to be and not of demoralising boredom, is not the schools' alone, but clearly education can play a key part.[1]

Introduction

When members of the Newsom Committee enjoined teachers to accept the preparation of young people for leisure as an important educational task, they did not do so from fear than many young people would, on leaving school, join the dole queue. Indeed, their proposals were premissed on the assumption that future patterns of employment would require a larger pool of talent of which 'average' and 'below average' pupils were an essential part. Technological advance and automation, they asserted, would require higher levels of skill and, contrary to popular belief, would not lead to high levels of unemployment. As I write today, less than twenty years after the Newsom Report, many pundits expect the already high unemployment figures to rise to four million by the middle of the 1980s and perhaps to five million by the end of the decade. Young people are amongst the most vulnerable groups: one in six of the unemployed is 19 years old or less and those who live in Northern Ireland, South Wales, and the North of England, and those who are black, are disproportionately represented in these depressing statistics. This rise in youth unemployment, dramatic though it is, becomes partially masked by the increasing number who avoid the labour market by staying on at school or by entering further education or by joining one of the various Youth Opportunity Programmes. In response to the riots in Brixton, Toxteth, and Moss Side, in the summer of 1981, Prime Minister Thatcher announced an increase in YOP places of 110,000 bringing the total number to almost half a million.

Since the causes of current unemployment levels remain obscure and controversial, predictions for the future cannot be made with confidence. This does not deter our many sociological and economic seers who are adept at presenting plausible sketches of future possibilities in the guise of highly probable predictions. It can be argued that the young unemployed are unfortunate victims of Mrs Thatcher's monetarist policies and that these policies can and will be changed soon. Or it can be argued that the recession is more permanent, even irreversible; the 'oil crisis' of 1973 was but the first in a series of demands from the Third World for a more equal share in the developed world's affluence. A third argument suggests that labour is now being permanently displaced by technological advance, by the new information technology, the microprocessor, and the industrial robot. Stonier, for example, claims that just as the industrial society shifted the labour force away from agriculture (80 per cent of the labour force at the beginning of the eighteenth century), the post-industrial society will shift the labour force away from manufacturing industry. He estimates that by early in the next century no more than 10 per cent of the labour force will be needed to provide for all our material needs.[2] This prognostication cannot fully be trusted; but then neither can the Labour Party's commitment to a speedy return to full employment. It may be that forecasts about high unemployment, like those about overpopulation, are wild exaggerations based on unreliable extrapolations. Nevertheless, it is very likely that in future most people will spend less of their time in paid employment, if only because they will start their careers later, retire sooner and live longer: the debate is not about the fact of less time in paid employment, but about its extent and its distribution.

Attitudes to work and leisure

For many people, retirement from full-time paid employment is seen as a release from work; at least they so perceive it until their own turn to retire finally comes. On this view, to be retired is to be freed from work and one becomes a person of leisure. Paid employment is an unpleasant duty and to be allowed to escape is merited by age. Like an ageing workhorse, one is put out to grass after dutiful service. Common perceptions of the unemployed, however, are of a different character, even when unemployment is involuntary. The unemployed are held to be blameworthy, to be lazy, to be scroungers on the welfare state who live at the expense of decent people who work for a living. Perhaps the present high level of unemployment is beginning to temper such accusations of parasitism; but an increase in popular sympathy does little to mitigate the sense of stigma which overwhelms most of the unemployed, for they now take to themselves the very attitudes they formerly took to the unemployed.

Even in these times, unemployment and redundancy come as a shock to most people; like a cancer, it is supposed to happen to someone else. Very quickly they feel the sense of shame, degradation, failure, and uselessness.[3] And so it will be as long as the working population adheres so comfortably to the work ethic. Of course part of the distress experienced by the unemployed is a direct product of the severe reduction in income; even the sick are better off than the unemployed.[4] But poverty is no more than one of a constellation of problems. Our identities are sustained in and through the work ethic. For most of us our occupation is one of the master categories of our self-definition. Our surnames often reflect ancestral occupations; and when we retire we define ourselves not by what we are but by what occupation we once pursued. To be denied an occupational status in midlife is to be denied a meaningful identity and a recognized social location. And this probably affects the young unemployed as much as the older unemployed. Very little of our secondary education is strictly vocational; schools are more oriented towards public examinations than towards jobs. Yet for those who leave school at 16, a job is the natural next step, one that has been awaited with eagerness for it signifies independence and adult standing. Teachers insist that the results of public examinations at 16 are 'qualifications', and for most of the pupils and their parents this means qualifications for a job. (If they are not, what are they qualifications for?) In reality they are very rarely occupational qualifications. But by calling them 'qualifications' teachers make examination results seem vocationally relevant and examinations can be used as a pseudo-vocational incentive for adolescent pupils to work hard and behave well in school. When employment is then denied to the young school-leaver, with his or her scroll of 'qualifications', the reaction is naturally one of shock and disappointment, personal crisis and social dislocation.

Within the framework of the work ethic, then, to be denied paid employment is to be rendered not fully human. People complain and grumble about their work, yet they seem willing to spend long hours in its pursuit. Surveys indicate surprisingly high levels of work satisfaction, even among manual workers who exercise little skill or responsibility.[5] In one survey the respondents were asked whether or not they would continue to work if they inherited enough money to live comfortably without paid employment. Eighty per cent – and almost all the younger respondents – said that they would continue in their jobs; and a further study of factory workers who won large sums on the football pools showed a return to work after a short period of extended holiday.[6] This addiction to paid employment is not easily explained, either by the inherent interest of the work or by the compulsive psychology of the work ethic. Paid employment gets people out of the confines of the home into other social worlds, a simple fact which is taken for granted by men but an obvious benefit of paid employment in the eyes of married women at home with children. Employment is often a major source of friendships: the importance of social life at work sometimes exceeds that of both the home and the neighbourhood. The potential loss of friends is one of the deepest anxieties about retirement. And work structures one's time. Regular hours and routines provide an ordered timetable for the day, the week, the year; though the routines are sometimes tedious, they also discipline us against our mood or the inclination of the moment and we are glad of it. Most activities, including leisure, are organized around the central time structures imposed by employment. Even if the unemployed enjoyed more adequate incomes, many would still find it difficult to provide alternative life schedules once that hub of social identity and time organization, paid employment, had disappeared.

New definitions of work and leisure

In an age of high unemployment the conventional distinction between work and leisure does not seem to be one which is useful to the analysis of the problem or to the generation of solutions. Perhaps the concept of leisure has outlived its usefulness and can be discarded; certainly the concept of work will have to be transformed and disconnected from paid employment. Perhaps it would be easier to speak of 'ways of life' or 'life styles'.[7] At least we might then review the issues unencumbered by concepts which may well restrict our imagination. Should we not now be working out what we mean by a 'life ethic' to displace the 'work ethic'? Is it not important to consider how people can lead a 'full life', rather than worrying about how to return to 'full employment'?[8] If we confine discussion to 'the unemployment problem' and an ensuing 'leisure problem' we are in danger of excluding from the agenda the wider social, political, and economic – as well as educational – matters which must be raised if we are to speak sensibly about the future of society.

By aiming to be 'down to earth' and 'practical' these solutions are tied to the social structures and attitudes which generated the original problem; they seem to be 'reasonable' solutions, but they are trapped within the conventional definition of work and leisure.

Take one of the most 'obvious' solutions: the redistribution of work. If paid employment is so very popular, why don't we introduce compulsory work-sharing so that no one is denied the opportunity to work? Employers do not like it, of course, since there are no obvious advantages for them. Nor are the unions any more enthusiastic. If their primary function is to defend and advance the interests of their members, then they will naturally tend to strive for job protection and to do so against the new technology, against other efforts towards increased productivity, and against job-sharing. Of course the unions will make the usual vigorous protestations about the plight of the unemployed; but it will always be somebody else who is to blame – the employers, the government and, if all else fails, foreigners. It has been suggested that trade unions should now place a higher priority on their secondary function, that of promoting social justice.[9] But how can they do so when this acknowledged secondary function conflicts so deeply with their primary function? Union leaders cannot diverge too far from the self-interest of the members.

The same kind of objection can be brought against another 'obvious' solution, by which we can pay the unemployed a decent income. The pressure to do so will obviously increase as the gap between a reducing but relatively wealthy labour force and an expanding but penurious body of unemployed grows even wider. But the notion of being paid to enjoy leisure conflicts so deeply with the work ethic of popular opinion that it is difficult to know how we shall ever be able to get the unemployed much above subsistence level: the work ethic requires the unemployed to be poor. Thus it is that the unemployed themselves are much more ready to speak of their rights to work than of their rights to a decent standard of living. The notion that the trades unionists are likely to play a significant role in helping to secure a guaranteed income for all, when to do so would inevitably involve an erosion of their own living standards, seems naive.

Education and the problem of work and leisure

Education is seen by most commentators as an important element in the solution to the 'problem' of work and leisure. But again the solution seems locked into the conventional definitions and the changes are portrayed as relatively painless adaptations of, or extensions to, some current trends rather than as fundamental assaults on our present values and social structures. Educational solutions are usually proposed in two forms: education *as* leisure and education *for* leisure.

The concept of education as leisure covers a wide range of ideas. At one extreme is the use of secondary schools and adult and further education as a convenient and relatively cheap method of 'mopping up' the embarrassingly high youth unemployment figures, in the hope that the problem can be solved when the recession has ended, or at least postponed until later. This was Mrs Thatcher's panic solution in 1981. At the other extreme is a vision of lifelong education, or recurrent education, in which everyone makes a more systematic, sustained, and repeated use of the educational system, for occupational retraining, for sabbaticals, or simply for pleasure. This system can be defended on egalitarian grounds, since those who under our present system obtain least, the school-leavers at 16, could in principle preserve their rights to education until a later stage in their lives. A massive increase in education would probably be popular with most teachers for it would be a happy reversal of their recent fortunes. Stonier believes that education is the principal solution to the vast unemployment created by technological advance. He argues that a hugely ex-panded educational system will provide hundreds of thousands of teaching jobs to cope with the bulk of the unemployed.[10] The flaw in this argument is that the majority of pupils do not desire more formal education; and if education were to become an alternative to employment, rather than now as a means to it, they would want less of it than they now have, not more. And if this new education became compulsory rather than voluntary, the teachers' enthusiasm would vanish in a flash. In any case many of us would demand some compelling arguments to be persuaded that a heavier dose of formal education is the best means of enhancing the quality of life for most of our citizens; I think the proposition extremely dubious.

Education for leisure is a much more limited notion, which is founded on the assumption that the secondary school curriculum fails to prepare people for leisure as it does to prepare them for work. Once this assumption is granted – and I believe it may be – then it is said that schools could and should play a more active role in leisure preparation. It is perfectly possible to construct specific syllabuses which are designed to provide pupils with leisure skills. But who would take such courses? If leisure studies are designed for those who are most vulnerable to unemployment (the most likely trend), then teachers would have to select or 'guide' the appropriate pupils; inevitably they would be the 'less able' who are considered unsuitable for public examinations in academic subjects. In making such predictions, teachers might well create a self-fulfilling prophecy whereby those expected to be unemployed (and so kitted out with leisure skills) would in fact become unemployable. Teachers lack the power to predict exactly who will become unemployed, at what stage, and for how long. If, on the other hand, every pupil is seen as a possible candidate for unemployment and every pupil is seen as in need of leisure education, then leisure studies would have to be a central element in a compulsory, core curriculum – and such an intrusion would be resisted by the academic subjects which now rule the curricular roost. My serious objection, however, is that it is quite absurd to separate in such an artificial way 'leisure studies' or 'leisure skills' from the rest of the curriculum and the whole range of skills schools seek to develop in pupils. Much of the present curriculum has considerable relevance for leisure; as Entwistle points out, a leisure oriented curriculum points directly to the traditional, humanistic, liberal curriculum of the British secondary school.[11]

Leisure and the social structure

I fear that whenever education is proffered as the major solution to the problems of unemployment and leisure, whether in the form of education as leisure or education for leisure, the plan never amounts to more than an ill-conceived palliative which distracts us from the need for more fundamental thinking. The solutions to unemployment and leisure will surely only be found when we radically restructure our society. Only by contemplating how we can restructure society can we transcend the conventional distinction between work and leisure and develop educational policies for such a society.

One possible answer was provided many years ago by Erich Fromm.[12] He argued that we can become a sane and civilized society only when we abandon what he called the receptive orientation of passive and alienated consumerism, which complements the marketing orientation of advanced capitalist societies. The receptive orientation characterizes capitalist man both at work and at leisure. Leisure time cannot be used actively or creatively, whatever teachers say and do, in a society where men and women work without genuine relatedness to what they do and to whom they do it. If men and women are to lead 'full lives' they must (by definition) adopt the productive orientation in which they transcend alienation as defined by Marx: man will be actively and creatively related to himself, to his activities and to his fellow men. This productive orientation can be generated in Fromm's view, only in a society which is restructured in terms of a humanistic communitarianism. Neither Soviet communism nor British socialism has realized such a society. State socialism merely becomes the new and ever more despotic tyrant. Modern industrial societies have to be rationalized and controlled and so generate strong centralization, bureaucratization, specialization, fragmentation, and hierarchy: this was the direction more astutely predicted by Weber than by Marx or Durkheim. For Fromm, recovering much of the optimistic idealism of Marx and Durkheim, people become active and responsible when they exert a genuine influence on the decisions which affect them at home, at work and in all aspects of communal life. The essential reforms for Fromm are a massive increase both in the decentralization of government and administration, and in popular participation in community structures.

Of the recent writing by politicians on the theme of work and leisure none impresses me more than that of Clemitson and Rogers.[13] Although they show no awareness of Fromm's writing, many of the fundamental reforms they advocate are consonant with Fromm's humanistic communitarianism. They share Fromm's conviction that social reform must be concerned with structural and attitudinal change. Their commitment to industrial democracy along the lines of the Bullock Report, and their advocacy of forms of common ownership other than nationalization, are both in tune with Fromm's thinking – and in conflict with conventional thinking in the Labour Party. Many similar ideas are to be found in Luard's defence of community socialism, with its emphasis on decentralization and increasing autonomy and diversity for local units in which men and women take greater control over the whole of their lives.[14] As the two major political parties in Britain polarize, the freezing of one set of orthodoxies unfreezes the thinking of many individuals who have to define themselves in relation to the changing party political boundaries and loyalties.

Social reconstruction

I have not space to elaborate, let alone defend, the idea of humanistic communitarianism. I take it just as one example of a possible social reconstruction – and it is obviously one with which I am in sympathy – to make the more general point that almost any social reconstruction would change our understanding of the relations between education, work, and leisure. A society with humanistic communitarianism as its goal would clearly decentralize many problems (and solutions) to smaller communities: governments and trades unions and employers would not be expected to come up with general solutions. Whilst regional interdependence is essential, with richer regions helping poorer ones, it would be for regions and districts to define their own needs and the means of realizing them. Community needs would tend to transcend the conventional gap between 'paid employment' and other kinds of activity, such as leisure or voluntary work. The meeting of needs would call for an increase in individual responsibility, effort, commitment and creativity. It would not be a society free of conflict; and there would still be problems of the distribution of wealth. But the productive orientation, by cutting through the conventional work ethic and definition of work and leisure, ensures that the resolution of conflict and the solution to wealth distribution can be sought in more auspicious and less threatening and dehumanizing social conditions.

Once we have determined, with Fromm, that our major social objectives should be the generation of decentralized communities in which men and women are active participants exercising genuine power and influence, then it becomes immediately apparent that one of the primary educational tasks is the preparation of young people for life in these communities. Community education under such a system would have to be more than the shared used of premises by schools, colleges of further education, the local library, and the leisure centre; it would have to be more than some advance in the democratization of teacher–pupil and teacher–parent relationships.[15] The dissolution of boundaries which these reforms signify is certainly important; but true community education must have a distinctive style which prepares young people for new community structures, of which they will soon become members. Schools in such a society would need to give young people a rich and active experience of participation in multiple communities and at the same time provide the vital skills by which conflicts between different communities can be resolved. At the root of such an education would be the development of the productive orientation on which community participation and control hinges.

The school curriculum and the work ethic

This is an awesome task for the schools and one for which they are not now fitted. Most of our secondary schools are steeped in hierarchy; they foster individualism and instrumentalism; and they are heavily pervaded by the very work ethic which is alien to the productive orientation. That is not to say the schools are now actively preparing young people for jobs – occasional lessons labelled 'careers' are common, whereas intensive vocational education is rare. I mean, rather, that schools are very successful at inculcating the work ethic and the conventional definition of work and leisure. The curriculum is imposed and evaluated unilaterally by the teacher, rather than chosen, organized, judged by, or even debated with, the pupils themselves. It is quickly defined as 'work' and soon becomes linked in pupils' minds with an unpleasant obligation which is fulfilled only under the ever-watchful and mistrustful eye of the supervising teacher. Every day in all our schools teachers utter thousands of statements of the type: 'Stop wasting time and get down to your work', or 'You come into my classroom not to play around but to do some serious work', or 'If you don't get on with your work now you have to stay at playtime and do it then, and you won't like that.' Effort soon becomes associated with 'work' which becomes associated with the imposed official curriculum; in its turn that curriculum is instrumental to the passing of examinations which in their turn are instrumental to the acquisition of paid employment. In this lesson, which even the 'least able' pupils learn so very thoroughly, resides that powerful dichotomy between work (high effort, boredom, low autonomy, discipline and constraint, seriousness, competitive individualism, long-term goals) and leisure (low effort, relaxation and idleness, passivity, pleasure, non-seriousness, immediacy, spontaneity, freedom, social co-operation).

Entwistle may be right in claiming that the liberal curriculum is the best preparation for leisure, but he ignores Peterson's just comment that when we move from content to method, from curriculum to pedagogy, it is the work-oriented approach which is dominant if not exclusive.[16] The work ethic is transmitted through pedagogy rather than curriculum content; but the pedagogy also destroys much learner interest in that context. The best way to kill young people's interest in an activity is for teachers to insert it into the formal curriculum and teachers have always been willing to raid young people's natural leisure pursuits as potential curriculum fodder. Thus, as Gathorne-Hardy observes,[17] games in the public schools were originally played voluntarily and purely for pleasure. It was inconceivable that they should be taught. But then games were taken over by the teachers and had to be played compulsorily for defined educational functions – to keep pupils fit or to instil team spirit or to sublimate sexual energy – and much of the original fun vanished. For surprisingly many secondary school children those aspects of the formal curriculum which are most relevant for the 'full life' (or for leisure, if you will) become associated with the unpleasant work of the imposed curriculum and so are disliked and rejected.

Community schools

With the decline of paid employment, then, there will be greater demands on our educational institutions. If formal education is genuinely to help people lead fuller lives and transcend the conventional distinction between work and leisure, then schools must be community schools which help to foster two things: first, the skills that are important to community participation and control; and second, the productive orientation. Schools are not ready for this task because the dominant pedagogies transmit the work ethic which is antithetical to the productive orientation. Schools may select an appropriate curriculum – the liberal curriculum with perhaps a renewed emphasis on literature, music, the visual and plastic arts, drama, dance, sport, etc. – but the pedagogy inoculates many pupils against such a curriculum.

I believe that we already know, in broad outline, how teaching needs to change and improve so that the productive orientation can be fostered in pupils: teachers need actively to help pupils to retain their original and near universal childhood conviction that learning and exploration are inherently pleasurable and the more pleasurable when high effort is involved; teachers need to help pupils to develop their own co-operative ways of working without constant supervision; they need to encourage self-evaluation rather than dependence on teacher evaluation; they need to foster intrinsic learning for its own sake; they need to regard the curriculum as the product of negotiation and joint contributions. Such good teaching has to displace our present tendencies as teachers to impose on pupils a predetermined curriculum; to instruct rather than to collaborate; to make all the main decisions which deny responsibility to pupils; to be the mistrustful overseer; to demand learning for extrinsic motives and because it is instrumental to examination success.

As often in fields of study such as 'education' and 'leisure' the most powerful ideas are the least pretentious. Perhaps today we are ready for John Leigh's insights that the primary skills in which schools must train young people are social organizational ones.[18] His main concern was education for leisure and he understood that to follow many leisure pursuits a person must have the skills to participate in, and sustain, the social organization devoted to that leisure pursuit – or if need be to generate such a social organization. Any education for leisure worthy of the name must draw upon and develop skills in pupils whilst they are still at school; the teacher becomes the facilitator of social organization, not its designer and director.[19] But more than this. If such skills are transferable between different leisure activities, then they can be transferred to activities that have little to do with leisure. They are

skills which relate to groups of people whatever activity they are pursuing. Such skills have to be taught through a particular activity but their application is general; what is taught in connection with football has at least some relevance to active participation in the union or the party political association. What the teacher has to communicate here is some sense of the possibility of social organisation, that it doesn't all depend on 'sir'. He has to provide for the possibility of success and foster a sense of the enormous strength that reposes in united group action. At the same time, in order to teach skill, he has to illustrate gently the pitfalls and difficulties. Often these difficulties will relate to communication, aims and allocation of responsibility; matters which are both complex in nature and often emotionally charged and there is no denying that to carry such theory into practice with, say, 4C on a bad Monday morning, is something which requires a high degree of skill.[20]

But we have to face the fact that John Leigh's ideas have had very little influence, so far as I can tell, on educational practice. Nor do I think they ever will until we reconceptualize the relationship between education and society and that in turn will not come about until we begin to restructure society. We cannot, in other words, reasonably expect education of itself to change society. Certainly education has a uniquely important role to play in a society which is undergoing major social reconstruction but it can never be a substitute for direct political action.

Conclusion

For these reasons I warmly welcome Stan Parker's insistence that 'It is about time we recognised the political implications of leisure', though I have reservations about the directions in which his argument then moves. For Parker unashamedly reintroduces the idea of socialism, but recognizes that in so doing he is on delicate ground. He does not, he assures us, want socialism to be taken to mean 'state ownership, nationalisation, drab equality, totalitarianism, East European society, the end of freedom' – and we all readily say amen to that – but he then redefines socialism and reasserts Fromm's excellent ideas. The weakness of the argument is obvious. Parker's redefinition of socialism disconnects the argument from contemporary party politics. In this he follows Fromm, whose ideas have been popular, I suspect, precisely because he avoids the term 'socialism' or other party political labels.[21]

Parker's argument can be reduced in this way: (a) he wants us to accept that leisure must be seen in a political context, but (b) he prefers to avoid ties to contemporary party politics. I do not see how we come to terms with the political aspects of leisure, and certainly how we can influence political and social reform, unless we are prepared at the same time to come to terms in some way with present party political realities. Unless we are ready to help the politicians to learn and in our turn to learn from the politicians, then the prospects for the next decade look gloomy indeed. At least three British politicians I have quoted in this paper – Luard,

Clemitson and Rogers – are informed, imaginative, and ready for discussion. There must be many others like them. Are we ready to take up the challenge?

Notes

1 Newsom Report, *Half Our Futures*, London, HMSO, 1963.
2 T. Stonier, 'Technological change and the future' in G. Cherry and T. Travis (eds), *Leisure in the 1980s: Alternative Futures*, Leisure Studies Association, 1980 (see chapter 2 above).
3 M. Jahoda, 'The impact of unemployment in the 1930s and the 1970s', Bulletin of the British Psychological Society, 32, 1979, pp. 309–14; A. Sinfield, *What Unemployment Means*, Oxford, Martin Robertson, 1981; J. Hayes and P. Nutman, *Understanding the Unemployed*, London, Tavistock, 1981.
4 Sinfield, op. cit.
5 Jahoda, op. cit.
6 Hayes and Nutman, op. cit.
7 H. Entwhistle, *Education, Work and Leisure*, London, Routledge & Kegan Paul, 1970; H. Entwhistle, 'Work, leisure and life-styles' in B. Simon and W. Taylor (eds), *Education in the Eighties*, London, Batsford, 1981.
8 I. Clemitson and G. Rogers, *A Life to Live: Beyond Full Employment*, London, Junction Books, 1981.
9 ibid.
10 Stonier, op. cit.
11 Entwhistle, *Education, Work and Leisure*.
12 E. Fromm, *The Sane Society*, London, Routledge & Kegan Paul, 1956; E. Fromm, *To Have or To Be*, London, Cape and Abacus Books, 1978.
13 Clemitson and Rogers, op. cit.
14 E. Luard, *Socialism Without the State*, London, Macmillan, 1979.
15 A. Skrimshaw, 'Community schools and the education of the "social individual" ', *Oxford Review of Education*, vol. 7(1), 1981, pp. 53–65.
16 A. P. C. Peterson, 'Education for work or for leisure?' in J. T. Haworth and M. A. Smith (eds), *Work and Leisure*, London, Lepus Books, 1975.
17 J. Gathorne-Hardy, *The Public School Phenomenon*, London, Penguin, 1977; D. Hargreaves, *The Challenge for the Comprehensive School*, London, Routledge & Kegan Paul, 1982.
18 J. Leigh, *Young People and Leisure*, London, Routledge & Kegan Paul, 1971.
19 Newsom Report, para 231.
20 Leigh, op. cit.
21 S. Parker, 'Learning to leisure in a more socialist society' in W. Bacon (ed.), *Leisure and Learning in the 1980s*, Leisure Studies Association, 1981.

15

Education for leisure: a case study from the Netherlands (1981)

GEORGE DE VINK

The cultural background

The Netherlands is a society which has been extensively permeated by the mores of the 'protestant ethic'. The idea that it was morally right that social life should be dominated by work became integrated into the mental life of the Dutch people. Work was not only seen as harsh necessity, it was also seen as a morally good thing in its own right and consequently, non-working, idle, or free time was seen as an evil which must be eschewed at all costs. Moreover, since the ideas of Calvin have strongly influenced religious life and thought in the Netherlands, then the ascendancy of the belief that 'only a laborious life can lead to God', also meant that non-working and non-productive social activities also became synonymous with perceptions of evil and spiritual emptiness. In turn, and in contrast with the Anglo-Saxon cultural tradition which is more extensively permeated by the hedonistic values associated with aristocratic traditions and the popular folk culture of 'Merrie England', the Dutch language does not contain a word which is synonymous with the English term 'leisure'. Rather we commonly refer to 'free time' following the German usage *'freizeit'*.

Of course, in the last two decades wider technological and social developments have in the Netherlands, as elsewhere in the world, led to a re-evaluation of traditional attitudes to work and non-work. Thus free-time activities are now viewed in a more positive way and seen as a social good: 'good for one's health, work, and self-actualization'. In turn a person's contribution to society is no longer exclusively measured through his or her contribution to productive

238

Education for leisure: the Netherlands

Table 15.1 *Estimated average number of working hours and (public) holidays of adult male workers in industry*

Year	Average working week (hours)[1]	Average number of (public) holidays (days per year)[2]
1870	70	7
1910	60	8
1922	48	9
1950	48	17.5
1960	47.8	21
1969	43.7	22

Notes: 1 From 1922 onwards the number of normal working hours as per collective agreement.
2 With the start of the five-day working week in 1961 the number of holidays reduced somewhat in various collective agreements.
Source: CBS Sociale Maandstatistiek, November 1969.

labour, rather more and more attention is being paid to those social activities contributing to the happiness and well-being of the society. Free time, or leisure activities are increasingly being seen as important factors in this process of development.

Technological developments in productivity

Many of these recent cultural developments have reflected wider technological developments in productivity. In the Netherlands, as elsewhere in the modern industrial world, the amount of time spend in productive labour has gradually declined in the twentieth century. As we can see from Table 15.1, this decline was particularly rapid in the interwar years. However, since then the trend downwards has continued in a slow but inexorable manner. Thus, by 1979, the average working week of manual workers was down to forty-one hours, while the average number of holidays had increased to thirty days a year. At the same time, technological change has also led to a surge in enforced 'free time' as jobs disappear from the economy, and the Dutch unemployment rate is now running at 11 per cent of the labour force. Many people cannot find temporary or permanent work and since they have internalized the mores of a still predominantly protestant and work-oriented society, naturally experience feelings of monotony, uselessness, and a wasted life. In turn these feelings are intensified

239

by the fact that many people have been educated in preparation for a world dominated by work and domestic or leisure consumption at the weekend or holiday time, and not for a world dominated by an inevitable increase in 'free time'. Moreover, any political or social programme which is put forward to cope with the problem of unemployment (job-sharing, early retirement, longer holidays, shorter working weeks) will inevitably involve a redistribution of resources, more inexpensive leisure activities, and an increase in the non-working time of the bulk of the working population.

Social policy and the state

In contrast with the situation in France or Germany, leisure was not an explicit policy-related issue in the Netherlands in the prewar years and the bulk of free-time provisions was either left to the commercial sector or to voluntary and private associations, often with strongly religious connections. None the less following the period of social and economic reconstruction contingent upon the ending of hostilities in 1945, various sectors of the state became more closely concerned with, and involved in, various aspects of the 'free-time' activities of the population. However, as was also the case in the United Kingdom, this involvement developed in a largely accidental and incremental manner and was not, as was the case in Nazi Germany, the consequence of a clearly articulated and conscious national leisure policy. Let me now turn to trace two of the most important of these developments.

Education

Immediately after the end of the war a new 'Further Education' sector of the former Ministry of Education, Arts, and Science was founded, with the brief of looking after the education of young people. This important development modelled on the British legislation incorporated in the Butler Act of 1944, gave a new status to the sphere of post-secondary or further education and to the role of community and adult education in the growth of personal development. The officials of the Dutch Ministry of Education were particularly interested in the concept of 'learning for leisure', and in 1952 a separate bureau of the Ministry was established with the primary task of promoting the recreational and educational use of free time of young people.

Outdoor recreations

During the early 1950s it was becoming apparent that there was a serious shortage of outdoor recreational areas in the Netherlands and consequently public policies were pursued to remedy this deficiency and to co-ordinate a more 'space-oriented' physical planning response to the phenomenon of leisure which gradually came to supersede the initial educational approach. In 1958 a new Department of Outdoor Recreation was created and in turn during the 1960s this agency widened its scope from a purely physical planning to a more active educational and training role. More recently its staff have shown an increasing interest in the concept of 'continuing or permanent education' and work with all members of the general public, particularly in the fields of nature preservation and the promotion of 'environment-friendly' behaviour.

Apart from these two examples a variety of other public agencies have some concern with the free-time activities of the populace. However, that being said, the most explicit policy orientations have increasingly been with the sphere of 'outdoor', 'natural', or country-side recreation. Therefore, while in the immediate postwar period the primary public interest was a concern with general leisure problems, the pedagogical and those of human development, there has been a subsequent shift in the period to a more physical and facility-oriented approach emphasizing a particularistic concern with outdoor recreation *per se*. Thus the only Ministry with Recreation in its name – the Ministry of Culture, Recreation, and Social Welfare – which was established in 1965, has always had a strong bias towards the provision of outdoor recreation and it is only recently that a more integrated planning system approach at a regional level has become visible.

The schools and leisure

While, as we have seen, the officials of the Dutch educational system were alerted to the phenomenon of leisure in the immediate postwar era, at the same time this concern has not been translated into any substantial curriculum initiatives. Thus the 'explicit curriculum' of the school 'subject content' and the 'hidden curriculum' of the school as a social institution are still posited on the traditional Calvinist ideal that 'people in the first place are working people'. In turn education is seen as a mechanism which is to prepare young people for a position in working life. Of course one cannot deny the importance and necessity of work in society. However, there are other spheres of life which are equally vital to the individual and leisure is clearly one of these. Unfortunately, preparation for social activity in one's leisure time is under-developed in the Dutch schooling system and is limited to a concern with a few specific subjects such as sport, music, handicrafts, and school trips or visits. In short then, there is a discrepancy in our society between what one could call the objectives of schooling and the social reality of education. Our schooling system aims to provide its pupils with a system of knowledge that can be used mainly for a professional career, while the social reality asks for knowledge that can also be useful for leisure purposes.

Of course, some people are suspicious of the concept of education for leisure. They raise the quite legitimate question of whether it is in fact necessary to be educated for leisure. After all, leisure implies freedom of choice and this may be contradicted by the necessary constraining circumstances of an educational system. However, while nobody needs to be 'educated for freedom', clearly there are all sorts of social and other constraints that limit a person's freedom of choice in their leisure. One of these is lack of knowledge concerning the leisure facilities and processes which are available. Leisure behaviour is in fact a process of choice out of a number of more or less established social and cultural patterns. Of course one's social position and one's life-cycle stage influence the choice of possibilities, but irrespective of this one also requires a certain amount of general and specific knowledge about the kinds of leisure facilities which are available. Reciprocally, one must learn how to use this knowledge effectively. Of course not all our leisure learning processes take place within the educational system or the schoolroom. Such areas as the family, the community, the world of commercial recreation, the mass media, and so on, are equally significant. However, in view of the fact that school experiences clearly play a critical role in later life, both at work and at play, then we decided at The Stichting Recreatie to choose the school as a focus on which to carry out an experimental project in the field of 'education for leisure'. Let us now turn to examine this in more detail.

An experiment in education for leisure

We started our work with the assumption that leisure education in schools should aim to provide young people with an awareness of, and ability to choose from, a wide range of alternative possibilities.

Because of this, it is not only necessary to inform children of the range of 'leisure choices' available to them, but it is also necessary to provide them with the skills, and practice-test acquired skills, and make effective choices. Of course many of these skills can be acquired in the family and in the community. However since, as I have already suggested, many adults have internalized a work-oriented culture and have not received any 'leisure-oriented' education in their own childhood, then schools have an important role to play in stimulating the latent curiosity and creativity of the pupils *vis à vis* the development of a more leisure-oriented culture.

In order to extend our theoretical ideas into effective practice, we developed a package of material on leisure education and choices under the title 'We are Going Out' (*Wij gaan uit*) and sent it out to 250 Dutch primary schools. The material was designed to give children a good deal of information about leisure, facilities and opportunities: where to go, addresses of useful organizations, and so on. In turn the children were encouraged to develop independence and autonomy. Young people are well able to organize their own school, class, or group outing, or any other leisure activity if they have sufficient material and personal support to aid them in the organizing process.

The material in the 'We are Going Out' Project was organized into four sequential phases as follows:

Phase 1

To be able to organize a leisure activity it is important to be as honest as possible. That means for instance that the group knows all the constraints and limitations from the start. We have categorized those limitations as: what is allowed and possible; what is absolutely impossible; who can join the activity; how much money is available. The meaning of this phase is to make clear that the 'authorities', including school board, teachers, and parents, can make conditions determining the leisure behaviour and choices of children.

Phase 2

The objective of this second phase is to agree on and decide what to do in principle. This, of course, is not an easy matter and the teacher should see to it that it remains a group event and that no single boy or girl dominates the decision-making. Supervision, therefore, is necessary but one has to be careful not to underestimate the capability of the pupils.

Questions to be answered in this phase are: How long can we go? (day, week etc.); When can we go? (summer, winter etc.); How do we travel? and, if necessary, How do we stay there? It may be possible that subgroups tackle various questions and then report to the others in plenary sessions.

Phase 3

The decision has been made. Now the hard work begins. Individuals or small groups write letters to organizations, collect information leaflets, brochures and useful addresses.

What has been done is written down and is reported back to the whole group and of course every now and then there are plenary sessions. All activities lead to a final session where the definite decisions are made.

Phase 4

This phase does not follow the third one, but starts somewhere during Phase 3. In this phase questions have to be answered, such as: What do we do when we are back or when the activity is over? What do we tell the other pupils or parents and how do we tell it? Do we show things? etc., etc. It is a phase of evaluation and rethinking and especially suitable for increasing learning effects.

Evaluations

Naturally, we were anxious to find out how this project worked out in practice and what people thought of our work. To this end we organized a number of meetings with parents, teachers, and students from the schools we had contacted. The results of all of these discussions confirmed our earlier impressions that there was a need for leisure education amongst primary school children, although school is not the only place for it. However, at present leisure education is given only marginal attention in Dutch schools. Nevertheless teaching styles are changing and the idea that teachers and children must work together and find out new things by exploration is becoming more popular. This new approach could well complement the development of leisure education since in both cases young people are confronted with the problems of decision-making and the choice of alternatives.

At the same time we were warned by our informants that a number of teachers felt uncertain about these new developments. Sometimes they begin to think they 'have it done all wrong' up to now. Furthermore, one warned us to be very careful with the introduction of our project because the schools were replete with new ideas, projects, and experiments. Some teachers gained the impression that for every social problem the school must provide the answer, and this sometimes scared them off starting another special programme.

Parents and teachers thought it important, especially in the case of leisure education, that the parents and the community participated as much as possible in school-work. In such a way, society and school interpenetrate. In short, integration rather than separation was emphasized.

Finally our informants stressed that they did not want leisure education to become a separate subject, but rather thought it should be an integral element in the curriculum as a whole. In other words they wanted the educational system to be 'tuned into leisure'.

Following our meeting with parents, students, and teachers a group of 'sociology of leisure' students from Breda conducted a more extensive survey of the 250 schools we had involved in the 'We are Going Out' project. The questions in this evaluation included the following:

Is leisure education necessary in connection with developments in society?

Is the primary school an appropriate educational environment for leisure education?

Which problems occur in attempting to integrate leisure education?

What do users think about the usefulness of the material of the project 'We are Going Out'?

Although at the time of the survey, six months after the schools had the project, only 20 per cent of them were actually using the material, we were able to get an impression of what the users thought about it. On the whole there was agreement that leisure education is a good thing. Leisure education can prepare people for the leisure part of life. Therefore, people should become acquainted with the many leisure activities and possibilities. Value judgements as such must be made by the people themselves. Leisure education should not categorize leisure activities into good and bad ones. But to gain familiarity with possibilities is not enough.

Leisure education must also provide criteria that can guide the choice of leisure activities. Our informants thought primary school level a useful environment for leisure education, because on that level one has a good opportunity to reach the population of the future. However, more parent participation may be needed because of the important link of leisure education in school and elsewhere. Also a further change towards a system of learning through exploring and learning by doing is desirable. Some teachers may also have difficulties with this because at present teacher-training courses pay little attention to leisure education. It may be possible to integrate leisure education in the present school curricula, although much will depend on the creativity of the school staff. Again it is emphasized that the teachers lack in their training the opportunities to get acquainted with leisure and thus have to find out themselves.

The school system and leisure education

Finally our work also indicated that school systems themselves constrain the innovative capacity of teachers and possibility of developing leisure education in the primary curriculum. From a theoretical perspective one may distinguish two contrasting types of institutions, namely 'open' and 'closed' schools. In closed situations teachers follow the established curriculum precisely. The central value is the academic content of the subject matter. There is little scope for innovation, social interactions, or Socratic dialogue between teacher and pupil and a high value is placed upon grading, examinations, and individual success. In an open situation the development of the individual child is the central value. There is scope for individual innovation, experiment, and the emphasis is put on learning to work and live together; knowledge is not an inert substance which has to be learnt, but rather is something which is negotiable, dynamic, and above all relevant to the lives of the children. Obviously within the closed school system guidance, including leisure advice and counselling, tends to be based upon authoritarian situations requiring strict rules and regulations, while in the more open system guidance is offered within a sound context of dialogue, co-operation, and pupil participation. We found that leisure education was more likely to develop in an effective manner within a democratic and open schooling system.

16

Early retirement: a new leisure opportunity?[1] (1982)

ANN McGOLDRICK

Introduction

In the 1960s in the United Kingdom early retirement was comparatively rare, except in cases of disability.[2] The early 1970s saw
compulsory early retirement used, together with redundancy
schemes, as a means to reduce numbers and deal with staffing
'bulges' in a wide range of industries.[3] In the later 1970s, while some
compulsory schemes continued, the intervention of unions and the
growing need within organizations to introduce wider manpower
planning and staffing reduction programmes, which were acceptable to their workforces, gave rise to a variety of special voluntary
early retirement 'schemes' and 'exercises'.[4]

At the same time, pension schemes were more generally being
adapted to permit earlier retirement at the initiative of the
individual, 'by consent' of the employer or 'by right' of the employee
on request.[5] The government introduced the Job Release Scheme,
subsequently modified, as a mechanism to assist the reduction of
unemployment levels, by encouraging those nearing state re-
tirement/pension age to leave the labour force earlier to free jobs for
younger workers.[6]

This trend towards earlier retirement is not only a feature of the
UK employment scene. It follows a similar and better documented
trend in the US in the later 1960s and early 1970s.[7] Similarly, other
European countries are monitoring such developments and, in some
cases, giving them national support. The Commission of the
European Communities has explicitly encouraged moves towards
more flexible retirement policies in member countries, emphasizing

the need for earlier options, work sharing, and job change to help alleviate economic/employment problems in the 1980s and 1990s.[8] In the UK, the Social Services Committee has been carrying out an inquiry into 'The Age of Retirement' for the House of Commons.

In the US, a more flexible system of retirement ages has been encouraged, with upward as well as downward age mobility, by the introduction and extension of the Age Discrimination Act (1967 and 1978). This now permits employees the opportunity to elect to continue in their job until 70 years of age.[9] In the UK, however, such upward flexibility seems unlikely at the present time, although our own pilot work at the University of Manchester Institute of Science and Technology (UMIST) and other studies would suggest that this would be the situation preferred by older employees themselves. In response to the continuing economic recession, it is, however, likely that more workers will be facing pressures to retire early or to change the nature of their work as they grow older.

These trends towards earlier retirement also appear to be occurring within a more positive climate of social opinion generally towards the idea of retirement and leisure. Better financial security from state and company pensions is frequently combined with generous financial settlements and 'liberalized' benefits for those who opt to take special early retirement offers. At the same time, increases in life expectancy and medical advances are helping to break down the traditional association of retirement with the end of useful working life – inactivity, poverty, sickness, disability and death. Studies in both the US and the UK have shown that retirement can be positively perceived by growing numbers of workers at all levels of employment, if they are able to look forward to an active and secure period of their lives.[10] While the recession and current rates of inflation continue to affect pensions and savings, recent evidence suggests that even this does not necessarily affect people's desire for earlier retirement or their plans to leave their main occupation at an earlier stage.[11]

The Early Retirement Study

The study set out to examine the decision to retire early and the experience of early retirement for men in the United Kingdom who had retired in response to a variety of special schemes and options. The work was organized in two main stages:

1. Detailed tape-recorded interviews with a sample of 120 male early retirees and their wives. Respondents also completed an extensive set of questionnaires.
2. A national questionnaire survey of 1,800 early retired men and their wives from a wide variety of industries and organizations and from all job levels.

The early retirees

Response rate : 1,207 men
Age range   :   45 to 64 years
Retired   :   3 months to 16 years

Before discussing the results of the study, it is necessary to describe certain characteristics of the sample in order that the correct focus can be placed on data presented:

Type of early retirement

Respondents had retired under a wide range of circumstances: compulsory ER (10 per cent), compulsory ER willingly or by request (12 per cent), ER instead of redeployment or in rundowns (12 per cent), various types of voluntary ER schemes (46 per cent), ER on completion of pension scheme (6 per cent), free choice ER at own request with pension as earned (14 per cent). Groups excluded from the study as requiring separate enquiry were those leaving on full disability terms and employees leaving with Job Release Scheme benefits only. Attention was thus focused on response to the various special early retirement options and early retirement arrangements under existing pension terms.

Financial terms on retirement

Companies employing early retirement options tend to be those with well established pension schemes. While terms offered vary considerably between companies according to type of retirement and individual circumstances, certain patterns are discernible. Those leaving at the time of special compulsory or voluntary schemes usually receive generous financial treatment, according to age and company service. This can include full or supplemented pension credits instead of actuarial reduction, and/or a severance payment or 'golden handshake'. Those leaving under ordinary pension terms are less generously treated. They tend to receive actuarially reduced benefits if they have insufficient service years for full pension credits; although commutation can provide a lump sum, and an earlier retirement may have been planned and prepared for well in advance. The vast majority of these early retirees receive pensions from the time of their early retirement.

The retirees discussed here are thus a special group, which does not correspond to 'the retired' in general in the United Kingdom, as surveyed recently, for example, by the Office of Population Censuses and Surveys on behalf of the Department of Employment and the Department of Health & Social Security.[12] In this survey, it was found that especially great hardship could result for employees forced to retire early on ill-health grounds, those with only enforced redundancy terms or without adequate company pension. Declining health and the effects of ageing can contribute frequently to the decision to retire early for the retirees discussed here and the majority of the sample referred to were feeling the effects of inflation on their financial situation. They must be considered, however, a 'healthier' and 'wealthier' group generally, who had special financial provision for their early retirement and most frequently volunteered to retire early. Thus they tended to be satisfied with life after their retirement and viewed positively the opportunities that early retirement could bring.

The opportunity to leave the job – a strategy for coping

For many older workers, early retirement can present an opportunity to escape from negative aspects of their work situation. Some of these can be connected with personal changes and the effects of ageing; while others relate to changes in technology and within industry itself, which can become increasingly difficult for the older worker to cope with.

While the sample contacted generally described themselves as satisfied with their working lives, a notable deterioration was found in the later years at work, when satisfaction and job involvement declined and their diminishing ability to cope with their jobs was a factor of concern for many. Forty-three per cent described themselves as experiencing less satisfaction at work in the years before their early retirement and 38 per cent stated that they were coping less well with their job. This, in fact, probably underestimates the true extent of such feelings, since when asked to indicate various dissatisfactions and stresses within their work

Table 16.1 *Dissatisfactions and concerns at work in years preceding early retirement (%)*

Work and job	
1. Pressures and stresses of job	39
2. Travel to/at work	23
3. Technological change (e.g. computers, new techniques etc.)	17
4. Over-worked	15
5. Unpleasant aspects of working/job (e.g. conditions, shifts etc.)	15
6. Bored/not enough to do	13
7. Hard to keep up	13
People at work	
1. Immediate boss(es)	22
2. Younger workers' attitudes	16
3. People directly worked with	11
4. People responsible for	10
5. Fellow workers generally	8

situation at this time, the vast majority of early retirees responded to several items.

Work dissatisfactions

It is not possible to discuss in detail here all the dissatisfactions and concerns experienced. Table 16.1, however, summarizes the main dissatisfactions in the work situation relating to the job and other people at work, experienced during the years immediately preceding early retirement, which respondents regarded as strong enough to form an inducement towards an earlier retirement.

The interviewees contacted at the outset of the study gave many examples of such concerns. A few such comments illustrate their feelings in relation to the pressures and stresses they had experienced:

'Changes in technology, such as in the law, national insurance and tax, made the job so much more complex that it became unmanageable.'

'The working environment had changed in the last few years and in my opinion can be likened to life in high-rise flats – I wanted out!'

'I became very dissatisfied with the apparent lack of human feelings on the part of Senior Management. A feature of the large company it had become.'

Table 16.2 *Concerns about changes in years preceding early retirement (%)*

Changes	
1. Changes in company structure/management	37
2. Changes in the job	21
3. Company running down	17
4. Union influence	16
5. Unpleasant company atmosphere	13
6. Need to change job	11
7. Insecurity of job or company	8
8. Need to move to new location	8

Changes at work

Changes in the company and certain aspects of company life or the need to change job or location were similarly concerns. These are summarized in Table 16.2 and some qualitative commentary follows.

'My job changed. I was selling not designing and making. I knew all the faults and better products of competitors! Also – I was no salesman.'

'The company was taken over. I had been a Marketing Assistant but I became an Accounts Payable Clerk. Also I had been in Birmingham for only three years and I didn't like it. Then they said I'd have to move again.'

'There was a general lack of enthusiasm about the place. Most people were fed up and worked on mainly for the money.'

Health factors

Health too was a significant factor for many of the retirees. While this was not so severe that it determined a disability retirement, poor health and other health factors were major areas of consideration. 'Tiredness' and 'feeling the effects of ageing' were noted but positive feelings towards the desirability of earlier retirement in maintaining health, in fact, rated highest in their considerations. Table 16.3 shows the range of health factors considered by the retirees.

'It was preventative. I was feeling pressure and I didn't want to work until I was too old to enjoy it.'

Table 16.3 *Health factors in early retirement (%)*

1. Wanted healthier/more active retirement	46
2. Prevent future health problems	36
3. Tiredness	26
4. Feeling effects of getting older	25
5. Poor health	24
6. Job affecting health	22
7. Wife's health	17

'I had slightly high blood pressure at the time so I had to take tablets. It has been better since I retired and I never go to a doctor now.'

'I had no reason to suspect the condition of my health but I felt strongly that the older we get the more we push our luck. To opt out of the "rat-race" might prolong my expectation of life.'

The opportunity for a new life-style – a development strategy

For the vast majority of the retirees negative aspects of work were not the only considerations in their early retirement. The financial inducements offered (75 per cent) and the appropriateness of their own savings and finances (58 per cent) made it possible for them to consider the benefits of increased freedom and new activities. While some had felt pressures towards early retirement from company and management (21 per cent), more importantly they had been influenced by their own positive perceptions of the early retirement experience. A long-term positive belief in the benefits of earlier retirement was stated by 68 per cent of respondents, who also frequently felt that they had 'worked long enough' or 'deserved retirement' (54 per cent).

Their intentions with regard to time-spending and life-style after early retirement varied very considerably, however. While some sought time for relaxation and leisure activities, others looked for opportunities for self-development, community participation or for further work or a new career. Before taking early retirement about half of the retirees had placed emphasis on the value of 'increased free time,' of 'rest and relaxation', 'time for hobbies and recreation' and 'time with family and friends'. Smaller numbers had intended to follow more active retirement pursuits: voluntary work (12 per cent), committees and societies (12 per cent) and further education

(10 per cent). The attraction of further paid employment with reduced working hours or on a part-time basis existed for 21 per cent. Fourteen per cent had seen in early retirement a chance of a new full-time job or an entirely new career, while 6 per cent saw it as an opportunity to become self-employed in some way and to start their own business.

Life-styles after retiring early

In this section, a brief summary is presented of the types of life-styles followed by the early retirees, based on the interview programme carried out at the beginning of the study and sub-sequently confirmed in the survey analysis. Emphasis is placed on 'The Opportunists', who saw benefits and challenges in their new experience. But for smaller numbers of retirees, whom I have called the 'The Disenchanted', early retirement did not present opportunities and was a negative experience. The categories and 'types' of life-styles suggested are not, of course, in practice mutually exclusive. They are presented here as a mechanism to examine response to early retirement.

'The Rest and Relaxers' For many early retirees rest and relaxation were of great appeal, the freedom to do as they pleased and to do as much or as little as they pleased. These early retirees followed the more traditional retirement patterns: newspapers, TV and radio, the garden, walks out during the day, trips in the car, and domestic activities. In retiring early, they felt the advantages of increased time in retirement years and at an earlier stage, when they could enjoy healthier, more contented years. Those who were nearer to normal retirement age at the time of their early retirement and retirees from manual occupations predominated in this group. As they grew older retirees might move into this category:

'It's nice to turn over for an extra hour during the winter months and to be able to do as you please all day.'

'I no longer have to work or to meet rigid timetables, I can take it easy. I'm never bored, it's too comfortable.'

Although the vast majority found this 'freedom' (77 per cent) the 'relaxation' (70 per cent) and 'doing as they pleased' (78 per cent) an advantage of early retirement, other life-styles could be combined with this slower pace.

'The Home and Family Men' Seventy-five per cent of the respondents found 'more time at home' to be a direct advantage of their early retirement. Numbers experiencing difficulties personally from being at home too much or in respect of the marital relationships were, in fact, small after an initial adjustment period. Similarly, over two-thirds valued increased time with their wives and families: time to spend with their wives in various activities (67 per cent), with children and grandchildren (61 per cent), seeing more of relatives (38 per cent) and in assisting with and sharing domestic chores (60 per cent). Smaller numbers used early retirement as an opportunity to travel more frequently to see distant family. Others moved house to be close to children and relatives, often assisting in bringing up their grandchildren, while their own children were working. Looking after grandchildren was a frequently mentioned pleasurable activity for retirees, as well as a way in which they felt they could support their families. For some retirees, these were the predominant activities of early retired life. Again, manual workers and those who were already slowing down were more likely to adhere to this type of life-style:

> 'I'm young enough to enjoy my retirement along with my wife. It's good to feel that we can still be of some use to our families, friends and neighbours now that we have more time available and we are not yet too decrepit, either mentally or physically, to help.'

> 'I have the freedom to travel as I like and visit my son and daughter, who live away, when invited – which is frequent.'

'The Hobbyists' Many retirees had looked to early retirement as a time to pursue or develop hobbies and interests for which they had found insufficient time in their later years at work. Such recreational activities, both inside and outside the home, were seen as an advantage by some 65 per cent overall. For some retirees, however, they were the main focus of their retirement time and a wide variety of such pursuits was described in detail by the interviewees. They ranged from the more traditional hobbies, such as DIY, philately, bird-watching, golf, and fishing, to various more specialized undertakings:

> 'I can now follow my hobbies properly. In my case it's music. My days are so filled that I could not fit in the Adult Education course I intended to follow.'

'About eighteen months before I retired my wife suggested I turn the small bedroom into my hobbies room. Between that, the garden, and the greenhouse my time is taken up. To me retirement means freedom.'

'The Good Timers' Early retirement can mean leisure time at an age which permits activities that retirees believed would not be possible at a traditional retirement age. Some respondents took the opportunity of this time to enhance their social life and spend time with friends (42 per cent), go out in the evenings (30 per cent), travel and take more holidays and time away from home (45 per cent). In some cases, lump-sum payments were used to finance the sort of trip that had not been possible in working years. One shop-floor foreman from an oil company, for example, went on a six-month trip with his wife to Australia and New Zealand – a lifelong ambition. Many more followed the philosophy of living to the full and for the present. Perhaps in this category too are the small number of retirees (some twenty in the survey) who decided to take a permanent or semi-permanent early retirement holiday by moving abroad, and the larger number who saw early retirement as an opportunity to move to the country and the seaside (approximately 18 per cent of the survey sample):

'Travelling is one of our major interests and we've had two major holidays already this year.'

'We've moved to Australia, about 240 miles from Sydney in a "holiday area" with a relaxing atmosphere. It's not conducive to work but it's great for the 55s and over!'

'Work is not everything. Life's there to enjoy. I would have retired even earlier if it had been possible.'

'The Committee and Society Men' Twenty four per cent of the respondents found increased participation in societies and committee work a major advantage of retiring early. In many cases, these were areas of involvement before retirement for which there had been insufficient time, and they sometimes developed to activities approximating to a full-time job. The organizations were extremely varied, as was level of participation, but retirees thus involved were frequently highly committed to their pursuits as a way of life:

'I have had long-standing appointments as Chairman, Trustee, and Vice President of various bodies. It keeps me busy, feeling "usefulness" to others and maintaining all my former contacts.'

'I am Chairman of two local bodies and treasurer of another, so I'm not idle for much of the time. They need my time.'

'The Volunteers' Retirees who spent time in voluntary work could again develop their early retirement occupation into the status of a full-time job. Many, however, preferred to combine voluntary and community activities, which helped them to retain their sense of purpose and usefulness, with more relaxed retirement occupations. The types of voluntary work engaged in ranged between helping friends and neighbours to full-time commitment to various charities and organizations, as well as involvement in a wide variety of social and environmental pursuits:

'I am founder chairman of the local branch of the Multiple Sclerosis Society and also on a committee to build a new home for the disabled. A proper level of commitment involves spending considerable time on the various aspects of these ventures and this would not have been possible if I was working.'

Nineteen per cent of the sample had participated in voluntary work at some level after retirement, 6 per cent of these being involved to such an extent that for them it was an entirely new life-style.

'The Further Education Men' Involvement in further education ranged from attendance at local college courses for hobbies and interests to Open University Degrees and MSc and PhD courses at various universities. The latter were less frequent, and might be associated with retraining for a new career. Nine per cent overall, however, participated in some type of educational activity and saw this as an opportunity provided by their early retirement:

'Since leaving my old firm I have enrolled at the local University to keep the old brain ticking over!'

'I'm learning French and Spanish – great help for my holidays.'

'I've gone back to school again. I'm balancing my Engineering training with a degree in Humanities at the Open University.'

'The Part-time Jobbers' While some retirees were forced back into various types of work by financial problems, many had intended to take part-time paid employment both as a way of filling their time

and as a supplementary source of income. Some 15 per cent had worked part-time, 6 per cent had engaged in occasional or freelance work and about 3 per cent had done odd jobs for payment. Others intended to look for part-time work when their year of unemployment benefit ended. They were mostly satisfied with their new jobs and often valued the extra income these provided until they became eligible for the State Retirement Pension. Some retirees had deliberately chosen to use early retirement as an opportunity to 'phase' themselves into retirement proper, even reducing their hours more than once or moving between types of work to accomplish this end:

> 'My activities from the time of retiring include helping to start a new business, followed by consultancy work, then part-time work designing and building fireplaces. I would like to add that I have not enjoyed myself so much for years."

> 'A part-time job is an immense benefit – it's a hedge against inflation and keeps one active mentally.'

'The New Jobbers'   This category covers several related types of early retirees. 'The Easier Jobbers' are retirees who take on full-time work again but of a less demanding or less stressful nature. While their pay will be less, early retirement benefits can buffer their financial situation. Thus early retirement provides the opportunity to remain in full-time employment but 'tone down', without serious consequences to their finances and standard of living. 'The Other Job Men' are those retirees who look for new jobs equivalent to those they retire from. Since they receive early retirement benefits as well as a new salary, their financial position can thus be enhanced.

'The Second Career Men' are those retirees who use early retirement as an opportunity to move to an entirely new career, possibly after a period of retraining. Examples within the survey were managers and engineers who became teachers, university lecturers, or even entered the Church. Finally, 'The Entrepreneurs' are those retirees who use early retirement as an opportunity to start their own business and become self-employed. In this respect, lump-sum financial payments can be important and retirees sometimes 'pool' resources to start in business together. The projects varied considerably in scope and complexity, from home-based businesses in car repairs, decorating, and gardening to setting up full-scale professional businesses. Similarly, they varied

in the amount of time devoted to the business, frequently involving longer holidays and more time away from work. In the case of one shared business, for example, it was agreed to close completely for the cricket season!

One early retired executive moved to a rival company on a four-day week basis. Two years later he moved again on a part-time consultancy basis to a third company. This freed time to prepare his new home in Scotland for retirement proper, which he planned for the age of 62 – although he thought he might take on the odd project from time to time 'to keep his hand in'.

> 'I finished work on Friday night and started my new job on the following Monday – it's congenial and, although the money earned is not nearly so great, the satisfaction is greater.'

> 'Leaving the company was a wrench after 36 years. Outside those gates stood a new life. I left on a reasonable pension and became a teacher and I think it was the best move of my life.'

Overall, some 23 per cent had worked again at some point in a full-time job. Five per cent had been self-employed. The figures show that more retirees had returned to full-time work than originally intended to do so, while fewer had entered part-time work. This related both to availablity of employment opportunities and financial requirements. It should be noted that the retirees finding the type of employment desired were among the most satisfied in the sample overall. Those not finding suitable work or forced back into employment against their plans tended to be among the least satisfied.

Early retirement – an appropriate strategy?

In discussing the data obtained from the study of this special group of retirees, it has been argued that a financially secure earlier retirement option can provide opportunities for the older employee. These relate both to opportunities to escape from negative aspects of the work situation and to a variety of positive opportunities in early retirement life. For each individual, the decision to retire early must be a balance of personal, social, and institutional factors. Similarly, the opportunities individuals perceive in an earlier retirement will vary. While for some retirees early retirement brings the opportunity for continuation or development of leisure pursuits, for others it is an opportunity for further paid employment or a change of working life-style.

The early retirees discussed here tended to be satisfied with their early retirement experience. Satisfaction related closely to their ability to carry out retirement plans. Overall, 80 per cent were pleased with their early retirement and only 6 per cent described themselves as displeased. Seventy-four per cent stated that they would retire early again, with 8 per cent being unsure and 18 per cent preferring to continue at work. The main reason given was insufficiency of finances to take advantage of early retirement opportunities. Compulsory retirees were less satisfied than the volunteers, although their satisfaction similarly tended to increase over time.

Retirees noted significant advantages in relation both to leaving and negative aspects of their jobs. For example, they described themselves as 'less tired' (48 per cent), 'more at ease' (70 per cent), and as in 'better general health' (52 per cent), with 'less stress and strain' (75 per cent), 'less worries' (68 per cent). They also valued the positive opportunities of early retirement, whatever approach they adopted towards it.

While here the emphasis has been on the successes of the early retirement experience, this must be balanced against the problems which occurred and the retirees who were dissatisfied with their new life-styles. These 'disenchanted' retirees were in the minority, particularly amongst volunteers. The most disillusioned tended to be those who were sick, those with financial problems, some compulsory retirees, and those who were lonely, depressed, and bored in retirement. Retirees who were forced back into work by financial necessity, or who had to take jobs that were ill paid or which they regarded negatively, as well as those who could not find further employment could become extremely disillusioned. While their retirement problems did not always relate directly to early retirement, for them early retirement provided no opportunities and was negatively perceived.

The views of older employees

In conclusion, it seems likely that more employees in the UK will have the opportunity to retire early over the next decade. Evidence from a pilot study for research currently in progress suggests that many older workers look forward to the prospect and positively perceive an earlier retirement. This new study has consisted of an informal interview programme and a pilot questionnaire sample of 192 employees over 45 years of age and their spouses. Sixty-three per cent felt that the stresses and problems of older workers in the employment situation were a cause of concern. Such attitudes increased with age, and the majority of workers in their later 50s and 60s expressed personal concern in this respect. While 86 per cent still found their jobs in many ways rewarding, 56 per cent thought that it is more difficult to cope with work as one grows older:

'As you get older, you are expected to work at the same speed as people a lot younger. You can do it, but it takes a hell of a lot out of you!'

Specifically noted were the current rates of technological change: new production techniques, computerization, the metric system, and the dreaded 'microchip':

'Younger people for fresher ideas. Metric systems, decimal money, microchips mean that youngsters have the right to press on and let older ones step down.'

'Chips with everything – phew!!'

While respondents were adamant that new ideas were necessary and would bring positive benefits for future generations, their own position in relation to them was one of uncertainty. Similarly, they felt guilt at remaining in employment at times of redundancy/unemployment and felt the need to make way for younger workers.

Some employees already felt that their work was affecting their health and disturbing family life and their marital relationship. Forty-two per cent were experiencing tiredness as a result of their jobs, which increased home tensions. Again, effects significantly increased with age. The workers, in fact, strongly favoured a flexible retirement policy which they felt would permit individuals to cope with such changes, rather than a fixed company/state age (79 per cent). Sixty-six per cent positively viewed a financially secure early retirement and 89 per cent indicated that they would wish to take an earlier retirement if it was financially feasible. In general terms they favoured the flexibility which permits individuals to assess their own personal, physical, mental, financial, and social circumstances. 'Phasing' into retirement was similarly preferred.

The final comment should be given to one of the employees interviewed:

'For the individual, flexibility would be ideal. Some people only live to work, while others work to live.'

Notes

1 This chapter presents some of the findings of a research project undertaken to investigate the effects of early retirement for men retiring under a variety of special arrangements and schemes. The study was funded by a grant from the Social Science Research Council and the work was undertaken between February 1978 and October 1981.

2 See for example: British Institute of Management, *Company Retirement Policies*, Information Summary 128, London, BIM, 1967.

3 C. M. Smith, *Retirement: The Organisation and the Individual*, Management Survey Report no. 23, London, British Institute of Management, 1974.

4 Examples can be found in various management surveys. For example: Industrial Relations Review, 'Early retirement pension arrangements and company practice', in *Industrial Relations Review Report* no. 141, December 1976; Incomes Data Services, *Early Retirement*, IDS Study, series no. 152, August 1977.

5 See for example the surveys of the National Association of Pension Funds, *Survey of Occupational Pension Schemes*, London, NAPF, 1975 onwards.

6 For example: Department of Employment, 'Measures to alleviate unemployment in the medium term: early retirement', in *The Department of Employment Gazette*, March 1978, pp. 283–5; Department of Employment, *Evaluation of the Job Release Scheme*, Research Paper no. 13, London, HMSO, July 1980.

7 Discussion of the trends in the United States and of research undertaken can be found in A. E. McGoldrick, and C. L. Cooper, 'Early retirement for managers in the US and the UK', in *Management International Review*, August 1978, pp. 35–42.

8 Commission of the European Communities, *Communication from the Commission to the Council on Work-sharing*, CEC, COM(79), 188 Final, Brussels, 7 May 1979; *Community Guidelines on Flexible Retirement*, CEC, COM(80), 393 Final, Brussels, 14 July 1980.

9 For discussion of employment and retirement patterns in the United States see: K. R. Brousseau, 'After age forty: employment patterns and practices in the United States', ch. 10 in C. L. Cooper and D. P. Torrington, (eds), *After Forty*, London, Wiley, 1981.

10 Discussion of attitudes towards retirement in the US and the UK and reference to studies undertaken is given in: A. E. McGoldrick and C. L. Cooper, 'Early retirement: the appeal and the reality', in *Personnel Management*, July 1978, pp. 25–7 and 41.

11 See for example: J. Morgan 'What with inflation . . . who can afford to

retire'? in M. W. Riley (ed), *Aging from Birth to Death – Interdisciplinary Perspectives*, AAAS Selected Symposium, Boulder, Colorado, Westview Press, 1979.

12 S. R. Parker *Older Workers and Retirement*, Office of Population Censuses and Surveys, London, HMSO, 1980.

17

Leisure and the future: considering the options (1984)

A. J. VEAL

Introduction

One of the least sophisticated techniques available in forecasting is the simple extrapolation of existing trends. If the trickle of publications on the future of work and leisure produced in the 1970s is extrapolated through the current flood of such publications, it is possible that there will be no leisure because the whole of the population will be engaged in either writing or printing such works. In Britain the best known books on the subject are Jenkins and Sherman's *The Collapse of Work* and *The Leisure Shock*. Others have included Clemitson and Rogers' *A Life to Live*, Allen *et al.*'s *The Shattered Dream*, Merritt's *World out of Work*, Martin and Mason's *Leisure and Work – the Choices for 1991 and 2001*, a number of conference reports from the Leisure Studies Association, a contribution from Australia in the form of Jones's *Sleepers Wake!*, Stonier's *The Wealth of Information*, Clarke's *Work in Crisis*, and, the latest contribution, Handy's *The Future of Work*.[1] Curiously, no American title appears in this list – either this is not an issue in the United States or the relevant publications have simply not reached European shores.

This plethora of literature on work and leisure is supplemented by an even greater volume of material on microelectronic technology, which deals to varying extents with the social, including leisure, consequences.[2] Other futurist literature of the post Second World War era has paid varying attention to the leisure issue,[3] and even in the 1930s eminent thinkers were writing about possible major changes in the relationship between work and leisure.[4]

Leisure and the future

The current crop of literature is characterized by the attention given to the topic of work–leisure relationships and by the degree of consensus among the authors about the nature and seriousness of the problem facing advanced industrial nations. They are virtually all of the view that high levels of unemployment are here to stay, and indeed are likely to increase, and that a variety of dramatic changes in attitude and economic practices are necessary in order to survive. The only exception to the generally pessimistic outlook would appear to be Tom Stonier who, while not minimizing the scale of change to be expected, nevertheless seems to believe that the new 'information economy' can provide full employment.

Another consensus should also be mentioned: that is the consensus among governments and major political parties that there is no insoluble employment problem; that the 'correct' economic policies – of left, right, or centre – will restore full employment to levels experienced in the 1950s and 1960s. In Britain two 'wets' from the Conservative government have made statements to the effect that the importance of work and the 'work ethic' will be reduced in future, but there is no sign of their views being adopted by the party at large, let alone the government.[5] There would appear to be more noise from the left on the subject: Jenkins and Sherman are trade union officials; Clemitson and Rogers are Labour politicians, and their book even sports a foreword by Neil Kinnock, written before he became leader of the Labour Party. A former General Secretary of the Trades Union Congress made a speech suggesting that new approaches to work are required and the TUC supports the European trade union campaign for a 35-hour working week.[6] Even the secretary of the Fabian Society has called for a change in the Labour movement's attitude towards work.[7] But the official policies of the Labour Party do not reflect these ideas.

Contemporary commentators on the future of work and leisure are generally prescriptive: they cast themselves in the role of prophets with dire warnings for society and numerous penances which must be paid if purgatory is to be avoided. My purpose is to review some of these prescriptions and ask some questions about their possible effects and the likelihood of their being adopted. But first some consideration is given to why the existence of the 'problem' and the prophets' definition of it is generally rejected by governments.

The problem and its definition

Perhaps the first reason why governments ignore the warnings of the prophets is that the future has arrived and it has not turned out nearly as badly as the prophets had predicted. When Jenkins and Sherman published their first book on the subject in 1978/79 unemployment stood at 1.5 million.[8] Talk of three and four million unemployed by the end of the 1980s appeared alarmist. If anything, Jenkins and Sherman's estimates of the level of future unemployment were on the low side. But even with over three million unemployed there are no signs of the widespread social unrest which, only a few years ago, might have been expected. Various job creation schemes keep many of the restless young occupied, and North Sea oil pays the unemployment benefits. Sitting tight and hoping that the problem will go away therefore seems a reasonable strategy.

Secondly, the experience of the United States over the last year or so suggests that fast economic growth can produce new jobs on a substantial scale, at least in the short term. Which leads to the third reason for the politicians' deafness to the prophets' warnings: this is that accepting the inevitability of chronically high unemployment appears to strike at the very heart of most governments' main virility symbol: the achievement of high economic growth. Economic growth is seen as the solution to all problems; so to admit to a chronic problem of unemployment would be to admit that high economic growth was not achievable or to accept that it had lost some of its magic. So the prophets continue to cry in the wilderness.

The policy measures and other remedies proposed by the prophets can be divided into three groups. The first concerns social attitudes; the second consists of a set of possible ways of spreading the available work, and leisure, around; and the third group is concerned with the ways in which the economic structure might or should change.

Changing attitudes

The idea that societies should change their attitudes towards work and leisure as a solution to the looming problem of unemployment is at the same time the most prevalent and the most enigmatic of the proposals we shall discuss. Basically it suggests that societies should abandon the 'work ethic' and adopt some new ethic. Jenkins and Sherman espouse the idea of a 'usefulness ethic' to replace the work ethic:

> If it appears, as we suggest that it does, that society, both individually and collectively, would be happier, would be more harmonious and would have fewer problems if the work ethic were either destroyed or reconstructed, then why should it not be done?

266

... The need to be wanted is, we believe, the true human condition; the need for formal work is but a perversion of this, so that the concept of usefulness rather than work must be the future ethic.[9]

Clemitson and Rogers see the alternative as a 'life ethic':

In short, we need to develop a 'life ethic' rather than a work ethic and the corresponding concept of a 'full life' rather than 'full employment'. Such an ethic would be concerned with the full development of human beings and human potential ... a life ethic would cease to see a person's only and major contribution to society as being made through his or her employment.[10]

Clarke, on the other hand, coins the term 'contribution ethic':

Perhaps out of the ashes of the Work Ethic, which is seriously challenged by the loss of the ideal of Full Employment, there will emerge the concept of a Contribution Ethic – a belief that our humanity does find fulfilment in doing things for others. That God is glorified through our being of service to our fellows whether that be through employee/customer relationships in the paid economy or whether that service, that giving of ourselves, is manifested in some other way quite outwith the paid economy.[11]

The idea that something called the 'work ethic' is preventing people from adjusting to modern economic realities is presumably based on the assumption that the work ethic exists as an important force in modern society. There is considerable evidence to suggest that this is not the case in Britain, and indeed in other western societies. Research on attitudes to work has raised considerable doubts about the centrality of work in the lives of workers in contemporary industrial societies.[12] For many years press and some political comment have suggested that one of the key reasons for Britain's relative economic decline is that British workers are not prepared to work as hard as their German or Japanese counterparts – hardly indicating that a powerful 'work ethic' is at large. Part of the reason for the belief in the existence of a work ethic is based on the well researched experiences of the unemployed and, to some extent, of the retired.[13] However, one of the main features of both of these states is a substantial loss of income. While there may be plenty of evidence to show that people find total loss of work combined with a substantial loss of income distressing, there is no evidence to suggest that a reduction in work combined with a safeguarded income would be at all distasteful. While attitudes towards 'scroungers' living on social security might be cited as evidence of the existence of a work ethic, it could, if indeed it is widespread, be seen in quite the opposite light: that those in work resent having to work to support others living an (enviable) life of idleness.

The possibility remains, however, that the work ethic exists within the culture – not necessarily in the hearts and minds of the workers, but among the media, educationists, the ruling classes, and so on. Thus it has an official existence, rather like an established religion, without being embraced by the population as a whole. In that case, it could be hindering progress towards a more 'leisured' society.

Nevertheless, the idea that the 'work ethic' could be replaced by another 'ethic' seems naive. It implies that some sort of missionary force could be brought into being to go around 'converting' people to the new ethic. It seems more likely that any new ethic will emerge as a result of change rather than as an agent of change.

Spreading the work around

Many of the commentators on the future of work and leisure have suggested that if there is to be less work available in future then at least the work that is available should be shared out equitably, so that the average worker spends less time in work and has more leisure, and unemployment is minimized. Thus there are proposals to reduce the working day, the working week, the working year, and the working life.

The first three of these have of course been taking place slowly ever since the turn of the century. Over the last thirty years, since the achievement of the basic 40-hour week, most of the reductions in work time have been in the form of a longer holiday rather than a shorter working week. On the other hand, it is of interest to note that while West German metal workers have just concluded a two-month strike to achieve a 38½-hour week, millions of office workers have enjoyed a 37½-hour week for many years. American research and the tendency for holidays to increase rather than the working week to decline, suggest that most workers would prefer to see any reductions in working hours in the form of a smaller number of larger 'chunks' of time, rather than a larger number of marginal reductions.[14] This suggests that, unless something like a 4½-day week is in prospect, the emphasis of future collective bargaining will continue to be on the extension of the annual holiday entitlement.

Other things being equal, a reduction of one hour in the work week or an increase of one week in holiday time will lead to approximately

2½ per cent increase in jobs. It would take an across-the-board 7-hour reduction in the work week to abolish Britain's dole queues on this basis. Both workers and employers tend to agree to reductions in working hours only in conditions of rising productivity and rising output, so that the worker also achieves an increase in pay and the employers' costs do not increase in real terms. Again, American research suggests workers' preference for income increases over time off is in the ratio of three to one.[15] If this is true here then productivity would have to rise by over 70 per cent and output by over 50 per cent to achieve the reduction in unemployment discussed above. While this is extremely unlikely in the foreseeable future, it is nevertheless true that every reduction in working hours negotiated has a positive effect on the number of jobs, either by increasing the number of jobs available or by preventing a reduction in the number of jobs.

Job-sharing is an alternative way in which work can be shared around by reducing the average working week. In this case the individual worker does take a cut in pay because the salary is shared as well as the work. While other changes discussed are likely to remain the province of collective bargaining with little direct government intervention, governments could intervene in the area of job-sharing to make it a right for those who want it.

Reducing the working lifetime can happen in three different ways: by lowering the retirement age, by raising the age at which young people leave full-time education, or by introducing some kind of sabbatical or retraining system so that people leave the workforce for periods during their working lives. The de facto average retirement age is falling because of voluntary early retirement schemes and the fact that redundant older workers have only a poor chance of regaining employment. While the retirement age is a matter of negotiation in some industries, such as mining, for most the question is determined by the state through state retirement pensions and, increasingly, through the minimum rules imposed with regard to occupational pension schemes.

Similarly the state has a great deal of influence over the education system. It is of interest to note that, in the USA, some 80 per cent of young people receive education to the age of 18, and some 50 per cent receive higher education. The provision of that scale of education would have a dramatic effect upon Britain's youth unemployment figures. It would also have a dramatic effect upon leisure activities in the sport and arts field, since those engaged in full-time education have high participation rates in these activities. In the UK, this is a more expensive option than in the United States, where a larger proportion of the costs of higher education falls on parents and the students themselves. Nevertheless, keeping young people out of the job market is cheaper than most of the other options available, and this seems to have been recognized by the current government which has invested heavily in job-creation and quasi-training programmes aimed at the school-leaver and organized by the Manpower Services Commission, at often controversially low costs. It would seem that such schemes are here to stay and that most young people will not in future be expected to enter the official job market before the age of 18. This has the effect of taking some 5 per cent of the potential labour force off the labour market. Logically the expansion of the higher education sector would seem a natural extension of this process, but under the current government, the opposite is happening.

The third option for reducing the working life is the idea of sabbaticals for all.[16] Such sabbaticals might be for a variety of purposes ranging from training to education to pure leisure. They might be funded through the education system – giving everyone the right to a certain amount of education after the age of, say, 21; or through the pension system – entitling people to a year or more of their pension 'early'. This is an area where governments could intervene to establish rights for workers, although the question of who would pay the costs is an open one.

The common problem with all the schemes discussed above is their cost. Where the costs fall on employers and workers (in terms of potential pay increases forgone) they are destined to be introduced only very slowly, if at all. In these instances the costs of not implementing the proposals, namely the high levels of unemployment, fall on the state. On the other hand, the net costs to government of implementing proposals in the area of education and earlier retirement are minimal.

One way of reducing average hours of work and producing financial savings to offset the measure is under active consideration in Belgium.[17] The concept of 'time management' involves reducing weekly working hours to three 9- or 10-hour days. Working hours per worker are therefore reduced by some 25 per cent and hence the number of jobs increases by a similar amount. The financial savings to pay for this generosity to the worker come from the fact that it is possible to use capital plant (such as factories, offices, and schools) for two 3-day shifts per week, thus making great savings in capital plant including transport. Alternatively, two 6-hour shifts could be worked for a 5-day week. Further research is being conducted in Belgium to explore the implications of the idea for work and leisure.

Changing economic structures

Finally we examine ideas that have been put forward to suggest how society might cope with the changes wrought by the new technology. The first of these ideas is that espoused by Stonier – the 'information economy' – and the second is Gershuny's idea of the 'self-service economy'.

The scenario which Stonier paints is one in which the new 'information economy' becomes enormously successful economically as a result of knowledge applied to productive and extractive processes. At one point he appears to draw an analogy with the productiveness of oil fields.[18] Here is a highly capital intensive, technologically advanced industry where the ratio of wealth production to staff numbers employed is enormous. As such the industry is very heavily taxed, producing vast government revenue which can be used to support government services or whatever. Other industries are, it seems, likely to emulate the oil industry as they become more technologically advanced and less labour intensive. But the revenues will be necessary to support a massive increase in the education system because such a technologically advanced system will only survive in a society where enormous resources are pumped into education, research, and sophisticated back-up services. Thus Stonier sees education as the major future user and employer of people's time, linked closely with the all-pervasive 'information industries'. He paints a picture of an 'Athens' of the future with machines taking the place of slaves, but where the leisured, cultured, educated 'Athenians' will be very necessary to develop the knowledge, science, and technology to maintain the mechanized and computerized 'slaves'.

Another view of the technological future is that, rather than a mass society of technologically literate and educated citizens, the system will be maintained by relatively few educated rulers. This scenario has been explored by, for instance, Kurt Vonnegut in his novel *Player Piano*.[19] But the next generation of computers will be able to think for themselves. Therefore, as has always been the case, the direction in which the system operates will be decided by those in power rather than by those with intellect. Either way a highly mechanized and computerized system of the future could dispense with much of human labour as we know it. Of course this will not happen overnight.

Gershuny does not relate the idea of the 'self-service' economy to such a futuristic scenario, but it is relevant.[20] The self-service economy is an alternative economy which develops alongside the official economy, but in which people do things largely for themselves. While self-service activities are not necessarily 'leisure' activities as usually conceived, the idea does represent a breakdown of the barriers between work and leisure. Are gardening, craft work, cooking, or DIY work or leisure? A hint of this type of relationship between a formal and an informal economy is provided by those who 'drop out' and go to live in the Welsh hills or similar locations. Minimal income from the 'formal' economy in the form of casual or freelance earnings or social security payments are sufficient to pay for those commodities such as transport and electricity, which must be obtained from the formal economy. For the rest, they engage in what Toffler calls 'prosuming'. The extent to which the movement towards a self-service economy is already happening is somewhat confused by conventional classification of non-work activities. Gardening and DIY are generally classified as leisure activities, whereas they can equally be seen as people working for themselves. The extent to which increased leisure time has been used for these activities rather than other, less instrumental, leisure activities is an indicator of the extent to which the move to a self-service economy is already spontaneously under way.

A proposal which links the abolition of the work ethic idea with proposals designed to reduce the labour input into the economy involves the institution of some form of 'social wage'. This is the idea that everyone should receive an income from the state regardless of whether they work in the formal economy or not. In this situation formal paid work becomes optional. Nearly all the commentators on the future of work and leisure referred to envisage this development in some form, such as 'negative income tax',[21] a 'guaranteed income for all',[22] or a 'national income scheme'.[23] The proposal links the work ethic issue with the reduction of labour inputs issue; it is normally discussed in the context of the need for a 'complete change of attitudes' where work is no longer the be-all and end-all of existence, and where 'work' in the formal economy becomes almost a privilege. To some extent the social security system serves as a 'social wage' system: the difference being that the social wage would certainly be higher than the average social security payment and would be an automatic right to all rather than a means-tested income of last resort. Few proposers of the social wage cost the results (the Ecology Party is an exception): it would certainly be expensive. In view of this and in view of the fact that the labour requirements of the economy are likely to be reduced only gradually overall, the proposals to lower the pensionable age, raise the age at which people leave full-time education, and introduce sabbaticals seem more likely to be implemented than the introduction of a social wage.

This paper has attempted to view the various proposals which have been introduced by a number of writers to cope with the future of work and leisure. The prospect of a 'leisure society' in the near future, though doubted by some,[24] is envisaged by many of these writers. But in view of the difficulties of introducing many of the proposals discussed and the virtual absence of these ideas from the agendas of the major political parties, it would seem that progress towards a society of leisure is far from certain.[25]

Notes

1 C. Jenkins and B. Sherman, *The Collapse of Work*, London, Eyre Methuen, 1979; Jenkins and Sherman, *The Leisure Shock*, London, Eyre Methuen, 1981; I. Clemitson and G. Rogers, *A Life to Live: Beyond Full Employment*, London, Junction Books, 1981; B. Allen, A. Bati, and J. Bragard, *The Shattered Dream*, London, Arrow Books, 1981; G. Merritt, *World Out of Work*, London, Collins, 1982; W. Martin and S. Mason, *Leisure and Work – the Choices for 1991 and 2001*, Leisure Consultants, Sudbury, Suffolk, 1981; G. E. Cherry and A. S. Travis, *Leisure in the 1980s: Alternative Futures*, London, Leisure Studies Association Conference Reports no. 11, 1980; Tourism and Recreation Research Unit (eds), *Work and Leisure: the Implications of Technological Change*, Leisure Studies Association, TRRU, University of Edinburgh, 1982; A. J. Veal, S. Parker, and F. Coalter (eds), *Work and Leisure: Unemployment, Technology and Life-Styles in the 1980s*, London, Leisure Studies Association, 1982; S. Glyptis (ed.), *Prospects for Work and Leisure*, London, Leisure Studies Association, 1983; B. Jones, *Sleepers Wake! Technology and the Future of Work*, London, Oxford University Press, 1982; T. Stonier, *The Wealth of Information: A Profile of the Post-Industrial Society*, London, Methuen, 1983; R. Clarke, *Work in Crisis*, Edinburgh, St Andrew's Press, 1982; C. Handy, *The Future of Work*, Oxford, Blackwell, 1984.

2 For example, I. Barron and R. Curnow, *The Future with Microelectronics*, Milton Keynes, Open University Press, 1979; T. Forester (ed.), *The Microelectronics Revolution*, Oxford, Blackwell, 1980; P. Large, *The Micro Revolution*, London, Fontana, 1980; P. Laurie, *The Micro Revolution*, London, Futura, 1980.

3 For example, D. Gabor, *Inventing the Future*, New York, Knopf, 1964; H. Kahn and A. J. Wiener, *The Year 2000: A Framework for Speculation on*

the Next Thirty-Three Years, London, Macmillan, 1967; A. Touraine, *The Post Industrial Society*, London, Wildwood, 1974; D. Bell, *The Coming of Post-Industrial Society*, London, Heinemann, 1974; A. Toffler, *Future Shock*, London, Pan, 1970; and A. Toffler, *The Third Wave*, London, Pan, 1981.

4 See, for example, B. Russell, *In Praise of Idleness and Other Essays*, London, Allen & Unwin, 1935.

5 P. Walker, 'The way ahead for a better life for all', *News of the World*, 19 November 1983; F. Pym, 'The revolution laissez-faire and socialism cannot handle', *The Guardian*, 10 October 1983.

6 L. Murray, 'Jobs for all is not the main goal', *The Guardian*, 26 August 1983; Trades Union Congress, *Work Time Action Checklist*, London, TUC, 1982.

7 D. Hayter, 'When work is a clean word', *The Guardian*, 1 November 1978.

8 Jenkins and Sherman, *The Collapse of Work*.

9 Jenkins and Sherman, *The Leisure Shock*, pp. 15, 185.

10 Clemitson and Rogers, op. cit., p. 13.

11 Clarke, op. cit., p. 196.

12 R. Dubin, 'Industrial workers' worlds: a study of the "central life interests" of industrial workers', *Social Problems*, vol. 3, January 1956; J. Goldthorpe, D. Lockwood, F. Bechhofer, and J. Platt, *The Affluent Worker*, Oxford, Oxford University Press, 1968.

13 A. Sinfield, *What Unemployment Means*, London, Martin Robertson, 1981; S. R. Parker, *Work and Retirement*, London, Allen & Unwin, 1983.

14 F. Best, *Flexible Life Scheduling: Breaking the Education-Work-Retirement Lockstep*, New York, Praeger, 1980.

15 ibid.

16 C. Goyder, *Sabbaticals for All*, London, NCLC Publishing Society Ltd, 1977.

17 W. Fache, 'Time management', paper to the ELRA meeting, Vaxjo, Sweden, May 1983.

18 Stonier, op. cit., p. 212.

19 K. Vonnegut, *Player Piano*, Macmillan, 1953.

20 J. Gershuny, *After Industrial Society? The Emerging Self-Service Economy*, London, Macmillan, 1978.

21 A. Toffler, *Previews and Premises*, London, Pan, 1984, p. 58; Stonier, op. cit., p. 213.

22 Clemitson and Rogers, op. cit., p. 93; Jones, op. cit., p. 243.

23 Handy, op. cit., p. 106; Ecology Party, *Working for a Future: An Ecological; Approach to Employment*, London, Ecology Party, 1981.

24 Ecology Party, op. cit.; K. Roberts, *Contemporary Society and the Growth of Leisure*, London, Longman, 1978.

25 For a more extensive treatment of these issues see A. J. Veal, *Leisure and the Future*, London, Allen & Unwin, 1987.

Index

275